THERAPIST TECHNIQUES AND CLIENT OUTCOMES

THERAPIST TECHNIQUES AND CLIENT OUTCOMES

Eight Cases of
Brief Psychotherapy

CLARA E. HILL

SAGE PUBLICATIONS
The Publishers of Professional Social Science
Newbury Park   London   New Delhi

To Jim, Kevin, and Kate

For information address:

SAGE Publications, Inc.
2111 West Hillcrest Drive
Newbury Park, California 91320

SAGE Publications Ltd.
28 Banner Street
London EC1Y 8QE
England

SAGE Publications India Pvt. Ltd.
M-32 Market
Greater Kailash I
New Delhi 110 048 India

Printed in the United States of America

Library of Congress Cataloging-in-Publication Data

Hill, Clara E.
    Therapist techniques and client outcomes : eight cases of brief
psychotherapy / Clara E. Hill.
        p.   cm.
    Bibliography: p.
    Includes index.
    ISBN 0-8039-3513-7. — ISBN 0-8039-3514-5 (pbk.)
    1. Brief psychotherapy—Case studies.   I. Title.
    RC480.55.H55   1989
    616.89'14—dc19   89-5893
                                                                          CIP

FIRST PRINTING, 1989

Contents

Clara E. Hill, Barbara J. Thompson,
& James R. Mahalik

Part IV: Conclusions

Preface

This book should be useful to therapists, therapists-in-training, clients, and psychotherapy researchers.

Therapists and therapists-in-training will find it helpful to learn what other therapists actually do in the therapy sessions. In reading the cases, therapists can identify similarities with their own clients and come up with new ways of approaching clinical situations with some clients. I would also hope that after reading this book, therapists will more often ask themselves what techniques they are using with clients, when they are most likely to use them, why they are using them, and what effect these techniques are having on the client. I believe that by examining their own behaviors in sessions, therapists can become more effective in their interventions.

There is also a lot in this book for clients. Most clients enter therapy, as did these clients, not knowing what to expect or how to behave. By reading these cases, clients can begin to see that a variety of things can occur in therapy. Of course, these things will not necessarily occur in any particular therapy, since each therapy is a unique combination of the specific therapist and client. This uniqueness is exactly what makes it so difficult to tell people what will happen in therapy, unless a very directive structured program is being offered.

For psychotherapy researchers, these cases represent a way of analyzing psychotherapy process and outcome that does not compromise the nature of the clinical interaction. In the methodology, we involved the therapist and client so that we could obtain their perspectives about the change process. We blended together both quantitative and qualitative techniques to arrive at conclusions about the cases. Thus, this study provides an exciting new methodology for determining how psychotherapy works.

I want to emphasize one aspect of the book that may not be readily apparent in the text. Therapists and clients reviewed drafts of the chapters of their cases, providing feedback about the accuracy of the conclusions and suggesting alternative ways of looking at the process. Asking the therapists and clients for feedback extended the collaborative process in which this project was conducted and, so, lessened the potential bias had I been the only one interpreting the data.

I hope that the readers are as stimulated by the cases as I have been. Having studied these cases for some five years now, I have learned a tremendous amount about psychotherapy. I hope that these learnings are communicated adequately enough in this book to enhance the delivery of psychotherapy and to stimulate new and better research on psychotherapy.

Acknowledgments

This project was aided by the continuing support of the National Institute of Mental Health through Research Grant MH-37837 to Clara E. Hill, Principal Investigator.

Many people devoted great amounts of time and energy to this project. First, I want to extend my gratitude to the therapists and clients who participated in this project. Each person dedicated not only time, but also a tremendous amount of energy and vitality to the project. I learned about psychotherapy process from the participants. I believe the openness and willingness of these persons to share their experiences is a lesson to us as researchers about how much the participants have to offer in helping us understand our subject.

I especially wish to acknowledge the original research team: Janet Helms, Sharon Spiegel, and Victoria Tichenor. In the text when I use the royal "we," I am referring to this research team. Our discussions of methodology and of the progress of the cases provided a wealth of material for this book.

A whole generation of students at the University of Maryland helped with this project. Every session and post-session therapist review was typed, corrected, and retyped until nearly perfect. Additionally, all the data had to be entered into the computer. Many people burned out doing these incredibly tedious tasks: Kay Anderson, Jacqueline Broddus, Katherine Brown, Michelle Burrus, Jeffrey Deutel, Jessica Giglio, Eunice Gill, Ellen Huberman, Jennifer Ireland, Isabella Jackson, Terry Jackson, Joyce Jennings, John Jordan, Karen Kane, Jeff Kaplan, Lisa Kamenir, Shelley Ossana, Cheryl Pressley, Pauline Price, Rosita Rodriquez, Dave Rosenberg, Suzanne

9

Ruddock, Randi Shaffer, Alicia Stephany, Priscilla Sheffield, Sandy Sherman, Maxine Siegel, Sherry Siegel, James Soden, and Robin Vinopal. Many students served as judges on the various process measures: Ira Abramowitz, Steven Bergman, Elena Cannady, Susan Carter, Elaine Chester, Rosemarie Cicarello, Mary Cogar, Deborah Dolan, Chris Duggan, Michael Genhart, Jeff Gould, Roderick Hall, Jeff Kaplan, Jim Mahalik, Janna McCargo, Garrett Moravec, Susan McCaa, Lisa Medoff, Peter Muehrer, Karen Paterson, Adria Pollack, Kathy O'Brien, Karen Rosenberg, Jacqueline Royal, Marie Sargent, Roy Sexton, Bruce Sharkin, Sandra Sherman, Jacqueline Smith, Barbara Thompson, and Leslie White.

I want to thank Elgin Perry at the University of Maryland Computer Center for helping me with the data analyses.

I would also like to thank Betty Clemmer, Jim Gormally, Karla Moras, Anne Regan, Barbara Thompson, and Victoria Tichenor for their invaluable feedback and encouragement based on reading drafts of chapters of this book.

Finally, I would like to thank my therapist, Dr. Rona Eisner, who not only helped me learn about therapy first hand, but also supported me through all the phases of this project.

PART I

INTRODUCTION

1

Introduction

I believe that therapist techniques are responsible for client change. Above and beyond being a nice person, a therapist must do something to help a client to change. Much like a surgeon has specific procedures and tools for conducting surgery, psychotherapists have specific techniques for helping clients.

The viewpoint that therapist techniques are the most powerful change agent within therapy has not received much support in the psychotherapy literature. Frank (1973) argued that client expectations and non-specific therapist factors are the factors leading to client change. In their review of the research, Bergin and Lambert (1978) concluded that techniques finished a distant third after client and therapist factors. They felt that techniques were crucial only for providing a credible rationale for the change agents and clients. Orlinsky and Howard (1978) concluded that techniques in and of themselves have not yet been shown to yield a consistently powerful differential effect on therapeutic outcome, but felt that without some techniques which feel right, therapists cannot participate confidently in treatment. Most recently, Lambert, Shapiro, and Bergin (1986) indicated that techniques were not irrelevant, but that their power for change was limited compared to that of the therapeutic relationship.

These reviewers have accurately summarized the existing research, but flaws in this research have limited the ability to determine the effects of techniques. To provide a rationale for the present study, I will review these methodological problems: the lack of a consistent definition of techniques, inadequate measurement of the impact of techniques, the use of group designs rather than case studies, and a lack of attention to moderating variables such as client and therapist factors, the therapeutic relationship, and external factors.

Definition of Techniques

From the inception of psychotherapy process research, definitional problems have plagued the study of techniques. Behaviors ranging from simple head nods or grammatical sentences to very abstract constructs such as analysis of transference have all been considered under the rubric of therapist techniques. The former types are observable, relatively discrete, and easy to measure. The latter are vague, have few operational anchors, may occur over long periods of time, may be manifest in many ways, and require more inference from raters. The issue for researchers has always been between choosing variables that are relatively easy to judge versus choosing ones which have clinical relevance.

I will operationalize therapist techniques through verbal response modes, which refer to the grammatical structure of the therapist's verbal response independent of the topic or content of the speech (Hill, 1982). Over 30 measures of therapist response modes have been developed, with the earliest systems developed by Porter (1943), Robinson (1950), Snyder (1945), and Strupp (1955). I will use the measure that I have developed (Hill, 1978, 1985, 1986), which compares favorably with other response modes systems (Elliott, Hill, Stiles, Friedlander, Mahrer, & Margison, 1987). Table 1.1 shows the categories and definitions for this system.

Several studies have examined the immediate effects of therapist response modes. Elliott, Barker, Caskey, and Pistrang (1982) found that clients rated interpretation and advisement as the most helpful and question as the least helpful response mode. Elliott (1985) found that general advisement, interpretation, and information were all positively correlated with ratings of client helpfulness. Hill, Carter, and O'Farrell (1983) and O'Farrell, Hill, and Patton (1986) found that therapist interpretation was associated with decreased client description of the problem and increased experiencing and insight. With immediate outcome as the criterion of effectiveness, interpretation was the only response mode that has been found to be effective across all studies. This supports other research on the efficacy of interpretation (Spiegel & Hill, 1989).

Table 1.1 Definitions of Response Modes

Approval: Provides emotional support, approval, reassurance, or reinforcement. It may imply sympathy or tend to alleviate anxiety by minimizing the client's problems.

Information: Supplies information in the form of data, facts, or resources. It may be related to the therapy process, the therapist's behavior, or therapy arrangements (time, fee, place).

Direct Guidance: These are directions or advice that the therapist suggests for the client either for what to do within the session or outside the session.

Closed Question: Gathers data or specific information. The client responses requested are limited and specific.

Open Question: Probes or requests for clarification or exploration by the client.

Paraphrase: Mirrors or summarizes what the client has been communicating either verbally or nonverbally. Does not "go beyond" what the client has said or add a new perspective or understanding to the client's statements or provide any explanations for the client's behavior. Includes restatement of content, reflection of feelings, nonverbal referent, and summary.

Interpretation: Goes beyond what the client has overtly recognized and provides reasons, alternative meanings, or new frameworks for feelings, behaviors, or personality. It may establish connections between seemingly isolated statements or events; interpret defenses, feelings, resistance, or transference; or indicate themes, patterns, or causal relationships in behavior or personality, related present events to past events.

Confrontation: Points out a discrepancy or contradiction but does not provide a reason for such a discrepancy. The discrepancy may be between words and behaviors, between two things the client has said, or between the client's and therapist's perceptions.

Self-Disclosure: Shares feelings or personal experiences.

NOTE: Definitions are taken from the Hill (1985) manual that is available from the author.

In past studies (Fuller & Hill, 1985; Hill & O'Grady, 1985) we have measured therapist techniques by examining therapist intentions or rationales for their interventions. Perhaps the most complete definition of techniques would include both intentions and response modes, thus including both why the therapist used a particular response as well as what the therapist did behaviorally. For the present analyses, however, I will focus only on the response modes because for several of the methods used to study techniques (described in the next section), there was no way of knowing what the therapist intention was. To be able to make comparisons across the different data sources, I used the definition of techniques that was common across all data sources.

Measuring the Impact of Techniques

The most typical method for studying the effects of therapist techniques has been to relate the frequency or proportion of occurrence of techniques to distal outcome, or change after therapy. Such correlational designs have been criticized (Gottman & Markman, 1978; Russell & Trull, 1986) because correlational designs cannot indicate whether certain response modes lead systematically to other behaviors. Further, correlational designs measure only the frequency of occurrence but ignore the quality. Using measures of immediate outcome obviates some of these problems, in that one can be more sure that the specific therapist response mode is at least partially causing the subsequent effect.

There are problems, however, with using immediate outcome measures. First, looking at the effects of all response modes of each type sums across all occurrences of the response modes, so that the general class of events is tested. This approach does not test the effects of a few critical incidents of the response mode. Secondly, not all of the impact of therapist techniques comes in the immediate moment. Often clients have a different reaction after they have had a chance to think about their reactions. Thus, it is important to measure the delayed effects and to focus on the participants' experience of the intervention to determine which techniques were heard and absorbed.

Some past research has used a more qualitative approach to gathering data about the participants' experiences of the therapy. Orlinsky and Howard (1975) used the Therapy Session Report to have therapists and client report on their experiences of sessions. Bogdan and Taylor (1975) and Miles and Huberman (1984) advocate interviewing participants about their experience.

In the present study, I will use immediate outcome measures to tap the subjective and objective reactions as well as questionnaire and interview data following sessions and treatment to tap the more delayed reactions to interventions.

Case Study Methodology

Hersen and Barlow (1976) contended that group comparisons distort useful data by averaging effects across clients. If a technique fails for one client, but succeeds for another, the resulting average for the two clients would be no effect for that technique. There is evidence that some clients get better whereas others get worse with any given treatment, but traditional group methodology is inadequate for answering the question of what leads to change for an individual in psychotherapy.

A case study approach has been advocated as a holistic methodology for studying how multiple variables interact to affect the process and outcome of psychotherapy for an individual (Bergin & Lambert, 1978; Gelso, 1979; Hersen & Barlow, 1976; Hill, 1982). From clinical experience we know that the change process does not occur in a logical, orderly fashion that is consistent across individuals. With one client, a therapist might use interpretation only after the relationship is established and when the client is searching actively for a greater understanding. With another client, the therapist might use interpretation at the beginning of treatment to demonstrate to the client that he or she understands and can help. Only by studying a case in all its complexity can we begin to discover why techniques are effective.

The drawback to studying a single case, of course, is that causal relationships are difficult to establish because of the interconnection of all of the variables and the lack of controls with unstructured treatments. Kazdin (1981) has stated that valid inferences can be drawn if a careful review of process data is done, competing hypotheses accounting for change are examined, and multiple cases are used to diminish the impact of a unique client's history and maturation. Use of multiple cases diminishes the impact of a particular case's idiosyncratic features and increases external validity (Hayes, 1981; Kazdin, 1981). Further, comparison of cases provides a stronger basis for making causal statements about the effects of the therapeutic treatment.

Historically, case studies of psychotherapy have been based on therapist self-report, with no empirical evidence. These case studies, for example Freud's case reports of Dora and the Rat Man, have had a tremendous impact on clinical practice. Unfortunately, when only the therapist's report is available, the case study has to be viewed with caution because the lack of corroborating evidence can lead to subjective distortions. From our own studies, we have evidence that clients and therapists perceive the therapeutic process in very different ways (Fuller & Hill, 1985; Hill, 1974), suggesting that examining only one perspective would yield a distorted picture of the process.

Thus, in the present study, I will examine eight cases of brief psychotherapy to determine which techniques replicate as effective across more than one case. Further, I will examine multiple perspectives on the cases to reduce bias.

Variables That Moderate the Effects of Techniques

Whether a technique is helpful depends on client and therapist characteristics, the relationship, and external factors.

Client Variables

Highlen and Hill (1984) reviewed several personality factors that have been found to be determinants of successful outcome. First, the client must be susceptible to interpersonal influence, get along with others, and be able to form a relationship. Antagonism or mistrust are contraindications for therapeutic success. Second, the client needs to be upset and in psychological distress. A certain amount of pain is a good motivator for changing, whereas persons who have mild, vague dissatisfactions are typically not easily persuaded to make the effort necessary to change. Third, the prognosis for treatment is more favorable if the distress is interpersonal rather than physical or somatic. Bodily complaints are often used as an attempt to retreat from others and not feel anxiety. Fourth, the client should have some coping capacity. Finally, client attractiveness and likability sometimes have been predictive of success.

Further, Highlen and Hill (1984) noted that there are specific skills involved in being a good client: verbal ability, capacity for self-understanding, and an ability to self-explore and focus. Klein, Mathieu-Coughlan, and Kiesler (1986) have found that client experiencing, which is similar to client involvement, is positively related to successful outcome in therapy. Strupp (1980) concluded that client involvement was the major predictor of which clients did well in therapy. Clients who were involved in the therapy process changed more in therapy.

Thus, to provide the best test of techniques, clients who are most likely to be responsive to techniques should be chosen. For this study, anxious and depressed clients who were motivated and able to form an interpersonal relationship, and who had problems with relationships and self-esteem, were selected.

Therapist Variables

Parloff, Waskow, and Wolfe (1978) noted that the literature recommends that therapists should possess the personal characteristics of security, objectivity, honesty, integrity, humanity, intuitiveness, perceptiveness, commitment to the client, patience, emotional freedom, creativity, and imagination. Strupp (1982) confined his list to maturity, skill, and sensitivity. Frank (1973) suggested persuasiveness and healing ability.

Equivocal findings have been produced for therapist gender, race, and age (Parloff et al., 1978). Beutler, Crago, and Arizmendi's (1986) review indicated that therapist age exerts only a weak effect on outcome, such that a therapist of a similar age is slightly better for younger clients with adjustment problems. Regarding gender, they noted that female therapists and/or therapists of the client's gender facilitate the treatment process if the therapist presents nonstereotypical sexual viewpoints, but effects on treatment outcome are less consistent. Regarding ethnicity, they concluded that attitude may be more important than ethnic origin.

Theoretical orientation, which represents a therapist's philosophical way of conceptualizing and thinking about therapy and client dynamics, exerts an influence on therapist behavior within sessions (Elliott et al., 1987; Hill & O'Grady, 1985; Hill, Thames, & Rardin, 1979; Stiles, 1979; Strupp, 1955). No evidence exists, however, that specific orientations result in better outcome (Smith, Glass, & Miller, 1980).

This literature, although interesting, gave few specific clues as to which therapists to select to provide the best test of therapist techniques. To find therapists who were most likely to use techniques appropriately, we selected experienced therapists who were nominated by their peers as the best therapists in the area.

Therapeutic Relationship

The therapeutic relationship has been defined as the feelings and attitudes that therapy participants hold toward one another and the manner in which these are expressed (Gelso & Carter, 1985). The relationship between the therapist and client has been posited by virtually all schools as either a necessary precondition or as the major change agent in psychotherapy (Gelso & Carter, 1985; Parloff et al., 1978). Much of the early empirical work was based on Roger's (1957) conceptualization of the therapist offering of facilitative conditions as the necessary and sufficient condition for successful therapy. Although the findings were initially very promising, numerous methodological problems and conflicting results have created doubt regarding the influence of facilitative conditions on therapeutic outcome (Lambert, DeJulio, & Stein, 1978; Parloff et al., 1978). Most theorists and researchers, however, continue to believe that the concept of the relationship is important, but needs to be redefined.

Recent conceptualizations have focused on the therapeutic or working alliance, which is the interaction between the therapist and client. Empirical evidence is promising in predicting outcome from working alliance (Gelso & Carter, 1985). Bordin (1979) theorized that the working alliance is composed of bond, agreement on goals, and agreement on tasks. A further important aspect of the working alliance discussed by Bordin is the concept of tear and repair. He theorized that every relationship has strains and problems, so whether the relationship has such tears is not as important as how the tears are repaired. Repairing the relationship can build a stronger working alliance.

Conceptually, problems still remain in teasing out the interaction between the relationship and techniques. Some would assert that it is the relationship itself that causes the change and that the techniques are used only to give the therapist something to do. Others would claim that it is the technical factors alone that lead to change. I believe that there is a complex interaction between the two factors. Certain techniques are used to build the relationship, for example support, listening, and empathy. Once the relationship is established, other techniques can be used to help the client change, for example interpretation. Of course, this does not hold true for all clients. Before some clients will trust and disclose to a therapist, they might need to be confronted to have proof that the therapist can see through their defenses. Thus, the interaction between techniques and the relationship probably depends on variables within cases.

External Factors

Much of psychotherapy research has examined only what occurs during the therapy hour itself. It is easy to study the therapy hour because we can gather complete information on it. Therapy, however, involves only 1 hour whereas there are 167 other hours in a week. Other events occur outside the therapy hour that impact on the clients and interact with the therapy process and outcome. Thus, we need to examine these other events to understand therapy. External factors can be divided into three areas: (a) extratherapy involvement, (b) supportive network, and (c) external events.

Extratherapy involvement. A major factor related to client motivation is what the client does outside of the therapy hour. For instance, a person might consciously think about what the therapist has said, talk with other people about it, and try new behaviors. Another person might go home and not think about the therapy. These behaviors probably affect the outcome of treatment.

Supportive network. O'Farrell et al. (1986) reported that differences in outcome between two clients seemed to be partially due to the fact that the more successful client had a supportive network towards which she could turn. The beneficial impact of a supportive network has been documented extensively, for example Cobb (1976). A client with other outlets for companionship is less likely to become dependent on the therapist. A further benefit of a supportive network for the therapy process is that clients can check out the therapist's feedback with friends.

Of course, the outside network can also work against the client's improvement. Family and friends can sabotage the client's changes. When a behavioral routine is upset, others often act to counteract the changes. Perhaps the classic example of this is the husband who brings chocolates for the wife who has just lost five pounds. Systems therapy (e.g., Haley, 1976; Minuchin, 1974) includes significant others in the therapy process so that they can be part of the change process rather than sabotage it.

External events. Inevitably, while a person is in therapy, outside events occur which have an impact on the change process. Events such as a new relationship, a job change, or the death of a loved one could have a major positive or negative impact on a person that would interact with the therapy process.

Preliminary Study

We did an analysis across the eight cases to determine whether there were any overall effects for the response modes (Hill, Helms, Tichenor, Spiegel, O'Grady, & Perry, 1988). Response modes had a significant impact on immediate outcome, accounting for about 1% of the variance. Self-disclosure, interpretation, approval, and paraphrase were the most helpful modes. Individual differences between clients accounted for 5% of the variance in client experiencing ratings, 36% in client helpfulness ratings, and 43% in therapist helpfulness ratings. What was effective in one case was not necessarily effective in another case, indicating the need for analyzing response modes using a case study approach.

Conclusions and Hypotheses

The purpose of the present study was to illustrate that techniques, as operationalized by therapist response modes, could be shown to be powerful agents of change if they were examined within a case study framework using careful measurement of the impact of techniques, and an explication of the moderating variables of therapist and client factors, the therapeutic relationship, and external factors.

Since increasing evidence (Budman, 1981; Budman & Gurman, 1988; Koss & Butcher, 1986) has accumulated suggesting the efficacy of brief therapy and because brief therapy presented a format amenable to this type of research, we studied these variables in a brief therapy format.

To provide the best test of the effectiveness of techniques, one has to ensure that techniques are delivered competently. Experienced therapists with good reputations were thus selected because they were most likely to have the clinical ability to select techniques that were appropriate for clients. Similarly, clients were selected who would be most likely to respond favorably to therapy.

My first hypothesis was that therapist techniques would be found to be effective in each of eight cases. Based on the past literature, I predicted that one of the most helpful techniques within each case would be interpretation.

My second hypothesis was that the effectiveness of specific techniques would vary across cases, with client and therapist factors, the therapeutic relationship, and external factors moderating which techniques were effective within cases.

2

Method

We used a collaborative model to collect data. We told our therapists that they were the experts from whom we wanted to learn as much as possible about how and why they did what they did. We told clients that they had valuable reactions to what the therapist did that would aid us in understanding therapy. Participants were instructed that there were no right or wrong answers, but that we were simply interested in what happened. We tried not to impose our biases on the data collection process.

Therapists

We chose experienced, master psychotherapists who believed in and were competent in time-limited therapy because we reasoned that they would be able to deliver appropriate techniques. To find such therapists, we asked colleagues to nominate the best therapists in the area. Those therapists who received the most nominations were invited to participate.

The eight therapists (4 men and 4 women) were all Ph.D. psychologists who ranged in age from 34 to 78 years ($M = 46.38$, $SD = 13.47$) and had 5 to 42 years of postdoctoral experience ($M = 18.50$, $SD = 10.85$). The therapists were paid \$40 per hour for their time (the going rate was \$60-75 per hour).

Clients

We chose to study anxious and depressed clients, who typically respond well to treatment. They were recruited through newspaper announcements that offered free individual psychotherapy for women over 25 years of age who had self-esteem and relationship problems, were available for three hours during the day, planned to remain in the area for at least one year, had no previous psychotherapy, and had no history of alcohol or drug abuse.

Of 94 appropriate telephone inquiries, 53 persons completed a battery of psychological tests (after being fully informed about selection procedures and signing consent forms). We interviewed the 15 persons with elevated scores on the MMPI scales of Depression and Psychasthenia. The selected clients were fully informed about the treatment procedures. The eight women who participated ranged from 32 to 60 years ($M = 42.38$, $SD = 9.41$). Clients were not paid for their participation.

Persons not selected were given referrals. Further details about why people volunteered to participate in this study are available in Tichenor, Hill, and Helms (in preparation).

Measures

In this section, I will describe the measures and summary data for the group on each measure. Table 2.1 presents a chart of which measures were collected during each phase of the therapy.

Process Measures

Therapist techniques were measured through the revised *Hill Counselor Verbal Response Category System* (Hill, 1985) which includes nine pantheoretical, nominal, mutually exclusive therapist verbal response modes (definitions were shown in Chapter 1). To correct for different amounts of talking, proportions of response modes were used rather than frequency. The average proportions of use for the eight therapists were: approval ($M = .06$, $SD = .03$), information ($M = .24$, $SD = .06$), direct guidance ($M = .05$, $SD = .02$), closed question ($M = .19$, $SD = .05$), open question ($M = .13$, $SD = .05$), paraphrase ($M = .20$, $SD = .07$), interpretation ($M = .08$, $SD = .04$), confrontation ($M = .05$, $SD = .02$), and self-disclosure ($M = .01$, $SD = .01$). The proportions of response modes are similar to those reported in previous research (Hill, 1978; Hill et al., 1979; Hill et al., 1983; O'Farrell et al., 1986).

TABLE 2.1 Chart of When Measures Were Administered

Time	Client Measures	Therapist Measures
Pre-Therapy	MMPI SCL-90-R Tennessee Self Concept Scale Target Complaints Hamilton Depression and Anxiety	Target Complaints
Each Session	WAI SEQ Post-Session Questionnaire Helpfulness Ratings Reactions Experiencing	WAI SEQ Post-Session Interview Helpfulness Ratings Intentions Response Modes
Fifth Session	Target Complaints	Target Complaints
Termination	MMPI SCL-90-R Tennessee Self Concept Scale Target Complaints Hamilton Depression and Anxiety Post-Therapy Interview	Target Complaints Post-Therapy Interview
Six Months	SCL-90-R Tennessee Self Concept Scale Target Complaints Follow-up Interview	
One Year	SCL-90-R Tennessee Self Concept Scale Target Complaints Follow-up Questionnaire	

Activity level. Therapist activity level was determined by counting the number of response units (essentially grammatical sentences) in sessions. This index of activity excluded therapist minimal encouragers (e.g., "MmHmm") but included silences attributed to the therapist. The average number of response units per session was 92.36 (*SD* = 19.58).

Therapists and clients rated the helpfulness of each therapist speaking turn using the *Helpfulness Scale* (Elliott, 1985) with a 9-point Likert-type scale (9 = extremely helpful). Elliott (1986) reported adequate reliability and validity for this measure.

The *Client Reactions System* (Hill, Helms, Spiegel, & Tichenor, 1988) consists of 21 nominal, non-mutually exclusive reactions organized into five major clusters: *Supported* (Understood, Supported, Hopeful, Relief), *Therapeutic Work* (Negative Thoughts and Behaviors, Better Self-Understanding, Clear, Feelings, Responsibility, Unstuck, New Perspective, Educated, New Ways to Behave), *Challenged* (Challenged), *Negative Reactions* (Scared, Worse, Stuck, Lack Direction, Confused, Misunderstood), and *No Reaction* (No Reaction).

The *Client Experiencing Scale* (Klein, Mathieu, Gendlin, & Kiesler, 1970; Klein et al, 1986) is a 7-point scale used to describe a client's level of involvement in the therapy. At a low level, discourse is impersonal or superficial; at higher levels, feelings are explored and experiencing serves as the basic referent for problem-resolution and self-understanding. Klein et al. (1986) reported high interrater reliability for 15 previous studies and indicated that experiencing is related to self-exploration, insight. working through, absence of resistances, and high-quality free association.

The *Client Post-Session Questionnaire* asked clients about the most meaningful or important thing that happened during the session, the most hindering or harmful thing that happened, and what they liked most and least about the therapist. We used a questionnaire rather than an interview because it was less intrusive on the therapist-client relationship.

Using the *Therapist Post-Session Interview*, which had a semi-structured format, we questioned the therapists about their general strategies, how they were helpful to the clients, whether they made any mistakes, and the most meaningful events for the clients.

The *List of Helpful and Hindering Components in Psychotherapy* (Cogar & Hill, in preparation) was used by three judges to code all helpful and hindering events mentioned in the Client Post-Session Questionnaire and Therapist Post-Session Interview. The categories were divided into five clusters: *Therapist Techniques* (support, direct guidance, closed and open questions, paraphrase, interpretation, confrontation, and self-disclosure), *Therapist Manner* (involvement, empathy, expertness, attractiveness, trustworthiness, understanding), *Client Tasks* (insight, focus, experiencing, making changes), *Client Manner* (involved, attractive, likable, comfortable, optimistic, defenses) and *Working Alliance*. The proportion, or number of times each event was mentioned divided by the total number of events mentioned, was the summary figure.

Relationship Measure

The *Working Alliance Inventory* (WAI) (Horvath & Greenberg, 1986) measured client and therapist perspectives of the working alliance. The WAI has three scales (tasks, bonds, and goals), each with 12 items rated on 7-point Likert-type scales. The total score was used since intercorrelations between scales were high (.69 to .92). Internal consistency coefficients ranged from .69 to .92. Scores for the eight cases are shown in Table 2.2.

Session Outcome Measure

Clients and therapists completed the *Session Evaluation Questionnaire* (SEQ) (Stiles & Snow, 1984) Depth and Smoothness scales, which factor analyses have shown to be distinct orthogonal factors. Each scale has six bipolar adjectives arranged in 7-point semantic differential formats. Scores are shown in Table 2.2.

Treatment Outcome Measures

Several instruments were used to determine whether clients changed as a result of treatment. The MMPI, SCL-90-R, and Target Complaints were recommended by Waskow and Parloff (1975) for inclusion in batteries of outcome measures. The TSCS was added to measure positive mental health. The Hamilton Depression and Anxiety Scales were included to get a clinician's perspective on the specific problems we were investigating. The interviews were added to get the participants' subjective perspectives on changes.

The *Minnesota Multiphasic Personality Inventory* (MMPI) (Hathaway & McKinley, 1951) is the most widely used objective personality assessment instrument. The self-report measure includes 3 validity scales and 10 clinical scales (Hypochondriasis, Depression, Hysteria, Psychopathic Deviate, Masculinity-Femininity, Paranoia, Psychasthenia, Schizophrenia, Mania, and Social Introversion). The clients were depressed and anxious, as indicated by their scores on the Depression ($M = 76.12$, $SD = 5.64$) and Psychasthenia ($M = 70.12$, $SD = 6.45$) scales.

TABLE 2.2 Scores on the Working Alliance Inventory as well as the Depth and Smoothness Scales of the Session Evaluation Questionnaire for All Eight Clients

		Working Alliance Inventory		SEQ Depth		SEQ Smoothness	
		M	*SD*	*M*	*SD*	*M*	*SD*
Case 1:	Client	168.40	6.95	4.94	.79	3.94	.79
	Therapist	180.20	13.31	5.02	.42	4.41	1.09
Case 2:	Client	216.59	13.26	5.59	.51	4.67	1.39
	Therapist	209.94	8.95	5.02	1.07	4.69	.68
Case 3:	Client	175.94	10.53	4.85	.53	5.07	1.13
	Therapist	169.53	22.47	4.60	1.21	4.56	1.14
Case 4:	Client	150.75	18.14	3.99	1.16	3.85	1.12
	Therapist	203.83	13.53	6.39	1.00	5.83	.97
Case 5:	Client	163.65	10.58	5.00	.88	3.17	.65
	Therapist	192.06	12.09	4.92	.85	4.26	.93
Case 6:	Client	195.75	9.03	5.49	.80	3.54	.93
	Therapist	181.95	8.44	5.05	.95	4.26	.63
Case 7:	Client	189.83	7.37	4.79	.71	4.26	1.16
	Therapist	184.50	10.31	4.68	.33	3.67	.39
Case 8:	Client	200.00	16.54	5.49	1.05	3.96	1.38
	Therapist	189.58	13.86	5.01	1.01	4.24	1.24
Total:	Client	182.60	21.71	5.02	.52	4.07	.60
	Therapist	188.85	12.94	5.08	.55	4.50	.62
Norms:	Client	195.13	33.08	5.06	1.00	4.21	1.43
	Therapist	192.47	25.27	4.62	1.08	4.01	1.12

NOTE: The norms for the WAI are based on Horvath and Greenberg's (1986, p. 546) data which I transformed from their older 5-point version to their newer 7-point version. The data for the SEQ is based on Stiles and Snow (1984).

The *Hopkins Symptom Checklist-90*-R (SCL-90-R) (Derogatis, Rickels, & Rock, 1976) is a self-report measure of symptomatology. We used the Global Severity Index (GSI) as our summary index. Scores were converted to *T* scores based on an outpatient female population. The SCL-90-R has been used extensively and has adequate reliability and validity. Means on the GSI for our eight clients at pre-therapy were 47.25 (*SD* = 3.06), indicating that our clients were within the average range of outpatients.

The *Tennessee Self Concept Scale* (TSCS) (Fitts, 1965) is a self-report measure of positive functioning. Scores were converted to *T* scores based on an outpatient female population. The TSCS has been used extensively and has adequate reliability and validity. The mean on the total scale for our eight clients at pre-therapy was 35.62 (*SD* = 5.55), indicating that they were low in self-esteem compared to outpatient clients.

Target Complaints (TC) (Battle, Imber, Hoehn-Saric, Stone, Nash, & Frank, 1965), is an individualized measure of problem severity. Clients described three target complaints in a clinical interview. Both client and therapist rated how much each problem currently bothered the client, using a 13-point scale (13 = worst possible functioning). Pre-therapy, the average client ratings were 10.04 (*SD* = 1.87) and therapist ratings were *M* = 9.67 (*SD* = 2.04).

The *Hamilton Depression and Anxiety Scales* (DiNardo, O'Brien, Barlow, Waddell, & Blanchard, 1983) were used to gain a clinician's perspective on anxiety and depression. On the Depression scale at pre-therapy, our clients averaged 17.25 (*SD* = 3.54), indicating that they were mildly depressed. On Anxiety, they averaged 16.25 (*SD* = 4.65), indicating that they were mildly anxious.

Post-therapy interviews. This semi-structured interview included questions about clients' and therapists' experiences of therapy, how clients changed as a result of treatment, and what caused these changes to come about.

Six-month client follow-up interview. This semi-structured interview included questions about what had happened to clients since termination, whether they planned to seek therapy again, and how satisfied they had been with treatment.

One-year client follow-up questionnaire. This questionnaire included questions about what had happened to the clients since termination, whether they planned to seek therapy again, and how satisfied they had been with treatment.

Procedures

Pre-treatment. Volunteers who met the screening criteria during a telephone interview were scheduled to complete the MMPI, SCL-90-R, and TSCS. Those volunteers whose MMPI scores most closely approximated our desired profile (*T* scores > 70 on scales 2, 7, and 0 and < 70 on 4, 6, and 8) returned to complete the Target Complaints and Hamilton Anxiety and Depression scales.

The selected clients were randomly assigned to therapists within the constraints of time availability. Prior to treatment, therapists were allowed to see their assigned client's MMPI profile and the Target Complaints (without the client's ratings of severity). To reduce the possibility of slanting the treatment towards change on the specific outcome measures, therapists were not allowed to see the SCL-90-R or TSCS.

Treatment. No attempt was made to change the manner in which therapists naturally did therapy. Therapists were allowed to use whatever techniques they believed were most effective.

After the first session, therapists rated their perceptions of the severity of the client's Target Complaints. Around the third session, therapists gave a DSM-III diagnosis on the client. During the fifth session, therapists and clients revised and rerated the Target Complaints. Around the eighth session, most therapists decided, either by themselves or in conjunction with the client, the exact number of sessions (between 12-20) they would have.

Treatment took place in a large room, with the therapist and client seated in armchairs facing each other at a distance of about 55 inches. The sessions were videotaped and monitored by a researcher from an adjacent room.

Post-session. After each session, clients went to a separate room and completed the SEQ, WAI, and Post-Session Questionnaire. Therapists completed the SEQ, WAI and the Post-Session Interview. Immediately following the therapist interview, the therapist and client were taken to another room to view the videotape. Both persons had to watch the videotape together to ensure that they were responding to the same portion of the videotape. Therefore, they were separated by a partition so that both could see the videotape and the researcher, but not see each other.

The researcher monitored the review, stopping the videotape after each therapist speaking turn. If the therapist speaking turn consisted of more than one distinct section (e.g., a summary followed by a change of topic), the researcher divided it into separate thought units. The researcher also wrote down the initial key words of the therapist speaking turn, along with the tape counter number, so that the transcribers could later locate the spot in the tape. Clients and therapists were instructed to review the tape and try to recall what they felt during the session rather than what they were feeling at the time of the review. Clients rated the helpfulness and wrote down the numbers of up to five reactions that described their feelings about the therapist intervention. Therapists rated the helpfulness of the intervention. During the review, all ratings were done in writing and talking was discouraged. Neither participant was allowed to see the post-session measures completed by the other participant.

Post-treatment. One to two weeks after treatment, clients completed the outcome measures and Client Post-Therapy Interview. In a separate session, the therapist completed the Target Complaints and the Therapist Post-Therapy Interview.

Six-month follow-up. The clients returned and completed the outcome measures and a structured interview about their progress.

One-Year Follow-up. The clients were contacted by mail and asked to complete and return all the outcome measures and a brief questionnaire about their progress.

Long-term follow-up. Three to four years after therapy, I called the clients to find out how they were doing. Additionally, I met with each therapist and client after they read drafts of the chapters of their completed case studies to get feedback about their reactions to the write-ups.

Data Preparation and Rating Procedures

Transcripts. Verbatim transcripts were obtained for each therapy session and therapist post-session interview. One person typed a rough draft while listening to the audiotape. Another person corrected the transcript by listening to the tape. A final check of the transcript was done against the videotape. The transcript was then unitized, according to guidelines in Hill (1985) for making grammatical sentences out of free-flowing speech.

Ratings of response modes. Nine (6 female and 3 male) undergraduate psychology majors judged therapist response modes. For training, which lasted about 20 hours until we had high agreement, judges read the manual (Hill, 1985), discussed each response mode, and rated transcripts from previous studies. Rotating teams of three judges independently categorized all therapist response units into one of the response modes categories. The master judgment was the category agreed upon by two judges or the category agreed upon after discussion for three-way disagreements. On three randomly selected transcripts from the cases rated by all nine judges, the average kappa (agreement corrected for chance) between raters for the independent (prior to discussion) judgments was .67.

Ratings on the experiencing scale. Six (4 female and 2 male) graduate students were trained using the transcripts and audiotapes provided in the Klein et al. (1970) manual. Following training, rotating sets of two judges used the transcripts and audiotapes of the session to rate each client speaking turn for the peak (highest) Experiencing level. An intraclass correlation using the alpha statistic on two randomly selected sessions rated by all six raters indicated an interrater reliability of .99.

Protection of Confidentiality

Participants were fully informed about all procedures, signed informed consent before and after the therapy, and read drafts of the chapters about their cases.

Analyses of Cases

For each of the case analyses presented in the next several chapters, the following procedures were used to analyze the descriptive measures, outcome, and therapist techniques.

Descriptive Measures

For the response modes, activity, WAI, and SEQ, the scores for each case were compared to the mean for all eight cases by using the standard deviation for the sample. Thus, the mean for a case had to be greater than (or less than) one standard deviation from the mean of the sample to be considered higher (or lower) than average.

Determination of Outcome

Change was judged from pre- to fifth session, pre- to post-therapy, post- to six-month follow-up, and six-month to one-year follow-up. To test whether each client changed on the SCL-90-R, TSCS, and Hamilton Depression and Anxiety Scales, Anastasi's (1982) formula was used. It corrects for measure reliability and uses the standard estimate of the difference between the two scores, treating pre- and post-scores as though they were different measures. The formula for determining the number of points necessary before we could say that change had occurred at the .05 (or .01, .001) level of significance was: 1.96 (or 2.58, 3.29) multiplied by (the standard deviation of scores in our sample) (square root of 2 minus 2 multiplied by the reliability of the measure). The index of reliability was the coefficient alpha if it was reported in the literature; if not available, split-half reliability or test-retest reliability was used. The number of points necessary for change at the .05, .01, and .001 levels on the SCL-90-R was 11, 15, and 19 points; on the TSCS was 8, 10, and 13 points; on the Hamilton Anxiety Scale was 5, 10, and 15 points; and on the Hamilton Depression Scale was 4, 9, and 12 points.

For the Target Complaints, an individualized change measure without traditional reliability data, change had to exceed the standard deviation of the sample. Thus, 3, 6, and 9 points were required for the .05, .01, and .001 levels respectively.

For the MMPI, change was considered to be 10 T score points. For outcome, I tabled the Depression and Psychasthenia scales since they were defined the target problems for our sample, as well as all scales with pre-therapy T scores > 70, and any other scales that changed significantly over treatment.

Analyses of Techniques

Separate analyses of variance were computed on therapist and client helpfulness ratings and client experiencing ratings to determine the impact of response modes for each case. When significant F values were found, post hoc analyses were used to determine differences between response modes.

Chi-square analyses (similar to sequential analyses) were used to determine whether response modes led systematically to client reactions for each case. When the chi square value was significant, cell chi square analyses were used to investigate which response modes led to which reactions, using an alpha of .05. For the present analyses, I considered the reactions of supported and therapeutic work as helpful, negative reactions as hindering, and challenged and no reaction as neutral.

To determine the most helpful and hindering events based on the post session reviews, I set an arbitrary cutoff of 5%, such that any given response mode was judged to be significantly helpful (or hindering) if it was recalled at least 5% of the time.

To determine the most helpful and hindering events recalled on the Client and Therapist Post Therapy Interviews, I simply counted all response modes that were mentioned at least once.

For a response mode to be considered as helpful and hindering in a particular case, that mode had to be significant in more than one of the eight different analyses.

PART II

CASE ANALYSES

3

Case 1: Men on Trial

"The heart has its reasons which reason does not understand."
Quote by client in session 14

This chapter will focus on the therapist techniques in the 20-session case conducted by Dr. A, a 47-year old, White, male psychologist with Sandy, a single, 35-year old Arabic woman.

Client

Sandy (a pseudonym) was the second born of two girls, with a sister who was one year older. Her family background was stormy and violent, with her parents fighting a lot between themselves and with her sister. She had a vivid recollection of an incident when she was sitting on her mother's lap when she was nine years old and her father hit her mother across the face without apparent provocation. Sandy described herself as the peacemaker, always trying to intervene in the fights. Sandy described her father, who was an administrative judge, as low key and easygoing on the outside, but tense on the inside. For the most part, he was affable, loving, and caring, but would occasionally and unpredictably have violent outbursts primarily directed at her mother. Her father was very close to his mother and would go to visit her in New England almost every weekend. Since Sandy's mother did not get along with his mother, she would not go along. Sandy felt torn apart by being forced to go with her father to New England and leaving her mother behind, typically after an abusive fight between her parents. Sandy's mother, a career woman, was described as outgoing, volatile, exciting, loving, accepting, and caring. Sandy said that her mother always gave her great support and much wisdom and love. She and her mother could disagree, blow up and scream and yell for a short period, but then they would resolve their fights and go back to being very close. Sandy's mother was very ill with rheumatoid arthritis from the time Sandy was about 12. She would spend up to six months at a time in the hospital. When Sandy was about 12, her dying grandmother also came to live with them and Sandy spent a great deal of time caring for her.

Sandy's sister had always been quite sullen and moody. Whereas Sandy had many friends, her sister had very few. In many ways, Sandy seemed more like the oldest whom everyone relied on. In fact, her parents often told her to take her sister along when she went out with her friends.

When Sandy was in high school, her father had a big fight with her sister and hit her. Her sister moved out for a month until the father decided to leave. Once the father left, his relationship with Sandy was very limited. He would occasionally have Sandy and her sister meet him and his friends at a fancy restaurant for dinner, but rarely did she have any time alone with him.

After graduating from college with a psychology major, Sandy spent several years in Vista as a community organizer and community college teacher. Her Vista career was very satisfying and stimulating to Sandy, filling her with idealism and energy to make the world a better place.

At 24 years of age, Sandy returned to the Washington area to take care of her mother right before she died. Having completed her Vista work, she was at a crossroads and had to decide on a career path. While in Vista, she realized that the people who had the power to make the decisions were lawyers. Because she wanted to have an impact on society, she decided to go to law school. Following law school, her father got her a clerkship in a law firm, where she was currently employed as an associate.

Sandy had dated in high school and college, but unlike many of her friends, had no desire to get married right after college. Since college, she had been in three long-term relationships with warm, caring, passive, unambitious men. Her pattern was that she would be attracted to these creative men, but after awhile she would get bored and break off the relationship.

Physical Functioning

Sandy reported health concerns of severe, constant muscle aches in her jaw, neck, shoulders, and back, for which she took aspirin and penicillin. Occasionally, her knee would swell up making it difficult for her to move. She had been inaccurately diagnosed at one point as having rheumatoid arthritis, of which her mother had died. Over the years, she had undergone surgery for tonsillectomy, deviated septum, appendectomy, and removal of fallopian tubes, and had also severely cut both hands walking through a sliding glass door, broken a toe, and broken a foot. Sandy did not always eat breakfast and dinner, drank a lot of coffee, sometimes used marijuana, and only occasionally exercised.

Pre-Therapy Expectations

Sandy had never been in therapy before. She thought therapy was for learning about yourself, discovering patterns, identifying problems and growth, and that a therapist should aid a client without having the client become dependent. She expected a therapist to be compassionate, honest, and respectful with good analytical skills and that the therapist would provide feedback and insight in an open, non-threatening environment.

Pre-Therapy Assessment

Sandy's scores on the pre-therapy assessment measures are shown in Table 3.3. On the MMPI, Sandy had normal validity scores and high scores on the Depression, Psychasthenia, and Paranoia scales. This MMPI profile was normal, indicating depression and anxiety with self-devaluation, intropunitiveness, and nervousness, as well as suggesting that she was sensitive and easily hurt, with complaints about other's shortcomings. Sandy's score on the Masculinity-Femininity scale was low ($T = 33$), which is typical of women who are passive, submissive, yielding, and demure. Sandy's behavior and her occupational choice did not demonstrate this stereotyped feminine pattern, but the results suggested that she may have had an underlying conflict about femininity.

Sandy's scores on symptomatology and self-esteem were about average for an outpatient population. She was functioning at an average level on her target complaints. The clinician judged her to be moderately anxious and depressed.

Consequently, Sandy was diagnosed by the research team as having a generalized anxiety disorder.

Target Complaints

Sandy's first complaint was that she did not currently have a good relationship with a man. Her second complaint was her professional identity. She felt that much of the work she did as a lawyer was routine and boring. She was expected to do most of the immigration work and felt isolated from the other lawyers. Further, she did not particularly like her male bosses. Sandy had not yet attained partner status and was not sure she wanted to remain in the law profession.

Her third complaint was her relationship with her roommate, a friend whom she had known since childhood. Communication had become very difficult. They were not able to have any open, honest discussion and resentments were building on both sides.

Summary of Client Pre-Therapy Characteristics

Sandy was likable, able to form a relationship, articulate, bright, and motivated to change. She was in some psychological pain, but her complaints were vague and mild. She had many bodily complaints, suggesting that she diverted her anxieties into symptomatology. She was insight-oriented, with a desire to understand who she was and where she was headed. Further, Sandy was functioning well in her job.

Therapist

After receiving his PhD in clinical psychology, Dr. A was on the faculty at a medical school for ten years. At the time of the study, he was an associate professor in clinical psychology with a specialty in marital and sex therapy. He had 19 journal articles and a book in progress. Further, Dr. A was very active and well-known for his contributions to professional psychology in both the state and national psychological organizations.

Dr. A was licensed, listed in the National Register of Health Service Providers in Psychology, and had a diploma from the American Board of Examiners in Professional Psychology in clinical psychology. Dr. A maintained an active private practice, seeing both individuals and couples between the ages of 15 and 55 years who were neurotic or had personality disorders. Brief therapy was his treatment of choice.

Using three 5-point (5 = high) scales for how much he believed in and adhered to each of three major orientations, Dr. A rated himself: psychoanalytic = 3, humanistic = 2, and behavioral = 4. In a written presentation of his theory, Dr. A stated:

> Behavior results from interactions between people and their environments. People consist of their current psychological (based partly on their prior learning experiencing) and biological states. Their environments consist of the meaning of particular situations to them, their active attempts to select or change these situations, and the "real" stimulus situation. Because I view our most important environments to be other people, I think of myself as an interpersonal theorist and therapist.
>
> People develop behavioral, cognitive, and/or affective styles, based on learning experiences over their lifespan and on the needs to maintain self-esteem and to protect against insecurity/anxiety (Sullivan, 1953). We can think of these styles as personality, which is a series of strategies based on maintaining self-esteem, a positive self-image, and freedom from anxiety/insecurity. We work within the limits of our styles to express our needs and to have them met. To maintain our preferred styles, we select, negotiate, and coerce others to play needed, complementary roles. People differ from one another in terms of the nature, the extremity, and the flexibility of their styles, so that some people have more flexibility to find complementary partners than others and to respond adequately and comfortably with a wide range of people.
>
> Individuals can also have a variety of skill deficits, such as not being able to communicate directly, not being able to manage conflict, having difficulty negotiating and bargaining with others, or not listening to others effectively. All these skill deficits may lead to troublesome interpersonal relationships. I intervene at the level of attempting to teach skills if a person is in a skill deficit situation rather than having some intrapsychic problem interfering with ability to use skills already present.

At the level of individual transactions, I have been very impressed with Lazarus' (1976) concept of the BASIC ID. In response to his or her environment, one has certain cognitions, images, affects, sensations, all of which may be affected or modified by one's biological state. These elements occur in a sequence which leads to behaviors in the interpersonal field. Anything which changes the intervening structure (e.g., affects) will end up changing the "pathological" behavior. The therapist intervenes at any place where he or she has skills and/or where the client can allow an intervention to take place.

Additionally, the individual needs to change perspectives through some sort of reframing, which changes the "situation" with a consequent change in behavior. One way that change occurs is for a particular sequence of cognitions, affects, etc., to be broken up and lead to different behaviors. Another way is for the individual to be forced into using an unfamiliar style which has some environmental payoff and thus may be rewarded and repeated.

The person's biological state is also important with respect to general physical health, the diet and exercise regime, and cognitive capacity. My approach is to refer people for help with the biological problems, but I help them recognize how their life styles can impact on both physical and psychological well being, and help them accept biological limitations imposed on them.

Treatment Process

The verbatim excerpt from the first few minutes of the first session illustrates the process between Sandy and Dr. A.

T: I don't know how much she told you and what your expectations are about being here and what we're going to do. Maybe we could start with that. And then I could tell you what I think. So we'll make sure we're . . .

C: Okay. Basically she told me that there would be 12 to 20 sessions (T: MmHmm) and that um we would just be working on problems that I had id- identified in my qu- questionnaire. (T: MmHmm) And that's about all I know. (T: Yeah) And also that there would be videotaping and to go over questionnaires before and after the videotaping (T: Right) and then go through the videotape and, and answer questions about my reactions to things that you've said.

T: MmHmm. Did she tell you anything about me or about who you'd be seeing or . . .

C: I asked her. She told me who, she, she gave me your name (T: MmHmm) and I said, "well who is he?" (C laughs) (T: Okay) (T laughs) And uh she told me that you're a professor here at the university (T: Right) and that uh there was a selection panel for all the therapists, a nominating panel (T: MmHmm) for all the therapists involved and that you were one of the therapists that was nominated and that you, that you were a very good therapist. (T: MmHmm) That's all I know about you.

T: Okay. Do you want me to give you the nickel version of me?

C: Yes, I would. That would be nice.

T: Okay. I'm a clinical psychologist. And uh, uh I work, I do work here full time. I also have a, a practice of probably about a day a week. I see individual clients and also see couples uh for marital therapy and some for sexual therapy, worked in a medical school setting for about ten years and then came here in 1972 and been here and teach graduate and undergraduate courses, these sorts of things. (C: MmHmm) Uh, I'll also give you a card in case you need to get ahold of me (C: Oh, all right) at any time. (C: Okay) Any questions about me that you've got?

C: Uh, well I, I'll tell you my first reaction. (T: Okay) My first reaction was when they said that uh, they told me your name, my, my reaction was, "oh, it's a guy" (both laugh) like yuck.

T: You, you're disappointed that it's a man.

C: Well, I'm not disappointed, you know, I just thought, you know, it would probably be a woman because I met [the researcher] and I, I liked, I liked her. (T: MmHmm) We had a nice conversation (T: MmHmm) when we were sitting there. And I'm not disappointed. But uh I think that I, I don't know, I was won-, I was asking myself "well do you think you would relate better to a woman," (T: MmHmm) because I feel very strongly and close, closer to women (T: MmHmm, MmHmm) than I do men. (T: MmHmm) But I don't know, I don't think it'll affect my relationship with you.

T: Hmm. In some ways then, it may be a problem in us relating. On the other hand, it may also give us the opportunity to work on some things. (C: Right, exactly. That's what I thought.) Well, let's keep that open and if, if that's a problem and let's, let's see how that goes.

C: I'll tell you if it's a problem, believe me. (C laughs)

T: Good, okay. Uh, I'm going to take notes as I go (C: Okay) and the reason I do that is because I like to have a chance before the next session to look back over what I've done and what we've talked about and so forth and sort of get, get my, get my head straight. (C: Okay). I won't

be able to take any notes in the sessions afterwards and so forth. So can
you tell me how come you're here and what's going on and all those
sorts of things?

This segment provides a good illustration of Dr. A's approach to
psychotherapy. He was very structured and wanted to let the client
know exactly who he was and what to expect from therapy. He
clearly established that he was going to take the lead and direct the
content of the sessions, rather than waiting for the client to decide
what to talk about. The segment also provided a good illustration of
Sandy's capacity for dealing with the relationship. She immediately
brought up her discomfort about being assigned to a male therapist
and indicated her willingness to examine her reactions to men.

Summary of Process

The first few sessions were devoted to an assessment of Sandy's
target complaints and family background. Dr. A did this assessment
to build an agenda about which issues they could deal with in the
therapy. Five themes predominated throughout the therapy: relationship with her roommate and sister, physical complaints, relationships
with men, job, and family. Strands of each of these themes were
discussed throughout the course of therapy, with one or two becoming the focus of each session.

The first major problem that the dyad dealt with was Sandy's
relationships with her sister and roommate. Her sister would call up
and ask for advice, but would get angry and hang up when Sandy
would tell her what to do. Likewise, her roommate was constantly
feeling angry and put upon by Sandy, even though they were good
friends. By using his own experience with Sandy and hearing her
descriptions of her interactions with these two people, Dr. A confronted Sandy with her tendency to not express her own feelings and
to take over and control people. Even though they seemed to ask for
advice, Dr. A suggested that what they actually wanted was a sym-
pathetic listening ear and for Sandy to share her feelings. He related
Sandy's position in her family as the person who always took care
of everyone to her current problems in taking care of others but not
letting anyone take care of her. When Sandy was able to follow
Dr. A's suggestions of listening and telling her feelings rather than

taking over, she began to have better relations wit
and roommate.

The next major area that the dyad worked on was San
ships with men. Although Sandy said that she wanted
relationship with a man, she got bored and broke off all re_   ..ps
after a period of time. They spent many sessions explor..g what
happened in each of the previous major relationships. Dr. A suggested that rather than bored, Sandy was actually enraged that she
did not get her needs met. As with her relationships with her female
friends, Sandy tended to take care of her boyfriends, helping them
in their careers. Her previous boyfriends all said that they had grown
a lot with her help. The end result of most of the discussions in
therapy on men was a feeling of being "stuck," which frustrated both
Dr. A and Sandy. After a number of sessions talking about men,
Sandy reported that she felt very depressed and irritable, feelings she
had rarely experienced and which were very uncomfortable.

They also discussed issues related to work. Sandy was feeling
isolated because she had been assigned to work on immigration
cases. Since no one else in her large firm had that specialty, she had
no mentors or advocates to advance her cause to get partnership. As
the only woman, she was treated as inconsequential in the office. She
sounded burned out and talked of wanting to take a year off to find
herself. One of her frustrations was that none of the men she had been
involved with made enough money to support her if she wanted to
drop out. Through therapy, Sandy learned that she needed to speak
up and tell the senior partners what she needed, rather than assuming
they would take care of her. She also started exploring other options,
such as going to school for massage therapy.

Another major theme in therapy was exploring Sandy's physical
complaints. Given her history of somatic complaints, Dr. A urged her
to go for a check-up. This caused considerable dissension from
Sandy, since she had experienced numerous hassles in her interactions with medical doctors before and had turned almost completely
to holistic medicine, acupuncture, and massage. She did eventually
go to a doctor referred by the research team, but as before got no
conclusive diagnoses on her physical complaints. Further, given her
complaints about soreness in her jaw from grinding her teeth, Dr. A
recommended relaxation exercises which Sandy already knew how
to do. During each session, he monitored how often she had been
doing the relaxation.

nally, a minor theme was discussing the family of origin. Although Sandy presented quite a bit of information about the family in the initial sessions, Dr. A did not integrate the family material with the present complaints except in the sixteenth session when Dr. A asked more about her father. Hearing about her father, Dr. A said that Sandy probably wouldn't want to have a relationship with someone like her father. Sandy agreed, saying why would anyone want to be around someone who beats you and is never around and gives you a hard time and shows off. In the next session, she felt sad and angry.

The final two sessions were spent in termination and thoroughly processing how Sandy had changed through therapy.

Client Behavior

Sandy came in well-prepared for each session with something specific to talk about. She was active and involved and articulate about her concerns. Her style was to explain a situation or problem in a story-telling fashion, giving a blow-by-blow description of what each person said. Sandy was more used to dealing with issues rationally rather than emotionally and had difficulty expressing her feelings. She was quite willing to deal with problems in the therapy relationship, however, and confronted the therapist when she was unhappy with things that he had done.

During the videotape reviews, she took notes so that she could remember what was said. In between sessions, she tried things that the therapist suggested and reported back on the results.

Therapist Behavior

For response modes, Dr. A used primarily information, paraphrase, and closed question. Compared to the other therapists, he used less interpretation. Dr. A was average in activity level. His style was oriented to assessing and solving problems.

Dr. A was casual and friendly, with a good sense of humor. He typically had an agenda of things he wanted to cover during a session, for example asking about her homework, but he also asked Sandy to add things to the agenda. He took notes and structured what should occur during sessions. He processed the relationship and the treatment thoroughly, asking her what she wanted to accomplish and how she felt about what they were doing in treatment.

Analyses of Therapist Techniques

Sandy and Dr. A talked about their reactions to the therapist techniques in the post-therapy interviews:

R: *What did Dr. A (or you) do to help changes come about?*

C: Therapy helped me change in the sense that the idea of coming in to talk to somebody weekly about issues that are causing you discomfort in your life allows me, if I choose to take it, the freedom to really try to explore in myself what that means and where it comes from. With the therapist giving me some prodding here, some suggestions here, some techniques here, allows your mind to receive it and to open up and use it in new ways that you haven't seen or used before, so that your concept of life becomes more open and you become more aware of what is going on with you. It's almost like putting yourself under a microscope and not being afraid to see what is there and saying this is an adventure for me and I'm going to use it to the best of my ability and I'll fall off the cliff and take the chance of feeling miserable because in that process is growth for you. It's not like you can come in and have somebody tell you what is the matter and solve your problems. I found myself becoming impatient, but then realized that you're not going to get there unless you go through the process. That's what therapy did for me. It allowed me the opportunity to explore. It gave me ways of looking at things that I hadn't looked at before. It gave me feedback about myself I hadn't known in an exchange where somebody wasn't telling me this is the answer. *I'm not hearing you say that the relationship helped you change. What do you think about that?* You can come in and say anything and that person is going to accept you no matter what you say. That does create the freedom for you to feel more comfortable, to explore because you have a partner that is there so that if you start to feel like you're falling off a cliff or too painful, this other person is there to hold your hand or bring you back to a certain sense of confidence. I don't know whether I'm minimizing the relationship, but I felt that it was more facilitative of allowing these other things to happen.

T: With the physical symptomatic changes, she went to a physician and a massage therapist and her level of tension decreased over time. She already knew how to do relaxation, so I renewed that and she was doing it at some point three or four times a week. So these things were helpful to her. *What was your part in that?* Defining it as a problem that we could work on in here and getting her motivated to actually do something about it. *What about the self-concept changes?* The process of therapy may have been helpful somewhat. She and I stood toe to toe a little bit and went after some things. My guess is that she feels she came out of that pretty well, that we liked and respected each other, and that there was a sense of really working on her problems. She probably feels pretty good about herself and what she could understand and the amount of work that she's willing and able to do on her problems. *So it wasn't just the relationship, but the process of dealing with issues in the relationship.* Right, I can't separate that from the relationship. The relationship was a working relationship. It wasn't just because we liked each other. I don't think that would have done anything. It was the process by which we both explored problems and she said some things she found very unattractive about herself. She also said some things about me that were relatively unattractive, but we worked with those things and didn't get overwhelmed by them. It was the engaging of one another, rather than my being accepting. She had some successes, with her sister and roommate and co-workers, which were helpful. She also narrowed down her sources of discontent with her job, which gave her an understanding about the specifics and made her feel that she had more of a handle on things. So there was a sense of internality, of her feeling more of a sense of self-mastery. *The interpersonal changes?* Part of that is skill change—communication, owning. *Did you directly teach that, is that how that came about?* A little bit, yeah. Also there was some insight involved in her recognizing her maternal, mediating role. *Well, you directly interpreted that.* Right, and she bought it, but not originally. We laughed about that some. She began to see that she was taking a very controlling role. She's probably a little less controlling at this point and more willing to see herself as somebody also who's needy and is not necessarily in that kind of superior role, at least with women. I don't know about men. With work, I think there was a sense of, through both interpretation and self-exploration, really coming up with specific factors that bothered her. The whole idea of not being compatible with the people traced back to her relationship with men to some extent and began to close a circle in terms of relationships with men, her family and the people at work. We didn't really deal at that level with her history.

R: *What did Dr. A (or you) do best with you (or Sandy)?*

C: Argued, in the sense of I could tell him something and he wouldn't shoot back with a statement, but would be more expansive or low key. He could have pushed me more. If he wanted to be bolder, it would have been all right. It was also helpful when he asked me how I felt and what things meant. It's easy to make a broad statement, but when you're asked about specifics about it, it really challenges you and causes you to think about what you're trying to say that is causing you to feel this way or to say that. I felt like he was pretty probing in a very low-key way.

T: Persistence. I developed a sort of focus and stayed with it. I was also useful to her in terms of knowing some things about interpersonal relating and teaching her those specific skills. Another thing had to do with being able to ride with where she was and try to keep her moving, but not get terribly discouraged or upset with her if she wouldn't go where I wanted her to go.

R: *Can you remember any specific therapist interpretations?*

C: At the beginning it happened with regard to being poised because he said it a few times and it was surprising to me. He said "you come across so poised that people don't know what you have to say." I thought about that a lot because I never viewed myself like that and I thought every-body always knew what I was saying. Also, when he asked me that question "What do you like about men?" because I couldn't think of anything to say. It sticks with me because it was such a simple, unas-suming question. But thinking about it was much more difficult and trying to answer it was extremely difficult. And going around talking to everybody else I know about it was even more exciting and I'm still asking the question. It has sparked a lot of interest and fun for me.

T: One had to do with her acting like a mother. That may have helped her redefine her relationship with her roommate and her sister. Also, the question about, "Is there anything good about men?" It was a challeng-ing question for her and shook her up and began to have her thinking in some different ways. Tying her job satisfaction to compatibility with men was probably helpful too.

R: *What did the therapist (or you) do least well?*

C: I think feedback. I felt the need to hear him say more about how he was viewing me and what was going on for him and how he saw me and what he heard me say. I also felt like I wanted him to put things together more, to tell me how he's put it together so I could react to it and agree or disagree, because it's more stimulating. I get stuck and I don't know any place to go with it and it's frustrating to hear him say "I'm stuck too." Not that he has to have all the answers, but . . .

T: Engaging her feeling-wise and us developing a really close, intimate relationship. I tend to be very task-focused and she tends to be very task-focused, so in that sense it was compatible for both of us. I think if I had been more feeling-oriented, and if we had managed to meet more affectively, that might have been helpful for her. I don't feel I did that very well. I don't think I did much with catharsis or hope.

Comment. The amount of agreement between the therapist and client in the post-therapy interviews was striking.

Quantitative Analyses

Table 3.1 shows the results of analyses for therapist response modes on the immediate outcome measures. Table 3.2 shows the codings of the post-session reviews. Both Dr. A and Sandy were very positive about the therapy, attributing most of the helpful events to therapist techniques.

Combining the results of the post-therapy interviews with the quantitative analyses shows that the most helpful techniques were open question, direct guidance, paraphrase, interpretation, approval, confrontation, and self-disclosure, whereas closed questions were not as helpful.

Discussion of Helpful Techniques

Open question. Sandy found it to be particularly helpful when Dr. A probed into how she felt and what she meant. The following excerpt from the 18th session presents an open question mentioned by both Sandy and Dr. A as being extremely helpful for forcing Sandy to confront herself:

> T: So one of the questions that that sort of brings up is that in a man, what do you need?
>
> C: That's a good question. I don't know. I don't really know. (Pause = 5 seconds) In a s-, I you know, I think about that. And you go, okay, well what do you need? And you say, well, I really don't need anything. But (C laughs) practically speaking seems like they're big headaches. But uh (C laughs)

Direct guidance. Direct guidance within the session, mostly involving structuring, was helpful for keeping Sandy on a particular topic and providing a plan for the 20 sessions. Advice for outside the session was helpful, especially in Dr. A's suggestions for Sandy to do relaxation exercises, practice communication skills, and monitor her behavior with others. Sandy consistently tried the various things that Dr. A suggested.

Table 3.1 Proportion of Occurrence, Client Helpfulness Ratings, Therapist Helpfulness Ratings, Client Experiencing, and Client Reactions for Therapist Response Modes in Case 1

Response Modes	%	Client Help Rating		Therapist Help Rating		Client Experiencing		Most Likely Reaction
		M	SD	M	SD	M	SD	
Approval	.09	7.10	1.44 B	5.76	.69 AB	2.53	.80 AB	Supported
Information	.24	6.88	1.48 BC	5.68	.68 AB	2.35	.69 B	Ther. Work
Direct Guidance	.04	6.92	1.44 BC	5.77	.61 AB	2.32	.67 B	
Closed Question	.20	6.63	1.46 C	5.75	.58 AB	2.33	.65 B	Negative No Reaction
Open Question	.11	7.28	1.48 AB	5.80	.64 A	2.63	.82 A	Ther. Work Challenged
Paraphrase	.23	7.35	1.41 AB	5.67	.64 AB	2.49	.77 AB	Supported
Interpretation	.04	7.74	1.34 A	5.76	.81 AB	2.51	.82 AB	
Confrontation	.03	7.29	1.35 AB	5.55	.75 B	2.31	.63 B	
Disclosure	.02	7.62	1.50 A	5.58	.78 AB	2.54	.79 AB	
TOTAL		7.06	1.45	5.71	.66	2.43	.73	

NOTE: Helpfulness was rated on 9-point scales (9 = extremely helpful); experiencing was rated on a 7-point scale (7 = high). ANOVAs indicated significant differences between therapist response modes for client helpfulness, $F_{(8, 2542)} = 14.24$, $p < .0001$, therapist helpfulness, $F_{(8, 2542)} = 2.57$, $p < .01$, and client experiencing, $F_{(8, 2542)} = 6.83$, $p < .0001$. Post hoc differences are indicated, such that response modes with the same letter (A-C) were not significantly different (A = highest ratings). The overall relationship between response modes and client reactions was significant, $X_2 (28) = 263.72$, $p < .0001$.

Paraphrase. Paraphrase, particularly focusing and clarifying what Sandy said, was helpful. Additionally, reflecting feelings was quite important for Sandy because she was not adept at recognizing her feelings. For example, Dr. A suggested that she was enraged rather than bored in her relationships with her friends. Many of the reflections were about anger, an emotion that Sandy was not comfortable with because of her father's violence when she was younger.

Table 3.2 Proportions of Helpful and Hindering Events in Post-Session Reviews in Case 1

	Client		Therapist	
	Helpful	Hindering	Helpful	Hindering
Therapist Techniques	.32	.15	.36	.03
Support	.02	.00	.06	.00
Direct Guidance	.05	.08	.08	.02
Closed Question	.00	.00	.00	.00
Open Question	.02	.01	.04	.00
Paraphrase	.07	.00	.09	.02
Interpretation	.06	.04	.03	.00
Confrontation	.03	.01	.06	.00
Disclosure	.05	.00	.01	.00
Therapist Manner	.19	.01	.14	.04
Client Tasks	.17	.01	.18	.02
Focus	.02	.00	.03	.01
Experiencing	.09	.00	.05	.01
Insight	.06	.01	.04	.00
Changes	.00	.00	.06	.00
Client Manner	.04	.02	.12	.02
Relationship/Alliance	.09	.00	.08	.01
TOTAL	.81	.19	.88	.12

Interpretation. One interpretation that was mentioned as quite helpful was when Dr. A reframed Sandy's behavior with her sister as maternal and suggested that she was this way because that was the role she had played in her family of origin. Thus, Sandy always took care of everyone else, at the same time acting as if she needed no one to take care of her. Because this behavior was so engrained, Sandy had been unaware that she came across this way and that it made others, particularly her sister and roommate, angry at her. This interpretative theme was brought up several times during the therapy and applied to a number of different relationships, so that Sandy was able to see how her behavior in many situations was putting people off. Sandy valued such insights and wished that Dr. A had helped her "put things together" more.

Approval. Approval was helpful in allowing Sandy to feel free to explore herself in a nonthreatening setting. Dr. A would reinforce Sandy for her courage in exploring difficult areas.

Confrontation. Confrontation and feedback about behavior were helpful in providing Sandy with information about how she came across. She seemed unaware of how others viewed her and valued hearing about how she affected others since her behaviors contributed to her problems in relationships. Additionally, Sandy wished Dr. A had confronted her more. A good example that was mentioned repeatedly as helpful occurred in the fifth session:

C: You asked me about not connecting with people. (T: Right) So I was thinking about that and I, I, I asked my friends about it (T: MmHmm) too because I talk to them about therapy. And I got some real good feedback. And, and I, I, I didn't think that I felt not connected with people. (T: MmHmm, MmHmm) But in discussing it with my friends, I don't feel like I'm not *not* connected to, to people. I think what I feel like is, I feel like I'm real connected to people, but I feel isolated in the sense that I don't get a lot of feedback from people. I don't get any feedback, I think mostly on my job I don't get feedback. And I don't really get too much feedback from my friends. (T: MmHmm) And I think that what may be, may be something that you might have been sensing (T: MmHmm) that I had, was just taking a look at (T: MmHmm) for myself, I mean because I didn't know it till I started talking to my friends about it. And we had a good exchange back (T: MmHmm) and forth and got some feedback from them.

T: Yeah, what and what, when you talk about feedback, I'm not sure exactly what that means in terms of your not getting feedback.

C: Well, I mean like you don't, yeah, I, I feel, and I've felt this way for, for I'd say, for a couple of years now. And I think a lot of it stemmed from work. I don't get any feedback about whether you're doing a good job or you're not doing a good (T: MmHmm) job at work, uh how they, how they view you. (T: MmHmm) You know (T: MmHmm) and the same with my friends, I mean I know that they like me and I have a lot of friends. Um, but I don't really get any, "Hey Sandy, you know, you're doing a good job" (T: MmHmm, MmHmm) or you know you're, you're, I don't feel like I get anything. (T: MmHmm) I feel like I get a lot out (T: MmHmm) and they, my friends agreed with me. I mean that, that was their suggestion. They said, "well, you know, you really give a lot out" (T: MmHmm, MmHmm) "and maybe what you, you might sense is that you don't really feel like you get a lot back." (T: MmHmm, MmHmm) Does that make sense? Is that (T: Yeah) somewhat clearer to you?

T: Yeah, let me tell, you know there's something that, that, that keys into in, in me, that o-, one of the things I guess that I've experienced with you is that you, you are so poised and so articulate. And it may be related to your style. It may be related to your family or it may be related to job training (C: MmHmm) in terms of, cause I assume that as an attorney you learn to be pretty direct and forthright. But for, for whatever, for wherever that came from, that a lot of times I, I hear you talking about things that you describe sort of as problems, but it's hard for me to experience those in some ways as problems so much because they're presented in such a forceful, direct, sort of way. (C: MmHmm) And I guess I don't, I don't experience much of your vulnerabilities. (C: MmHmm) And I don't know whether, so in that sense, it's sort of hard. It, it it's hard for me to, to, to give and to sort of (C: Yeah) say, it's hard for me to hear that you need.

C: You know it's interesting you mentioned the poise because that's something I noticed about myself looking at the videotape. (T: Mm-Hmm) I mean if anybody were to ask me to describe myself, poise would not have been one of the words I would have used, (T: Yes) but looking at the videotape, I do look poised.

The segment illustrates what Sandy meant by "feedback," how she used the videotape feedback, and how she checked out what Dr. A said by asking her friends how they felt about her behavior.

Self-disclosure. Self-disclosure was often beneficial in allowing open communication about the immediate relationship and in showing Sandy that Dr. A could be vulnerable. Dr. A used more disclosure than any other therapist, probably because of his interpersonal orientation (see Chapter 11). Although Sandy generally rated disclosures very highly, she did not like one specific disclosure when Dr. A told her that he was "stuck."

Discussion of Less Helpful Techniques

Closed question. Closed questions were consistently viewed as unhelpful. Dr. A gathered a lot of information, sometimes asking the same questions in successive sessions. For example, he asked a lot of details about Sandy's relationships with men, but was not able to use the information directly to help her in the session. He also asked a lot of questions about Sandy's physical functioning, which was not an expressed concern of hers for this therapy. Sandy said that she knew that Dr. A needed to know the information, but said it was boring to repeat the facts without exploring her feelings about them.

Process Issues

Dr. A was particularly good at dealing with Sandy's problems related to her sister and roommate. Sandy may have been motivated to work on these relationships because she had a lot of immediate difficulty dealing with these people in her everyday life. Perhaps another reason that treatment in these areas was effective was because they fit into Dr. A's preferred style of solving specific problems and understanding interpersonal interactions.

Two issues that Dr. A was not as successful in dealing with during treatment were Sandy's concerns about men and her concerns about her career. In the post-therapy interview, Sandy mentioned that both issues were related to her relationship with her father. Dr. A did give one interpretation relating Sandy's reluctance to get involved with men with her reactions to her father. Although this interpretation was explored only minimally, it seemed to fit for Sandy. Perhaps more exploration of her feelings about her father and her parent's relationship would have been helpful.

On the other hand, Sandy may not have been motivated to change in the areas of her career and relationships with men or on the job because she did not have a great deal of pain. She was mildly dissatisfied and unhappy but not in severe distress or crisis so she had no precipitating stress to impel her to change. Given that Sandy was not in a current relationship with a man, she was more unhappy with what she did not have rather than struggling in an untenable relationship. Likewise, in her job, Sandy was earning a decent salary and was competent. So even though she was dissatisfied, she had no current crises to deal with.

Moderating Variables

Therapist Factors

Dr. A was an experienced and caring therapist. His warmth, sensitivity, and sense of humor were particularly important given the client's difficulty in relating to men. In the post-session reviews, both persons indicated that the therapist's manner was helpful, but it was not mentioned as being helpful as often as were his techniques. Dr. A's use of techniques was undoubtedly influenced by his preference for using a problem-solving approach. However, he was also able to be flexible in using more of an insight-oriented approach to fit what Sandy wanted from therapy.

Client Factors

Sandy was motivated, involved, insightful, attractive, and likable. She worked hard at the task of therapy, both within the sessions and outside of therapy. She was extremely articulate, but more rational and intellectualizing rather than being aware of and expressing her immediate feelings. She diverted her anxieties into physical symptoms and was thus not in a great deal of psychological pain. Despite some existential unhappiness, however, she was functioning adequately in her life. Thus, perhaps because she was functioning at a pretty high level, Sandy was particularly receptive to high level therapist interventions such as interpretation and confrontation.

The Relationship

Scores on the WAI (see Chapter 2, Table 2.2) indicated that Sandy viewed the working alliance as very weak in the first few sessions, but as improving to a moderate level by the end of therapy. Dr. A's WAI scores indicated that he found the working alliance to be moderately strong throughout therapy.

Two questions from the post-therapy interviews shed light on the participants' views of the relationship.

R: *If a close friend were entering therapy with Dr. A and asked you to describe him, what would you say?*

C: I would feel very comfortable for them to do it. They would have the opportunity to come into an atmosphere with a man that was not going to be overpowering and would listen and have an understanding of what they were going through. His manner is very laid back and he's easy to talk to. He's not defensive. If it was a woman, I would definitely say that you could say anything you wanted to say.

R: *How would you (therapist) describe your relationship with Sandy?*

T: There was a sense of fondness about my feelings for her and I think her feelings about me. But there was also a distance between us in that our boundaries never merged. Sometimes I think she felt really close to me, but I think a lot of the times it was really clear that we were two separate individuals. We were working on her problems in an affectionate, at times humorous, context. But there was a sense of challenge that stayed there through the time.

Things began on a tense note for this relationship, as illustrated in the excerpt from the first session when Sandy told Dr. A that she was not sure she could relate to a male. They spent the first five sessions in a power struggle over who would control the therapy. Dr. A described it as "circling" or trying to negotiate whether they could work together. Perhaps the critical factor here was that the therapist discussed their differences openly and asked the client how she felt about all aspects of the treatment. Further, Sandy was able to interact with a man who was warm, caring, and empathic, yet, unlike her previous boyfriends, still strong. Dr. A was able to listen to her criticisms of men without becoming too defensive.

One interesting aspect of this dyad was their ability to negotiate. The client entered therapy wanting to have greater insight into her problems, whereas the therapist had a problem-solving orientation. He expressed early on that he wished she had more specific problems to deal with, rather than her vague complaints and wishes to understand herself more. They were able, however, to negotiate a stance whereby Dr. A tried to be more insight-oriented and Sandy was able to present some problems that were more clear-cut, for example her relationship with her sister. Although neither was able to do or get exactly what he or she wanted, they were each able to value what the other had to offer.

Further, they were a good match in many ways. Both liked to process their relationship thoroughly. Had Dr. A unilaterally decided what they were to do or taken a passive stance, Sandy would probably have been angry and battled with him. Because they processed the relationship, however, there were few secrets between them and they were clear on where they stood with each other.

In sum, Dr. A and Sandy were able to develop a warm, friendly working relationship that allowed them to work on some specific tasks within therapy, although they did not become very close. In discussing the effects of the relationship on the process of the therapy, both Dr. A and Sandy remarked that the relationship was crucial as a foundation, but that it was the specific therapist techniques that led to change. As Sandy said, the relationship created the freedom for her to explore because she had a partner who could hold her hand or bring her back if she started to feel like she was falling off a cliff. Thus, she felt that the relationship was facilitative of allowing other things to happen.

External Factors

Extratherapy involvement. Questions asked in the post-therapy interviews indicated that Sandy was actively engaged in working on her issues outside of therapy:

R: *How did you (or Sandy) use the therapy between sessions?*

C: I would go out and talk about it. I would tell my friends about it. I got a lot of feedback from them about what they thought, especially from one friend who's a social worker. She was real comforting in, "you're really going through a lot and learning a lot and you should be proud of yourself that you're going through this because it's not easy." So that was real helpful. She also said "Your therapist is probably having a real good time with you." I'd never thought about that. So she would give me a lot back that I would not have thought about myself. I really felt that not only did I have my therapy here, but when I came out and would come back and tell people, I would get even more feedback. So I felt like it was kind of an ongoing process even when I came home. And then I would take some of the things that I learned and try to use them so that it was kind of a snowball effect.

T: I think she worked her ass off between sessions. She tried out things we talked about. If I suggested things, she would go try it out or if I didn't suggest things to her she would often go out and ask people about things. She did a lot of bouncing off people, getting other people's opinions and really thinking about stuff.

Support network. Sandy had a wide support network. She was close to her sister and her sister's children and had a large circle of supportive female friends with whom she spent a lot of time. When the therapist gave her feedback about her behavior, she would ask her friends how they saw her. They would substantiate and expand on Dr. A's feedback, so that Sandy got validation from others in her environment. This undoubtedly had a facilitative effect on the process of therapy.

External events. This was a calm period within Sandy's life with no external events interfering with the process of therapy.

Outcome of Therapy

Session Outcome

Scores on the SEQ (see Chapter 2, Table 2.2) indicated that Sandy and Dr. A both viewed the sessions as being moderately deep and smooth.

Pre-Post Changes

Table 3.3 shows that Sandy was somewhat improved at the end of 20 sessions of treatment. On the MMPI, she was significantly improved on Depression, Hypochondriasis, and Social Introversion, with her MMPI profile completely within the normal range. Further, Sandy's symptomatology had decreased, her self-esteem had increased, she had improved in her relationship with her roommate, and was less anxious and depressed. She was unchanged in her relationships with men or in her professional identity issues.

In the post-therapy interviews excerpted below, the client and therapist agreed that Sandy changed most in her interpersonal relationships, with some changes in symptomatology and self-esteem.

R: *Did you (or the client) change in symptomatology?*

C: I felt a little less anxious, more of an internal at peace with yourself. I don't feel totally at peace with myself, but I feel like I'm less wired. I think my neck and my back feel better. *Any specific behavioral changes?* I can't think of any. *Self-concept changes?* I went through a few self-concept changes. In the middle of therapy, my self-concept was not very good. I was feeling very insecure, not attractive, not thinking

Table 3.3 Scores on Outcome Measures for Case 1

Measures	Pre	5th	Expect	Post	6 Mo	1 Year
Client-Rated Measures						
MMPI						
Depression	76			53**		
Psychasthenia	68			61		
Paranoia	65			59		
Hypochondriasis	62			50*		
Social Introversion	52			34*		
SCL-90-R GSI	50			37*	35	[42]
TSCS	43			55**	[51]	56
TC (1) Men	8	8	4	8	7	6
(2) Professional Identity	10	9	4	9	6*	[8]
(3) Roommate	9	[10]	2	2**	[3]	1
Satisfaction					8	8
Therapist-Rated Measures						
TC (1) Men	8		6	6		
(2) Professional Identity	10		5	8		
(3) Roommate	8		6	2**		
Researcher-Rated Measures						
Hamilton Anxiety	19			7**		
Hamilton Depression	18			4***		

NOTE: High T scores indicate high symptomatology on the SCL-90-R GSI, high self-esteem on the TSCS; worst functioning on the TC, higher satisfaction, and greater disturbance on the Hamilton scales. Expect = level expected after treatment. * = significant change at $p < .05$; ** = $p < .01$; *** = $p < .001$. Negative changes are in brackets.

I had anything important to say, not happy. Then I gradually started to feel better about myself and feel more grounded and realistic about who I am and in general feeling better and better self-concept from that period. *What do you mean by realistic?* I learned that it's okay to be angry. I never thought I was an angry person. I never wanted to say anything bad about anybody else. But the reality of life is that it's all right to be critical.

T: I don't know about her ability to concentrate, but she was waking up some at night and my guess is that she felt less sad and a little better about things, so that her depression is better. Also the physical things that she had probably lessened. *Any specific behavioral changes?* That overlaps a lot. Most of the things I think of as behavioral are also interpersonal. All we dealt with was interpersonal stuff, just about. *Self-Concept changes?* One of the problems she talked about at first was feeling negatively about herself. I have a feeling that she ended up feeling a little bit better about herself. I think the experience itself was one that she really tied into and probably felt good about how she did that. She saw the difficulty with the job as less of a personal failure on her part, and more a part of her differences with men and with these people, so my guess is she feels a little better about herself.

R: *Any changes in interpersonal relationships?*

C: In that one period I was fighting and having more tensions between myself and people. It was really disturbing because I had never felt that very much and I really didn't like the way I felt. But then I felt like at least I did talk about it, especially with the partners. That period was extremely critical and difficult and real uncomfortable. But I felt like I at least cracked the surface there in terms of how to relate to them. But now I see them in a different light too. With my sister, my relationship is much better and happier for both of us. A lot came from that one session when Dr. A said, "Well, do you want to be her mother?" I never thought of it like that. I thought I do sound just like her mother and I don't want to be her mother. And then having him say, "Have you ever told her how you really felt about it?" When I did tell her how I felt, it precipitated this horrible, uncomfortable thing for both of us. But from that point on, we've been able to relate on a better level. Also he said something about accepting people where they were. And it's true, you have to accept people where they are. You can't just expect them to be anything but what they are. And that really stuck out in my mind a lot. I feel like my relationship with [past roommate] has gotten more honest. I still have a problem talking to her sometimes like about the house. Other than that, I can say things I haven't been able to say before. My relationship with men is changing because I'm asking them this question about what is good about men and then having these conversations about it. So my relationships are more honest because right off the bat they know where I'm coming from. Not that I have any relationships going on right now, but just in general relationships. I think I would like to have a relationship but for the life of me I don't know why. *Have you changed with your father?* I've been clearer in trying to tell him how I feel.

T: There were a lot of things. It surprised me, but a lot of the therapy was really delving into that. First, she did some changing in her relationships, more with her sister than her roommate, but some with her roommate, where she was more direct, able to own and be non-attacking about the things she felt. Also, she played less of a maternal role, where she was able to either suggest things or ask for things rather than somehow being enormously protective and controlling. She's getting along better with her sister. Of course, she moved out with [roommate], so that's hard to tell, but it seemed to me she was getting along better with her also. In terms of her relationships with people at work, she probably always had done confronting, but I think probably her requests for help seemed to be much more direct and open, where she was willing to approach them in an open way rather than in a way where she was really angry. So she changed in some skill level things. In terms of her relationships with men, it's really hard to tell. She didn't hook up. So it's really hard for me to see that she made any specific behavioral changes there. But she certainly thought through and was really surprised by some of the things that she came up with. She got in touch with some of her negative feelings and her lack of positive feelings toward men. But whether that's going to affect her relationships with men is not clear to me.

R: *How satisfied are you with the nature and amount of change made in treatment?*

C: I feel pretty satisfied with it. I wish I had resolved these problems completely, but I also realize that it's unrealistic to believe that you could resolve these problems in 20 sessions.

T: I guess I would have liked her to change more. I'm glad she felt good about what happened. I would have liked there to be more definitive changes, but she didn't present the kind of symptomatology where there often are definitive changes. Where she presented it, fighting with her sister, neckaches, in fact she profited on. Where she presented, like not wanting to go to work, she still has a lot of concerns about. Her changes in that were understanding rather than behavioral changes. I would have liked to have gotten further with the relationship with men. I would have liked to have seen her hook up with a guy and be able for us to work through that. I also would like to have seen some more stuff done about work. In the time we had, I don't think we could have expected a great deal more change.

Sandy was also asked to talk about what caused and maintained one of her major problems. Her answer indicated that the therapy had helped her gain some insight that her difficulties in relating with men were a result of her family background.

C: I don't think I was ever willing to admit this before, but I think a lot of my problem in relationships with men does stem from my father, in the sense of just seeing this real physical brutality when we were growing up. And also always having him in a position to tell us what to do. My perspective of men, on the one side, was this real domineering force that could also flip out and become physically violent. But the other side of that, which is probably one of the sources of my confusion, is that he also is a real intelligent person and he is real low key and humble. And also when I argued with my father, I could not yell. He won't talk to you if you yell at him. So you had to sit down and have a conversation with him and articulate the problem. Also he was very loving, a real unconditional love that he did give amidst all that confusion and violence. He always gave us the feeling that "I am there for you and I love you." But it was confusing because he wasn't there a lot and because of all the other things that happened. *What about your mother?* She was always the domineering factor in raising us. She was always extremely aggressive. She was always there. She took care of us. She always gave us this sense of comfort and security even when she didn't know herself where her next dollar was coming from or whether she would even be here because she was so sick. She was protective but she was free enough that she would let you lead your own life. There wasn't a strong sense of discipline. It was more self-imposed. You knew that if you didn't come home at a certain time that was going to be a problem and you didn't want to disappoint her. There was a real close relationship with her because she provided support and understanding and caring and assurance. My feelings about women are clearer to me because she was always the stronger one for us and we could always lean on her and she was always there and she was fun and she was exciting and she was stylish and she was just a real whiz. She was just one of these real special people. It was like these two people were really wonderful people, but there was a lot of confusion and sorrow and pain. But there was also a lot of wonderfulness and security and stability and love. So I can see that in terms of my relationships with men that my ideals are extremely high and confused to a certain extent.

Six-Month Follow-Up

The client maintained the gains she made during therapy. She was improved in her professional identity, but was about the same as at post-testing on symptomatology, self-esteem, her relationships with men, and her relationship with her roommate.

In the interview, she said that work had been going better and that she had begun taking massage therapy classes at night. Also, she had begun dating a younger, Jewish man whom she liked. He was more similar to her than her previous boyfriends had been in that he was an achiever. She also reported that her relationships with her sister and her father continually improved.

One-Year Follow-Up

The scores at the one-year follow-up indicated that the client maintained the changes that she had made during therapy. Compared to her scores at pre-therapy, she was improved in self-esteem and her relationship with her roommate. She stated that things had been about the same. Work was "moving like a turtle" with regard to change and integration of her into the office, but generally she felt pretty good. She mentioned nothing specific about her relationships with men. She had not entered therapy, nor did she have any immediate plans to do so.

Long-Term Follow-Up

Three and a half years after termination, Sandy was feeling fairly good about herself. Having completed the schooling, she was now doing massage therapy a few hours a week. She was still with the law firm, but was working more independently. Further, she had been dating someone for a few months. Sandy had gone back into therapy for about a year with a prominent male gestalt therapist.

In the interview, Sandy mentioned that she was beginning to enjoy doing immigration law because she felt she was doing something for her people. I asked whether this was related to her relationships with men. Although Arabic, Sandy was born in this country and had always considered herself white. All her friends and boyfriends had been white. But perhaps she felt ambivalent about marrying a non-Arabic man. Her parents had been closely tied to their culture, but she had grown away from it during the assimilation process. It may have been, however, that she felt underlying conflicts about cross-cultural relationships as well as about male-female interactions based on her culture.

Summary

Evidence indicated that therapist techniques were the most helpful change agent in this therapy. Specifically, the techniques of open question, direct guidance, interpretation, self-disclosure, confrontation, and approval were helpful. Closed questions were not as helpful and the client wanted more confrontation.

All the moderating variables were favorable in this case. The client was functioning well and was able to respond to high-level therapeutic interventions. The therapist was open and active and could adapt his style to meet the client's needs. The relationship was adequate and supported the use of high-level interventions. Further, the client had a supportive network of friends and no interfering external events, making this an ideal period for change. Thus, these factors supported the use and facilitativeness of the techniques in this case.

4

Case 2: A Haven from Anxiety

This chapter will focus on the therapist techniques in the 17-session case conducted by Dr. B, a 47-year old, White, female psychologist with Molly, a 51-year old White, married woman.

Client

Molly (a pseudonym) was an only child whose parents divorced when she was four or five years old. After the divorce, she rarely saw her father until she was an adult. Both parents were rather loud, outspoken, and hard to live with. Further, her mother was strict, irascible, and unloving. Molly had only recently discovered that her mother had suffered from congenital syphilis, which accounted somewhat for her major physical complaints and irritability. As a child, Molly had been left on her own most of the time. She was not punished because she was a quiet, good girl who stayed out of everyone's way. The one bright spot was summers that she spent with grandparents, who were more benevolent.

Molly completed one year of college and then dropped out to get married. Her husband was a plumber whom she described as quiet, well-liked, and insensitive to her moods. Molly indicated that she and her husband were compatible in the areas of family and friends, but incompatible in the area of feelings.

Molly had worked part time as a secretary from the time her two sons went to school. Her oldest son was 32, married, and had a child. The youngest son, age 24, was still living at home.

About five years before therapy two significant events occurred, which Molly indicated were the precipitating events for her seeking therapy. Her husband had a major accident which left him bedridden for a year and her mother was dying. Molly chose to nurse her husband rather than take care of her mother, but then felt guilty that she had not done more for her mother.

While her husband was recovering, Molly began working part time as a secretary in a community mental health agency.

Physical Functioning

Physically, Molly was healthy, with no concerns about her physical health other than backaches and a poor appetite. She had undergone surgery to remove a benign breast tumor 22 years ago and for conization of her cervix 19 years ago. She was quite active with walking and house and yard work, but did no structured exercise. She frequently used alcohol, coffee, and cigarettes.

Pre-Therapy Expectations

Molly had never been in therapy before. She thought that therapy was to help gain insight into your problems and learn how to lessen or live with them. She thought that therapy should last about a year and that the ideal therapist should have sensitivity and a genuine interest in the client.

Pre-Therapy Assessment

Molly's scores on the pre-therapy assessment measures are shown in Table 4.3. On the MMPI, Molly had normal validity scores and high scores on the Depression, Paranoia, and Psychopathic Deviate scales. Her MMPI profile, which was normal, suggested an agitated depression with some sensitivity and guardedness.

Compared to an outpatient population, Molly's scores on symptomatology were average, but her self esteem was below average. She was functioning in the average range on her target complaints. The clinician judged her to be slightly anxious and depressed.

Hence, she was diagnosed by the research team as having a generalized anxiety disorder with an avoidant personality disorder.

Target Complaints

Molly's first complaint was feelings of guilt about her mother, with whom she had never gotten along. Toward the end of her life, her mother became very irritable and hostile, accusing Molly of taking things when she came to visit. Molly would force herself to visit her mother, but then get angry about her accusations and leave as quickly as she could. When her mother died, Molly felt that she should have done more for her.

Her second complaint was worry about her responsibilities for her father, who was 84, remarried, living in Florida, and very ill. After they had reestablished an ambivalent relationship, her father started demanding her attention. Recently he had told Molly that she ought to be grateful to him because her mother had wanted to get an abortion when she realized she was pregnant.

Her third complaint was difficulty communicating her needs to her sons. Her sons, like her husband, did not like to talk. Rather than ask her sons, particularly her youngest son, for help, Molly did everything herself.

During the fifth session, she added three more complaints: general levels of anxiety and tension, her relationships with others, and guilt and anger.

Summary of Client Pre-Therapy Characteristics

Molly was a quiet, phobic client, who was likable, able to form a relationship, and motivated to change because of an acute crisis situation. She had a high score on the Paranoia scale of the MMPI, which could have been a forewarning of her reticence and hesitance to trust a therapist. Her main complaints were feelings of anxiety, guilt, and anger, and her relationships with her family. She was not insight-oriented and believed that she should solve all of her problems by herself. She was in a stable marriage and worked part-time at a secretarial position, so she was functioning adequately in life.

Therapist

Dr. B was similar to Molly in terms of their age, graying hair, slim body build, and mannerisms.

Prior to her formal training in psychology, Dr. B taught junior high school. She completed her PhD in counseling psychology and then worked as a counselor at a university counseling center for 10 years. Given that the orientation of the counseling center shifted to a brief counseling model during that time, Dr. B had considerable experience in delivering brief (12 session) therapy. She left the counseling center position to establish and direct a doctoral program in counseling psychology, a position that she presently held. She had 24 publications and was quite active in university and professional activities.

Dr. B had recently completed a two-year training program in short-term psychoanalytically-oriented psychotherapy. She was licensed and listed in the National Register of Health Service Providers in Psychology and maintained an active private practice of individual psychotherapy with anxious and depressed neurotics.

Using three 5-point (5 = high) scales for how much she believed and adhered to each of three major orientations, Dr. B rated herself: psychoanalytic = 4, humanistic = 3, and behavioral = 2. In a written presentation of her theory, Dr. B stated:

> My basic view of persons is a positive one. I have positive expectations that neurotic conflicts can be resolved, that people can change with insight, integrated understandings, support, and a minimum amount of hopefulness.
>
> I view adult behavior and attitudes as a product of childhood experiences mixed with what are the *real* elements of our present day circumstances, such as economic factors, tragedies, etc. I don't see past experiences, however, as unduly determining our present but certainly as influencing our present. In that respect I feel optimistic about persons changing who want to change, as they work and expend energies in the service of understanding.
>
> For most persons who seek change through therapy, there is an important element of pain which is actually facilitative. For there to be no pain, it is not likely that someone would either seek therapy or be sustained in the struggles to change.
>
> Persons can and do eventually change through integrated understandings and perhaps, most importantly, through the love and care of the therapist. In that regard, I see therapy as a very special and significant relationship between client and therapist.

Treatment Process

The verbatim excerpt from the first few minutes of the first session illustrates the process between Molly and Dr. B.

T: I did have an opportunity to look at the information that you had filled out earlier. And so I have a general idea about why you're interested in therapy at this particular time. It would be helpful, I guess, though, if you would kind of give me an overview in your own words about what it is that um particularly contributed to your deciding to come into therapy at this particular time.

C: Um, well, I know I have a lot of anxiety which makes me uncomfortable. And I don't, (T: MmHmm) I don't like to be that way. Um, I don't think all the interpersonal relationships in my life are as good as I would like them to be. And I just thought that perhaps therapy could help me deal with those things to sort them out for myself.

T: MmHmm. Well, why don't we start maybe with the first thing you mentioned—the anxiety. Uh, could you tell me a little bit more about that?

C: Well, it's um, [Pause = 3 seconds] it's not all the time. It's just that um sometimes I get, well I think the doctor that I spoke to last time asked me if I had feelings of impending doom. And of course that, that is exactly what it is at different times, (T: MmHmm) for no particular reason, (T: MmHmm) and um which really does inhibit your life if you go around feeling like that for any length of time. (T: MmHmm) It's not constant. But um I can be by myself. I can be with other people. And it's just this vague anxious feeling. (T: MmHmm) I don't like to drive. I don't know whether that has anything to do with it or not. (T: MmHmm) Um, this, this is the farthest I drive from my house to here. (T: Hmm) I avoid going places that I have to drive alone. (T: MmHmm) And I don't know whether that's all connected or not. I don't know the reason for it. (T: MmHmm) Um, I don't have any uh fear or phobia about meeting new people or doing anything like that. But there's some things I just avoid. (T: MmHmm) And I really don't know why.

T: Hmm. Driving being one of the things that you tend to avoid (C: MmHmm) when you can. (C: MmHmm) Can you give me an example of other situations that you might feel avoidant about?

C: Um, things that I know that I can positively say, I'm sure there are a lot of other little things that would come to me. But I don't like to go to the grocery store. (T: MmHmm) And I really don't know why. (C laughs) (T: MmHmm) It's so silly because I've been going to the grocery store for 30 some years. (T: MmHmm) And all of a sudden, I, I used to go the same day all the time, had my little list in my hand. Now I go whenever I push myself, with no list, don't know what I'm doing in there. (T: MmHmm) Maybe it's because our family is smaller now. And no, I don't, I really don't know, I avoid that too. And this morning, before I came in here, even though I knew what time I was supposed to be here, I deliberately started on something. Well, it was silly. And I realized what I was doing. And I stopped. I was trying to fix a necklace that had been sitting in the drawer broken for a month. So I put that aside and got myself together to come.

T: And caught yourself getting (C: Yes) involved in something that would take you away (C: Yes) from coming here (C: Yes) which you were feeling.

C: Well, I intended to come here. It's not that I didn't. (T: Right) But um, and I'm very rarely late any place I go. I'm never late for work or anything like that. But it was just one of those little things that I find myself doing sometimes.

T: MmHmm. It's interesting that you caught yourself. You're kind of on to yourself a little bit then, huh?

C: Oh, I know, I know. And not always, but sometimes I am.

Dr. B initiated by asking the client to explain why she came. Then she sat back and probed, trying to assess the scope and depth of the client's problems, much as she did throughout the therapy.

Summary of Process

Initial sessions. During the first two sessions, the client explained her target complaints and discussed a current crisis with the severe illness (and death within a couple of weeks) of her stepmother. During the next three sessions, the therapist did a structured history taking, gently probing Molly about her childhood years and the last five years. Molly was reluctant to discuss the first 20 years of her married life, which she dismissed as idyllic.

Middle sessions. After the history, the therapist made a conscious shift to asking the client to determine the topics of the sessions. They talked about Molly's negative reactions to watching herself on videotape, feelings of guilt about her relationships with her mother and father, communication problems with her husband and sons, and reactions to her husband's accident which had dated the onset of many of Molly's current problems.

A considerable amount of time was devoted to arranging for vacations. Molly wanted the summer off from therapy so that she could go on long weekends with her husband. The therapist tried to deal with the ambivalence over therapy that was indicated by Molly's reluctance to attend sessions. They ultimately reached a compromise where the client attended sporadically over the summer. During these sporadic sessions, the client dealt with some of her most meaningful problems, particularly around her anxiety.

Termination. The final session was spent discussing the termination. The client maintained that although she found the therapy to be helpful, she would not be sorry that it was over because she could use the time. The therapist helped her examine her ambivalence and her difficulty expressing her emotions.

Client Behavior

Molly was late for several sessions. She was quite anxious at the beginning of therapy, sitting rigidly with closed posture on the edge of her chair. She spoke in a soft, phlegmatic voice and was self-deprecating, resigned, and martyrish. Opening up and talking about herself was difficult for Molly. She was passive during the sessions, waiting for direction from the therapist. When told to bring up topics, Molly did not plan anything to talk about, but brought up whatever she could think of at the moment. Once the topic was determined, however, she participated willingly.

In watching the videotape, observers frequently commented that the interaction was slow, monotonic, and boring because Molly was not outgoing, verbally expressive, or flamboyant. She seemed to dampen herself down to become inconspicuous. Reading the transcripts was more enjoyable than watching the tapes because Molly revealed a lot about important, fascinating issues and her monotonic, self-deprecating style was not as apparent.

Therapist Behavior

For response modes, Dr. B used primarily paraphrase, closed question, and information. Compared to the other therapists, she used more interpretation and less confrontation. Thus, Dr. B's style was oriented towards examining feelings and insight as well as giving and getting information.

Dr. B was very inactive during sessions. Rather than speaking much herself, she encouraged the client to talk.

Dr. B was somewhat formal, soft spoken, and reserved. In the therapy, she was very gentle, supportive, and reflective, primarily seeking to understand and clarify what the client was saying. Her major attribute was her patience with Molly. She seemed to accept and like Molly just as she was and felt no need to push her to go faster or be different from who she was. Dr. B mentioned that she often had a fiery temper outside of her therapy sessions, but that she felt very motherly with this client.

The therapist would usually begin the sessions by asking the client what she would like to talk about. No clear focus or agenda was established for what the dyad would be focusing on during the treatment. The therapist would typically end the sessions by encouraging the client to think about what they had talked about so that they could discuss it the next time.

The therapist was attentive to time, beginning and ending sessions promptly, even when the client was late. She also carefully planned for vacations and reminded the client of the number of sessions left in the therapy.

Analyses of Therapist Techniques

Molly and Dr. B talked about their reactions to the therapist techniques in the post-therapy interviews:

R: *What did Dr. B (or you) do to make those changes come about?*

C: I think basically just talking about things that I never talked about before with anyone else. Someone who can listen to it, without saying "That's not a good attitude" or "That is a good attitude" or "What could you possibly do different about this?" You sort of get a picture in your mind when somebody's talking to you about a particular problem of what you can do. You spend 50 minutes talking with Dr. B about something that with friends you might just say in a couple sentences. It would make me stop and think about things that I could do, even if Dr. B might not say a specific thing. The thought's put in your mind, "Now why do you think you do this? What do you think you could do that would be better?" Right away, I can see that it would be better if I would say what I thought in a reasonably intelligent way, rather than holding around and carrying it around for years. I would be the one that would stay late to do paperwork and then I would think for a week, "Why did I do that when I didn't even want to do it?" Nobody else did it. What's preventing me from saying, "It's just not convenient." I can do these things now and not feel guilty about it. I can express good thoughts and bad thoughts without carrying them around. Dr. B helped me see that it is possible and that people do those things. We discussed the fact that I didn't even know the words to say about a lot of things like, "It's not convenient for me to do this." If people like you less for that, then that's really their problem, not mine. *It's interesting that you didn't have assertiveness training or role playing, yet you changed just by her talking with you and giving you permission to ventilate your feelings and open up and think about what was going on.* There was a time in my life when I was slightly assertive, not totally, but I could say things. But then it went away and started doing this and I lost it. I was afraid to say anything to anybody and I just kind of withdrew. It was almost like I had permission to do those things and then I could find it for myself and do it. *So her part was what?* Getting me to talk about these things and leading me to believe that I could say these things. Lightning wasn't going to strike if I didn't agree with somebody about something or if I spoke up. *The driving phobia that you brought in initially was hardly ever discussed and yet, you feel real improvement in the anxious anticipation of driving. How do you understand that having happened?* Probably because the driving wasn't it at all. I never used to be like that. I could get in the car and go anywhere. I knew it was something that I had developed for some other reason, probably this withdrawal thing. If I didn't get in the car, I didn't have to go anywhere, right? I didn't have to deal with anything. Probably I was safer if I just stayed at home and did whatever it was I did. Getting into the car means going out, facing the world, talking to other people. And once I got a little more sure of myself, then that went a long way to being able to get into the car and go some place. *That's an interpretation I don't recall ever hearing Dr. B tell you.* No, she didn't tell me that. *You apparently did some thinking and came up with an understanding yourself?* Yeah. I wasn't born that way, so I had to have acquired that somewhere. Obviously, if I don't want to drive, I want to stay home. And when I stay home, I'm going to crawl up in a book because I feel safe there. So it was just a question of making myself stop doing this. I mean, I didn't all of a sudden one day say, "I'm going to get out in the car and I'm going to do this." A friend of mine volunteered to go shopping for me for a couple of weeks and that horrified me. It made me ill thinking that

I would be that bad off to have to have somebody do that. That gave me a level of shock to say this is just horrible. So I got in the car and went and I realized that I'm just going to have to do these things. But I also found something to do on the way that I wanted to do, like stop and have lunch, making it a little more pleasant, and that worked better.

T: One way I helped the change come about was by doing a brief history, getting enough background to be able to speculate about what in fact is her pattern of defenses and what might be some of the transference effects within therapy. The second way was by helping Molly make connections between the here and now and some antecedents to that behavior, which allowed her a certain level of understanding, and with that understanding I feel comes control. You can't control something you don't even know exists. That's where I see the importance of insight, understanding, making connections between the present and other things. *Say a little more about how you view insight being behind behavioral change.* I think she had a clearer understanding of why she did the things that she did. She came to understand, for example, the role that reading played in her life and how that was something that started back when she was a small child of 3, when she started reading. Up until that point, reading was just something that she always did. I think she was able to understand that reading played a particular role for her to isolate her when she felt threatened or insecure. It provided a haven for her. She also came to understand how that reading then took on a certain character as she was an adult. She had these rather macabre kinds of reading materials and that simply fed her anxiety. *How did change occur?* The actual experience she had with me and the therapy was significant and unlike any she had ever had. That allowed us to look at what she was feeling and what was happening as it occurred and have her better understand and not be so fearful. She was able to experience in the therapy a kind of tolerance and acceptance for her that was unusual. She probably has it with her husband but he doesn't seem to be very explicit about things like that. I was more explicit about that, which was helpful for her. The relationship helped her to feel better about herself because she got in touch with the positive parts of herself. *How did the symptom relief come about? Do you attribute that to the corrective emotional experience? You didn't spend that much time talking about it.* We never did relaxation exercises, that's for sure. It had more to do with the general catharsis. She was like a coiled wire emotionally. The relief that she was able to experience by identifying and then feeling her feelings probably accounts for a lot of the reduction of anxiety.

R: *What did Dr. B (or you) do best with you (or Molly)?*

C: Probably making me see exactly what it is I was trying to say without pushing me. It would just be, "Think about this and we'll talk about it next week." And just in that, I would put a lot of thought into some things that probably I wouldn't have just by her conversational suggestions. It wasn't, "Now I want you to think about what we just," it wasn't that kind of thing. It was just sort of, "Maybe we could think about this some more and talk about it next week," which works better for me than direction. *If someone were more confrontive or more homework-oriented, what does that do to you?* It goes right out of my mind. I don't want to do it. It's like a child. *What were some of the specific techniques that she used that were helpful?* By starting out and saying, "What do you remember about such and such a time," I would start on some obvious things and then get into things I'd forgotten. And tying certain things in one instance into certain things in another time, one thing would relate to another with her guiding me into it without directly saying "Do you think this was this?" I could form connections with her direction. I don't know if I could have put them together without her help. She would lead me into seeing what it was that we were doing or what I was talking about.

T: Being patient and not being put off by her avoidant behavior. I don't think there were any instances in which I felt that I was personalizing anything that occurred between Molly and me and that helped the work. I was able to set aside my impatience in the service of understanding. Also, being able to address those things that she's always been so fearful about addressing. Being very candid about what it is or was that was going on so that she would learn not to be fearful about addressing certain things, like feeling her feelings. *What techniques were most helpful?* Support, exploration of feelings, and interpretations.

R: *Do you remember any specific therapist interpretations, that is, feedback that helped you (or Molly) view yourself (herself) or your (her) situation in a different way?*

C: If I didn't like the way things were going, instead of confronting the business with family, friends whatever, I would just withdraw. By holding all these feelings in and not letting them out, you won't get any better, you just get a lot worse. I think I realized that I'm allowed to express my feelings if I want to instead of just taking off with them. *Anything else?* About me feeling guilty because my husband was in this accident. I was in the hospital at the time and he asked if he should stay with me. If I had insisted that he stay, which was probably in the back of my mind, if I had been a little more pushy and he hadn't gone, the whole thing wouldn't have happened. So I was angry because I may have felt part of it was my fault or that if he cared enough to stay with me in the hospital at the time it happened, none of it would have happened. It all boils down to, if you did this and I did this, none of this would have happened. And I would never have said that to anybody, but talking about it and getting it out in the open and seeing it was true, a lot of it dissipated.

T: Maybe the interpretations that were made about the readings, the role they play in isolating and separating her, providing a haven, and exacerbating her anxiety. *How did she demonstrate that the interpretation was heard and helped her reframe herself in a different light?* She stopped reading. *Since you have a psychodynamic view and elicit a lot of historical material, were there any historical interpretations that you can remember?* In the second to the last session, I made reference to her not always feeling comfortable and accepted by the mother and how that had some bearing on her looking for places of solace and how reading was an extension of that. And a couple times I mentioned her relationship with the mother not being all that she would have liked it to have been and how that had some effect on her which carried over into her adult life. *Did she show that she heard those interpretations?* Those were difficult interpretations for her to hear. She never picked up on those things to talk about. I think she had a fair amount of resistance to exploring that.

R: *Recall one session that was particularly satisfying and describe what stands out the most?*

C: The last when Dr. B said, "How do you feel about this being the last session?" As usual, I went around the other way by saying "I'm sure I will miss therapy," but I couldn't come right out and say, "I'll miss coming here and talking to you." And she said, "You said it but in a round about way." Dr. B smiled when she said that and I realized that I probably would miss coming here and having someone to talk to that I felt was paying attention or was listening. So that was best, not because it was last, but because I realized that it was too bad that it was the last and seemed like I was just getting familiar with working things out and it was time to stop. It took me a long time to not feel uncomfortable.

T: The last session because it was a good termination session. I was able to demonstrate what I thought was going to be problematic for her without clobbering her over the head in some discouraging way, but making a point that is how her feelings continue to be unavailable or inaccessible to her because she depresses feelings. *What technique did you use to help her express her feelings more openly?* I had to refocus her a number of times. One time she started telling me an anecdote and I could just visualize her going away and being completely off the point. So it was suggesting to her what might be something that she was feeling, allowing her then to respond in terms of the accuracy of that and encouraging her to explore those feelings.

R: *What did Dr. B (or you) do least well with you (Molly)?*

C: I can't think of anything. *This is not anything against her. Every relationship has pluses and minuses. Just try to think of something that you would change if you could.* I really can't think of anything, except when I was going to get off a few Mondays to do things and I thought maybe she was angry that I wasn't going to be here, but not in a nasty way. But I really wanted to do these Monday things that I had a chance to do and I was perfectly willing to make up the time. I couldn't come in here, but I felt that maybe I had to make too many excuses. I felt like a child saying, "But why can't I have another cookie?" That's the only thing. But I wasn't really angry or anything. I just felt maybe I wasn't allowed to deviate from this program one bit. That's all.

T: That's really hard to answer. I'm so blinded to myself. I don't know. One thing I noticed may have something to do with some anxiety that I feel in the session. It's not so intense, but gets demonstrated by my not saying things very clearly.

R: *Recall a session that was particularly unsatisfying.*

C: In the first session, I was feeling nervous because I knew the cameras were here. When I saw the film, I felt kind of nauseated, thinking "I don't like the way this looks. It's not going to work because I'm not going to be able to say anything because I know I'm going to have this film." I felt like I was going to have to be very guarded which I didn't want to do. But it didn't work out that way. After the first session, I was a little nervous and intimidated about the world seeing this film and seeing this silly woman up here complaining about nothing. I felt like I was wasting people's time and what was I doing here, and I was never going to get anything out of it, and I just felt very depressed. But I didn't feel that way after any of the other ones that I can recall. *Were there areas you thought needed more or different attention?* I thought of several small things that I never brought because we were too busy doing something else. I didn't want to confuse it with too many issues. *What were they?* Just about the way I am sometimes and what I can do differently. Sometimes I come across as Pollyanna and give the impression I was this really nice person all the time, but everybody was stepping on me—that's not true. Maybe I should have clarified more that I have a lot of bad things I do. It's not just other people picking on me.

T: It was the session before they were going on vacation and talking about the husband. My tack was to go with what she was indicating to be some positive aspects with the husband. In your [researcher's] questioning me after the session and our talking about it, I perceived you [researcher] as thinking that I had allowed her to avoid the issue of our separation, that it was going to be 3 weeks until I would see her again and I hadn't addressed her feelings about that. That felt to me like I had made a slight technical error. But I hadn't been feeling it during the session and it was only in your questioning that I felt your judgment that it would have been better to address the separation. That's the only session that I remember leaving with a sense of uneasiness. *Is there anything you wish you had pursued further with Molly?* Were I to work faster than I do, it would have been helpful to spend more time exploring the relationship with the mother and especially the father, since he is still alive and going to die soon. My constraints were that we had just so much time and there's a certain pacing that seems comfortable to me which didn't allow more focus on the mother and father.

Quantitative Analyses

Table 4.1 shows the results of analyses for therapist response modes on the immediate outcome measures. Table 4.2 shows the codings of the post-session reviews. Dr. B and Molly were both extremely positive, attributing most of the helpful events to therapist techniques and most of the few hindering events to the client.

Combining the results of the post-therapy interviews with the quantitative analyses indicates that the most helpful techniques were interpretation, approval, paraphrase, disclosure, and direct guidance. No consistent evidence was found that any techniques were hindering.

Discussion of Helpful Techniques

Interpretation. At the beginning of therapy, Molly was not particularly insight-oriented, but Dr. B taught her to become interested in understanding her behaviors. In the post-therapy interview, Molly mentioned that she had begun to question "why" she did things. The interpretations that were mentioned as the most effective regarded Molly's guilt over her supposed responsibility for her husband's accident, some connections with Molly's current behavior and the childhood antecedents to that behavior, and the function of reading horror books in fueling Molly's anxiety. A particularly poignant example from the 14th session of the interpretation of reading the horror books is excerpted below. Prior to this excerpt, the client was

TABLE 4.1 Proportion of Occurrence, Client Helpfulness Ratings, Therapist Helpfulness Ratings, Client Experiencing, and Client Reactions for Therapist Response Modes in Case 2

		Client Help Rating		Therapist Help Rating		Client Experiencing		Most Likely Reactions
Response Modes	%	M	SD	M	SD	M	SD	
Approval	.04	7.54	1.36 A	6.74	1.04 B	2.70	.84 B	
Information	.18	7.44	1.42 A	6.80	1.12 B	2.58	.86 B	No Reaction
Direct Guidance	.05	7.52	1.24 A	6.82	1.15 B	2.53	.75 B	No Reaction
Closed Question	.19	7.74	1.10 A	6.67	.99 B	2.53	.75 B	
Open Question	.12	7.67	.94 A	6.89	.96 B	2.77	.83 B	Challenged Negative
Paraphrase	.25	8.00	.86 A	6.96	.87 B	2.61	.79 B	
Interpretation	.14	8.19	.85 A	7.22	.73 B	2.64	.87 B	Ther. Work
Confrontation	.03	8.09	.64 A	7.09	.78 B	2.72	.96 B	
Disclosure	.00	8.00	.00 A	9.00	.00 A	4.00	.00 A	
TOTAL		7.80	1.05	6.89	.95	2.62	.81	

NOTE: Helpfulness was rated on 9-point scales (9 = extremely helpful); experiencing was rated on a 7-point scale (7 = high). ANOVAs indicated significant differences between therapist response modes for client helpfulness, $F_{(8, 1268)} = 9.14$, $p < .0001$, therapist helpfulness, $F_{(8, 1268)} = 5.70$, $p < .0001$, but nonsignificant differences for client experiencing, $F_{(8, 1268)} = 1.61$, NS. Post hoc differences are indicated, such that response modes with the same letter (A-B) were not significantly different (A = highest ratings). The overall relationship between response modes and client reactions was significant, $X^2_{(28)} = 146.42$, $p < .0001$.

discussing many things that make her anxious, such as worrying over the possibility of her grandson getting hurt on amusement parks' rides, her husband drowning in the ocean, and her son crashing in his car.

C: But why do I dwell on these ridiculous things, like I mean stupid things like riptides and which have nothing to do with everyday living. I always seem to grab, and all I read these days, all I've been reading for the past 4 years, I used to read a lot, are these horrible, disgusting horror novels, you know. Why do I do that? People say there's some-

TABLE 4.2 Proportions of Helpful and Hindering Events in Post-Session Reviews in Case 2

	Client		Therapist	
	Helpful	Hindering	Helpful	Hindering
Therapist Techniques	.47	.00	.31	.02
Support	.08	.00	.04	.00
Direct Guidance	.04	.00	.02	.01
Closed Question	.00	.00	.01	.00
Open Question	.00	.00	.01	.00
Paraphrase	.20	.00	.13	.01
Interpretation	.14	.00	.07	.00
Confrontation	.00	.00	.03	.00
Disclosure	.00	.00	.01	.00
Therapist Manner	.08	.00	.22	.00
Client Tasks	.22	.06	.19	.00
Focus	.00	.02	.04	.00
Experiencing	.14	.04	.04	.00
Insight	.08	.00	.07	.00
Changes	.00	.00	.04	.00
Client Manner	.16	.00	.16	.06
Relationship/Alliance	.00	.00	.03	.00
TOTAL	.93	.06	.91	.08

thing wrong with somebody that reads them. I don't think that. But that's all I read anymore. The, the more disgusting and horrible they are, the more I read them. (T: MmHmm) And I wonder about that too, because I didn't use to do that. I wonder if that (T: MmHmm) has anything to do with it. I don't know.

T: Well, what about reading the novels? How do those novels make you feel? I mean wha-, what's it like for you to read those kind of novels?

C: I, I don't know. They um, they're not, I don't believe them. You know, they're like um the Stephen King books and things like that. (T:

MmHmm) I, I don't know. They do, they do distract me. I um, but it's gotten so that that's solely the type of things I read.

T: MmHmm. Now they distract you. And what else do you think comes from reading them?

C: I don't, I don't know. People have asked me. I don't know, but I, that's it. I will go to the bookstore and bring home stacks like this of these um books about vampires and horrible things and um, (T: Mm-Hmm) I mean to the exclusion of oth-, other things. I used to read a little bit of everything, (T: MmHmm) but this, this is it. I'm bringing them home by the barrelful. (T: MmHmm) And just that, and nobody will borrow my books anymore because they don't like what I read, (T: MmHmm) not that I care about that. But I mean this just goes to show you that it's gotten to the point where friends who used to borrow books, or asked me if I had anything to read, don't ask.

A few minutes later: C: I just sometimes wonder (T: MmHmm) when I started doing this? (T: MmHmm) Why did I start doing this?

T: I suppose that kind of reading though does kind of um in some ways support or confirm uh what feels to you like the way things are anyway or can be. I mean when we think about your kind of carrying about an expectation that, that something horrible will happen, I mean it's as if those kinds of novels in some way fit in with what is your expectation. (C: That could be.) It's kind of a confirmation of what you think uh could probably happen anyway, I mean not literally, but . . .

C: Yeah, yeah, I know. Uh that's true because uh, uh, you know, things that um really are removed from most people's everyday life are things that I worry about anyhow. (T: MmHmm) So that's right, they probably do confirm it. Uh vampires can come in the window and kill everybody. And uh (T: MmHmm) or an axe murderer is going to get loose in your neighborhood (T: MmHmm) or something like that. Yes, um maybe, so maybe that's just confirming all the apprehension I feel anyway. I don't think I'm feeling the apprehension because I read the books, (T: Mm-Hmm, MmHmm) because I, I don't usually, never have done this. I don't see how that I think, (T: MmHmm) I think I read the books because I feel the apprehension.

A few minutes later: T: So the books, in a sense kind of feed this uh attitude or, or feeling, or predisposition that you have. It's the books almost end up nourishing or, or, or keeping you kind of um, your thinking focused in this kind of way.

C: That's true. (T: MmHmm) That's true. So I think I'll make an effort to uh read something else for awhile.

T: MmHmm. So it seems that maybe that might be something that you could do to not feed or intensify your, your more negativistic and anxious feelings.

The awareness that reading horror books led her to feel more anxious helped Molly decide to stop reading such books. Thus, insight led to change. The next two sessions were spent talking further about her reading habit and working through the new understandings about why Molly read the horror books.

Approval. Dr. B was incredibly patient with Molly. Even though Molly was sometimes withdrawn and defensive and boring to those observing, the therapist was able to listen and be very involved with her. Dr. B characterized it as mothering Molly as she had not been mothered as a child. She also gave the client lots of reinforcement for her ideas and attempts to change. The whole tone of the therapy was gentle and soothing.

Paraphrase. Paraphrase, particularly reflection of feelings, was helpful to get Molly in touch with her feelings. For most of her life, Molly had denied her feelings and the therapy provided a cathartic opportunity for her to express and accept her feelings.

Self-disclosure. Dr. B offered only one disclosure in the final session, but it was regarded as extremely helpful. In the excerpt below, Molly was talking about losses and how she could express feelings only to her grandchild because he was a baby. She had made no overt connection to the loss of therapy.

C: I guess I set up, a lot of people gave me those examples and I kind of followed along with it, um you know, if other people don't do, don't make a big, emotional show of anything, then I don't want to do it either. It's the same thing about being rejected or (T: MmHmm) or feelings being reciprocated or anything. I mean, you tend to follow examples (T: MmHmm) and I guess if you see that uh, I mean I can respond really well if somebody um, but somebody else has to do it first. (T: MmHmm) Uh I, I don't, I'm not usually the type to (T: initiate) to initiate anything like that.

T: MmHmm. Well, I'm glad we did talk about this though. So that in fact, uh kind of like a more, um, um, total uh picture in a sense. Um there's something that we looked at recognizing that having a last session carries with it a number of different feelings. And yes, on the one hand, there's a certain amount of relief that it does feel good or maybe even feels exciting to say "Okay, now I'm gonna try something out and I've learned some things and I'm eager to see now ah how I can take the learnings from this situation into, into my life." And also another part of it is that, that there's some sadness that when we have experiences or connectiveness with the person, that to give that, to give that up carries with it a sense of loss, or a certain amount of sadness. *And, and I must say, M. that I certainly have thought of this being our last session and it carrying for me a, a sense of loss. I think that you and I have worked well together. And I have felt uh, I have felt connected to you. And to give that up is, is uh, uh, is a loss.*

C: Yeah, I never really put it into my own words. I just, that the sense of loss is there, (T: MmHmm) a lot of times, with a lot of things, but I'm always hesitant to really put it into words, um.

T: Or maybe even hesitant to feel it, let alone put it into words, huh?

C: Well, I, I, I feel things, um (T: MmHmm) sometimes I try to push things aside and not, but you can't help feeling things. They're there. (T: MmHmm) Sometimes you just prefer not to deal with it. (T: Mm-Hmm) And it's almost like, you know like Scarlett O'Hara, "I'll think about it tomorrow." (laughs) (T: MmHmm) I mean, it's that kind of thing. (T: MmHmm) And if you keep doing that, then obviously it all piles up and you have a lot of things to sort out. And it's not, it's more uncomfortable doing it that way than if you deal with things as best you can when they happen.

Molly obviously had difficulty dealing with her feelings about the termination. Dr. B interpreted Molly's discussion during the entire session as a veiled reference to the termination and her statement immediately preceding the disclosure as inviting the therapist to initiate the discussion about the termination. Thus, Dr. B felt that Molly was ready for the disclosure. Molly seemed touched by but uncomfortable with the intimacy and backed away from the disclosure, yet still rated it as very helpful.

Direct guidance. Direct guidance within the session was also helpful in that the client had a tendency to become distracted and wander off into tangential topics. The therapist kept her focused so that they did not waste a lot of time. Further, Dr. B structured what would happen in the sessions. She tried to shape Molly's behavior by telling her that she should come prepared to talk, but Molly never did come in with specific things to discuss.

Techniques Not Used in This Therapy

Confrontation was seldom used in this case. In the post-therapy interview, the client said that she would not have liked a confrontive therapist because confrontation made her feel like a child asking for permission. She apparently communicated this to Dr. B during therapy. The therapist sensed the client's need not to be confronted and kept the therapy at a safe, gentle level where the client felt very supported. The only time that Dr. B challenged Molly was about taking time off of therapy for summer vacations and this confrontation was not well received by Molly.

Process Issues

This case was fascinating because the client changed in two specific areas, assertiveness and her driving phobia, that were not discussed in therapy. Early in therapy, the client reported that she had begun driving again. In the post-therapy review, she said that she overcame the driving phobia when she became aware that she was not really being afraid of driving but that her general anxiety kept her home and safe. Similarly, the client reported both in therapy and in the post-therapy interview that she was becoming more assertive at work and with her husband and friends.

My explanation of how she changed in these areas relates to the traumatic experience five years prior to therapy when her husband had the accident and her mother was dying. At that time, Molly stayed home for almost a year caring for her husband and avoiding going to help her mother. Her guilt over causing her husband's accident and over not getting along with her mother seemed to have precipitated her anxiety. She had no one to talk to and just felt she was a terrible person for having such feelings. Kept inside, they festered. She turned to reading horror books as an escape, which served several purposes. On a conscious level, it served to distract Molly from her own situation. The horror on the printed page kept her mind from the real horror of death and her sense of powerlessness. She unconsciously identified with the victim's powerlessness. The reading reinforced her fears and anxieties of the world as a dangerous place that she needed to avoid.

Molly had always felt that the world was a dangerous place. In her childhood, she had been abandoned by her father and inadequately cared for by her mother. When her own children were young, she was

constantly worried about their getting into danger. But these conflicts had been at a low level during the early years of her marriage
when things were fairly idyllic. The trauma of her husband's accident
and her mother's death triggered all the old conflicts to an intolerable
point.

Molly probably did not seek therapy earlier because she thought
she should be able to solve everything by herself and not ask for
anything, something she had learned early in childhood from not-
good-enough parents. Interestingly, when she went back to work, she
got a job as a part-time secretary in a community mental health
facility, perhaps as a way of being close to therapists. She talked
about not wanting to go to any of these therapists, however, because
they seemed so disorganized and ineffective.

The therapy taught her a new way of looking at herself by examining her thoughts and feelings and allowing herself to accept who
she was. She was then able to apply this new insight approach to her
problems with assertiveness and driving and understand why she had
those problems. She had the behaviors in her repertoire so that when
she had some insight into her problems, she could change very
rapidly. The follow-up data support that she was able to continue to
apply this approach and improve.

Another interesting issue is that career aspirations were never
discussed as potentially being responsible for part of Molly's depression and anxiety. Concurrent with her husband's accident and her
mother's death, her two sons had grown up. Molly had always held
part-time secretarial jobs, which were not intellectually stimulating.
During the long-term follow-up, Molly mentioned that she had no
purpose in life. Perhaps a more fulfilling career would be important
for her.

Moderating Variables

Client Factors

Despite a deprived childhood, Molly had good coping strategies
and had a fairly good adjustment with family, work, and friends. She
was in an acute crisis that had begun five years prior to therapy with
regard to her husband's accident and mother's death, which resulted
in a driving phobia, unassertiveness, and guilt feelings. She was

psychologically ready to change after having tried to cope on her own for five years. Although she was not insight-oriented prior to therapy, she was able to learn to be curious and came to value an insight approach to understanding herself.

The only factor that held Molly back from making more use of the therapist techniques was her defensiveness. She found it somewhat difficult to open up and believe that she could rely on someone else to help her with her problems. She required a lot of support and gentle encouragement. Molly was very clear that she did not want to be confronted. Had she been paired with a confrontive therapist, she probably would have terminated.

Therapist Factors

Perhaps primary to the change in this case was Dr. B's ability to form a caring, warm, safe, mothering relationship with Molly. She provided a non-anxious presence, which helped Molly feel accepted. This safe environment allowed the client to use the techniques that the therapist offered. Interestingly, Dr. B mentioned her own interpersonal manner as being helpful far more often than did Molly (see Table 4.2). In almost every post-session interview, Dr. B pointed out that Molly liked her a lot. Further, the matching between Dr. B and Molly on both gender and age was probably quite helpful in giving an immediate sense of similarity.

Dr. B's choice of techniques was clearly derived from her orientation. Her description of her theoretical orientation given prior to therapy is very similar to what she actually did in the therapy sessions, which suggests that Dr. B was able to use her preferred style of therapy with Molly.

The Relationship

Both Molly and Dr. B felt that the relationship was very strong and positive, as indicated by their high ratings on the WAI (see Chapter 2, Table 2.2). Further, both indicated that the working alliance increased across the treatment.

The client mentioned that Dr. B was exactly the type of therapist that she wanted. They seemed well matched in their expectations and preferences. Given that the pairings were random, this matching was in fact serendipitous.

Dr. B and Molly seemed to understand each other implicitly, without ever processing the relationship overtly. For example, Molly never overtly said, "Don't confront me," but Dr. B picked up the covert message and was always very gentle with her. Further, Molly agreed with how Dr. B structured the therapy.

This strong relationship undoubtedly provided Molly with the trust to incorporate the therapist's insight approach and use it to change specific aspects of her behavior, for example reading horror books and driving. Yet the relationship itself was seldom mentioned as a helpful component of the treatment in the post-session reviews.

External Factors

Extratherapy involvement. Comments in the post-therapy interviews indicated that both Dr. B and Molly felt that Molly worked hard outside of therapy:

R: *How did you (Molly) use the therapy between sessions?*

C: I spent over an hour a week thinking about it. When I was driving or not doing something else, I would think about things I could do to change or what we had discussed the previous week.

T: She was pretty gutsy, or perhaps a better word is feisty. She came in with more motivation than was apparent at the beginning because she hung in there. She clearly thought about things in between sessions, although she was not able to initiate bringing that into the next session. She seemed willing to make changes, to risk doing things differently. Now the reading, that was more a matter of being frightened out of reading. Once she addressed the reading and was hearing herself describe what she was doing, the denial dropped off and she got scared. I wonder how sustained the change in reading will be? I don't think she should not ever read, but I don't know if she should read that macabre, cannibalistic reading she was doing. I would wonder if what she has and knows at this point would be enough to make her stay away from using reading defensively at some future time. I thought she did some working in between sessions, especially more toward the end.

Support network. Molly claimed that she and her husband had a circle of friends and extended family with whom they socialized, but she never talked about any specific friends in therapy. She said that she never talked to any friends the way she talked with the therapist, indicating that her discussions with friends were relatively superficial. Further, although her relationship with her husband seemed stable, he was not a confidant for Molly. In fact, Molly was private, reserved, and a loner, spending a lot of time in solitary activities such as reading and gardening.

External events. At the beginning of therapy, Molly's stepmother died. Her father was also very ill and died after the therapy was over. Although Molly was not very close to her father and stepmother, she felt some guilt and obligation towards them. On the other hand, her immediate family was very stable, with no major events occurring during the therapy. Hence, external factors did not seem to play a major role in this therapy.

Outcome of Therapy

Session Outcome

According to the scores on the SEQ (see Chapter 2, Table 2.2), sessions were viewed as very deep and moderately smooth. Further, both Molly and Dr. B indicated that the sessions became deeper as the treatment progressed.

Pre-Post Changes

Molly was somewhat improved after 17 sessions of treatment (see Table 4.3). On the MMPI, Molly's post-therapy scale scores all remained within five points of the pre-therapy scores, indicating that there were no major changes. Further, she was higher in self-esteem, lower in depression, functioning better on most of her target complaints, and unchanged in symptomatology and anxiety. Change on two target complaints came early in treatment, as evidenced by the fifth session ratings.

In the post-therapy interviews excerpted below, both client and therapist noted behavioral changes (stopped reading horror books, improvement in the driving phobia), increased self-esteem, improved interpersonal relationships, and decreased anxiety.

R: *How have you (or has Molly) changed as a result of therapy?*

C: I'm able to express my feelings, negative or positive, to significant people. At work, when they ask if I'll stay late and work, I used to say "Yes" and I would stay late and do this work. All the time I was thinking

TABLE 4.3 Scores on Outcome Measures for Case 2

Measures	Pre	5th	Expect	Post	6 Mo	1 Yr
Client-Rated Measures						
MMPI						
Depression	68			68		
Paranoia	67			67		
Psychopathic Deviate	62			[63]		
Psychasthenia	58			[60]		
SCL-90-R GSI	45			43	37	31
TSCS	39			54***	[50]	56
TC (1) Guilt over mother	11	4*	3.5	4**	4	3
(2) Worry over father	9	5*	3.5	4*	1*	[2]
(3) Communicate to son	9	[11]	5	4 *	4	3
(4) Anxiety/Tension		11	4	5**	4	[6]
(5) Relationships		10	5	4**	4	4
(6) Guilt/Anger		8	1	6	6	4
Satisfaction					8.5	9
Therapist-Rated Measures						
TC (1) Guilt over mother	10	[11]	6	7*		
(2) Worry over father	11	7*	4.5	7*		
(3) Communicate to son	7	6	4.5	5		
(4) Anxiety/Tension		11	5	5**		
(5) Relationships		9	5	5*		
(6) Guilt/Anger		11	6	7*		
Researcher-Rated Measures						
Hamilton Anxiety	12			[13]		
Hamilton Depression	8			4**		

NOTE: High *T* scores indicate high symptomatology on the SCL-90-R GSI, high self-esteem on the TSCS; worst functioning on the TC, higher satisfaction, and greater disturbance on the Hamilton scales. Expect = level expected after treatment. * = significant change at $p < .05$; ** = $p < .01$; *** = $p < .001$. Negative changes are in brackets.

"Why me, God? Why do I have to do it?" Now I can say, "No, I really can't stay late and do the work. But let me know another time and I can space it out." I don't feel bad about it. With my family, my husband's off today and he said, "Are you going to have time to get my breakfast before you leave?" I said, "No, I'm really not, but there's such and such right there in the kitchen" and I didn't feel put upon to stay there and get his breakfast and be late. I can speak up for myself a little bit so I don't let people walk all over me and hold all this anger in and get anxious. *What about your driving anxiety?* It's still around a little bit, but I don't think about it as much. If I have to go some place, I get in the car and go there. I don't spend 20 minutes thinking, "I have to go and get in the car and go some place," which is what I did. I still don't really like to drive, but I just do it. If I don't think about it that much, it works out better. *How have your feelings about yourself changed?* The less anxiety I have, the more capable I feel to do the things that I want to do. I don't have to accomplish a lot. I'm trying to quit smoking right now, which is not easy, but I'm really giving it a try. And that's making me feel a little bit better about myself that I'm going to do something constructive and positive here. I'm probably grouchier, but I'm really going to try. *Other behavioral changes?* I haven't been reading as much. I've been doing more things, like cleaning out cupboards, refinishing furniture, raking leaves, rather than just sitting in a corner reading.

T: The therapy was definitely a corrective emotional experience for her. The relationship with me was one of the more important gains for her in that she finally had an opportunity and took some risks to identify and experience her feelings and to do that with somebody. In doing that, she experienced catharsis and relief that was somewhat novel for her. It strengthened her own sense of self-worth and self-esteem. Those two things contributed to her clearly optimistic expectation at the end, that she was going to be more open about her feelings and take more risks with people in terms of trying to connect with them and have some intimacy. *Did her relationships improve?* I think she thinks that is happening and will happen more than I do. The last session was a good example of how she is still so unaware of how defended she is and how that actually gets played out in her interpersonal behavior. Her feelings about ending the therapy were so unavailable to her and only became available by helping her to get in touch with them. That's not any different from how she's going to be with people in general, who aren't going to help her to identify those feelings and encourage her to own them and express them. So, although I understand her generally positive feelings and expectations about how she thinks this is going to have made a difference for her, I don't think the differences will be as great, behaviorally, as she expects. There probably will be something of a carryover with her feelings about herself. *Any other behavioral changes?* She seems more relaxed. She's acting or certainly feeling differently in the home. A definite behavioral change is her reading habits just went 180 degrees, so that she's not isolating herself by her reading as she had done before. Another change she reported was feeling more comfortable driving on the beltway and being in social situations.

R: *How satisfied do you feel with the nature and amount of change?*

C: I don't feel too anxious right now. I'll see how it goes, how long it lasts. Right now I feel that there's hope that I can stay reasonably calm and unanxious and manage things better.

T: I'm much more skeptical than I think she is about the stability of her gains. If I were seeing her in my private practice, I would not have stopped with her at 17 sessions. I would see much more work occurring now, given that we certainly did establish a therapeutic alliance and she's in a much better place to explore her resistances and to take behavioral risks than she was before.

Molly was also asked to talk about what caused and maintained one of her major problems. Her answer indicated that the therapy had helped her gain some insight into her problems:

C: I came from a family that never sat around and discussed things. Children were to be seen and not heard. With no brothers and sisters, I was just never a real talkative person. And you didn't have counselors. I probably wouldn't have gone to one anyway. But I grew up with the idea that you just did the best you can do and that's it. If something's wrong, that's too bad. You better take care of it yourself. And I'm sure that carried over all my life. *What maintains it currently?* Probably I maintain it, because certainly I have friends who are not like that.

Six-Month Follow-Up

Molly maintained the gains that she made during therapy. She was about the same as at post-testing on symptomatology, self-esteem, and on her target complaints, with continued improvement on one complaint. She gave very high ratings of satisfaction (8.5 on a 10-point scale) to her experience in therapy.

In the interview, Molly said that things were not too bad and that she was not very anxious. She felt more in control in general and still able to drive when she needed to. She reported that she had been more depressed during the winter, but kept herself busier and felt more resilient. She had visited her father shortly before he died and had been able to carry out the necessary decisions. Molly had one session with Dr. B during the six-month interval to deal with the stress of her father's illness.

One-Year Follow-Up

Molly maintained the gains that she made during therapy. In fact, by the one-year follow-up, she was significantly improved on all measures as compared to the pre-testing. Therefore, the therapy seemed to set the change process in motion in that Molly continued to change gradually when therapy terminated.

In the questionnaire, Molly again brought up that her father's death relieved her of the responsibility for him. She said that she felt she should have done more while he was alive, but felt free of some of the tension following his death. Asked to describe the changes made as a result of therapy, she replied that she had become more able to express her feelings to members of her family and more able to accept their feelings, which she attributed to feeling more confident in herself. She had not sought therapy.

Long-Term Follow-Up

Three and a half years after termination, Molly reported that she was feeling fairly good about herself. She was able to drive when she needed to. She was assertive, even though she was not completely comfortable being outspoken. She occasionally read horror books, but not exclusively as she had before. She had cut back to working 20 from 24 hours per week, so that she could have more time for herself. On the day I talked to her, which was one of the first nice days of spring, she had left the dishes in the sink and gone for a walk in the woods, something she would not have allowed herself to do a few years ago. Things were stable in her family, with her younger son still living at home. Although she had not sought out further therapy, she had developed a rewarding friendship with one of the therapists at work.

Summary

Therapist techniques were a helpful change agent in this therapy. Specifically, the techniques of interpretation, support, direct guidance within the session and gentle suggestions, paraphrase (reflection of feelings), open questions about her history and feelings, and self-disclosure were often helpful. Confrontation was seldom used.

Further, no consistent evidence could be found that any therapist techniques were unhelpful.

The relationship, client factors, and therapist factors all moderated the effects of the techniques. There was an ideal match and a warm, supportive relationship which helped the client hear the interventions. Similarly, the therapist was empathic, caring, and patient. Further, the client was in an acute crisis and ready for change as well as open to an insight-oriented approach to therapy. External factors did not exert much influence. Thus, the techniques were used within a facilitative situation.

5

Case 3: Free to Be Me

"It is only by risking our persons from one hour to another that we live at all."

William James quoted by client in the 14th session

This chapter will focus on the therapist techniques in the 17-session case conducted by Dr. H, a 43-year old, White, male psychologist with Lucille, a 60-year old, White woman.

Client

Lucille (a pseudonym) grew up in a small southern town during the depression. She was the second of two children, with a brother five years older. Her father was a bookkeeper/accountant, who was 20 years older than her mother. He had not been a dominant influence in her life, acting more like a grandfather than a father. With her mother in charge of family matters, there were no battles at home. Her mother had gotten a college degree but only started teaching piano lessons when her children were in school.

Lucille completed college, majoring in secretarial administration (now called business and economics). Her father then got her a job with a local department store as a bookkeeper. A year after Lucille finished college, her father died. Lucille remained at home with her mother. Meanwhile she worked her way up in the department store to be a buyer. In this position, she traveled frequently to New York City, where she developed a love for the arts. She felt, however, that being a buyer was a dead-end job and was glad to quit to marry her husband, a solid, dependable man, at age 26.

Right after she got married, Lucille's husband took a job in Texas, where they soon had their first child. They then moved back to their home, but soon moved again to the Washington, DC area, where her husband got a job as the manager of an ice cream manufacturing plant. These moves meant that Lucille was far away from her extended family. Another change was that Lucille switched from the Methodist church to her husband's Southern Baptist church, in which he was very active and a firm believer. Unfortunately, Lucille was never comfortable in this fundamentalist church.

Lucille described her husband as needing to be in control. For example, he insisted that she stay home to raise children. She, on the other hand, never felt okay about asking for things for herself. Although her children were a major source of joy for Lucille, the early years at home raising the children were quite confining. She described herself as changing from the strong, energetic person she was as a buyer to a meek, dependent wife and mother. Because she did not drive, she had little freedom.

She had three children, two daughters and a son. After her youngest child went to school, Lucille had a life crisis, in which she paused to consider where she was going with her life. Deciding to make some changes, she became more assertive, learned to drive, and demanded a car of her own. She also quit going to church as regularly. Lucille said that her husband was tolerant of these changes, although he felt that he had to make apologies for her absences from church by saying she was sick.

Seven years prior to the therapy, Lucille's husband died suddenly of a heart attack. At about the same time, her mother also died. Then, two years before the therapy, Lucille was mugged in the parking lot of a shopping center. As a final straw, a sister-in-law and her husband, who had been major sources of support, had recently moved across the country.

After her husband's death, Lucille lived on a smaller income but did not return to work. She had taken several community college courses including career planning, philosophy, and creative writing. Her interests were in the arts, especially songwriting.

Physical Functioning

Physically, Lucille was healthy. She ate regular meals for the most part, although she thought she ate too much junk food. She did not exercise but thought she should. She had undergone surgery for a tonsillectomy when she was three years old, for an appendectomy when she was 12 years old, and for removal of a breast lump when she was 29 years old. Lucille drank coffee quite often and used aspirin frequently for headaches.

Pre-Therapy Expectations

Lucille had never been in therapy before, other than for one session of family therapy. She believed that therapy was for discovering and understanding one's problems and searching for ways to resolve them. She thought that therapy should last until these things were accomplished. A therapist, she thought, should be objective, empathic, and sensitive.

Pre-Therapy Assessment

Lucille's scores on the pre-therapy assessment measures are shown in Table 5.3. On the MMPI, Lucille had normal validity scores and high scores on the Depression, Social Introversion, and Psychasthenia scales. This profile indicates that she was depressed, withdrawn, and anxious, with self-devaluation, self-punitiveness, nervousness, and perfectionism. She was extremely low on the Masculinity-Femininity scale ($T = 22$), which is typical for women who are passive, submissive, yielding, and demure, as well as constricted, self-pitying, and fault-finding.

Lucille was average in symptomatology, but below average in self-concept compared to an outpatient population. She was functioning at an average level on her target complaints. The clinician judged her to be moderately anxious and depressed.

Thus, Lucille was diagnosed by the research team as dysthymic.

Target Complaints

Lucille's first complaint was a lack of achievement. She wanted to live a more worthy, fulfilling life. Her second problem was driving anxiety. She wanted to get over her inability to go places, particularly at night, because of her fear of driving. Her third complaint was a lack of values. After breaking away from her husband's church and its "hypocritical" values, she felt a void in terms of values. In the interview to establish the target complaints, Lucille expressed concern about whether she was motivated enough to change.

In the fifth session, Lucille added the complaints of a tendency to dwell on negative, self-defeating feelings, a lack of self-confidence, and a lack of discipline.

Summary of Client Pre-Therapy Characteristics

Lucille was a self-pitying, depressed woman, who was struggling to stay involved in life. She was hypercritical of herself while idealizing others. The precipitating factors leading Lucille to seek treatment were her adjustment over the loss of her husband and mother and being mugged. She was having a hard time establishing who she was and what she wanted from the rest of her life. Lucille was not working, but was taking college classes.

Therapist

Dr. H had a PhD in clinical psychology and had worked as a counselor at a university counseling center for 18 years. He was licensed and listed in the National Register of Health Service Providers in Psychology. Dr. H was well-regarded by the counseling center staff and sought out by students as a therapist. He was also sought out as a supervisor by many counseling and clinical psychology graduate students. In addition to his counseling center position, Dr. H maintained a small private practice.

Using three 5-point (5 = high) scales for how much he believed in and adhered to three major orientations, Dr. H rated himself: psychoanalytic = 4, humanistic = 3, and behavioral = 4, describing himself as integrating psychoanalytic and behavioral theories.

The Treatment Process

The verbatim excerpt from the first few minutes of the first session illustrates the process between Lucille and Dr. H.

T: I'm going to have to ask quite a few questions today to . . .

C: Well, if you're a little bit sketchy about it, so am I. (T: Let me, let me . . .) That's, that's my problem.

T: Let me tell you the, the impression I got. And then you can take off from there. (C: Right) Um it seems like you're, you're not happy yourself right now, that you're experiencing some kind of down feelings or sadness or lethargy or something. And sounds, I got the impression you weren't doing much but sitting around and spacing out in front of the TV or something like that too much. Uh I got the impression that a daughter was not happy with that.

C: Well, all three children have expressed concern about . . .

T: Okay. And that uh, I, I know you lost your husband. But I don't know when that was.

C: Seven years ago.

T: Seven years ago, okay. Well I, I guess that wasn't real clear to me that you had picked yourself up and started over after that loss.

C: Um for a while I did, (T: You did, okay) for about three years. Well ah I had to pick up the pieces ah because he had taken care of everything before. And I also mentioned that my mother had died the same month that my husband did. And it was pretty emotionally devastating. Plus all the responsibilities then that came my way that had to be taken care of so . . .

T: Was that mostly, mostly new to you in some sense? Family, grand-children, etc., etc.?

C: Largely new, yes, or at least being responsible for taking care of them seemed to be. The there came a while where I managed to (Pause = 5 seconds) push myself out and enjoy doing what I did for awhile. I went back to school to a community college and took um about six different classes, (T: Hmm) was involved with some of the theatre there (T: Hmm) and um enjoyed that. Then I don't know, it seems like . . .

T: How long, I mean, (C: Um . . .) was that several, a couple of years?

C: The spring of '81, yeah, a couple of years, a year and a half. Then in the, in January of 1982 I was mugged and . . .

T: On campus?

C: Oh no. At the mall parking lot, and uh you know jumped on physically, (T:Yeah) which really, and you know, I lost my house keys and everything. Uh and it really made me quite paranoid in that I felt extremely vulnerable. Uh I mentioned in the interview I think that a woman alone, particularly an older woman alone, was almost like a target, a victim, a potential target or victim or whatever you know. And uh I think that really threw me back into the reclusiveness. (T: Mm-Hmm) And um I don't know whether biorhythms has anything to do with this or not. I seem to feel that now I'm beginning to come out of it somewhat and that, I just filled out this form you know about am I any better than I was before. I have, just recently I've begun a new class, which, I was doing my homework when you came in. Uh and that's stimulating.

T: What kind, what kind of class?

C: Creative writing. The, the arts in general appeal to me: theatre, music, reading, so forth and so on. I don't veg out in front of the TV all the time. (laughs) I do read and uh . . .

This segment illustrates Lucille's eagerness to talk and be involved in therapy and shows that Dr. H's approach was to get right into Lucille's problems rather than to structure the treatment or inform Lucille regarding what to expect.

Summary of Process

Initial sessions. There was a power struggle for who would control the topic. Both had agendas for what they wanted to talk about during the hour, such that they frequently interrupted each other and talked simultaneously.

After identifying Lucille's major problem as the absence of a good support system, Dr. H adopted a behavioral approach and suggested that Lucille join a community theatre, be more friendly with neighbors, and go to meetings of her interest areas. His rationale for using a behavioral approach during these early sessions was to push for rapid change and if that did not occur, to use her reaction to diagnose how resistant she would be to change efforts. Lucille responded to Dr. H's suggestions with "Yes, but," giving reasons why she could not do these things. She was full of self-pity and martyrdom. Her primary excuse was her driving phobia, which prevented her from going to events by herself at night. To suggestions about how she could find others to take her, she responded that she did not feel comfortable imposing on people. Lucille was not sure that she wanted to or could change.

Middle sessions. A turning point came when Dr. H gave Lucille a homework assignment at the end of the fifth session to think about whether she wanted to make a commitment to change. During the sixth session, she said that this confrontation had frightened her because she thought she had made that commitment by coming to therapy. After this, the process slowed down, with Dr. H and Lucille working together more productively.

Dr. H's overall strategy shifted from offering solutions to helping Lucille understand why it was so difficult for her to change. During this phase, Lucille revealed more of her childhood and marriage. From her family and church, Lucille had incorporated the belief that said that women were not to achieve but were to stay home and take care of their families and want nothing for themselves. Lucille had broken away enough to realize that she did want to achieve something, but could not progress beyond that.

Final sessions. These sessions, which were spread out because of Dr. H's frequent vacations, had a slow and companionable pace. Lucille would report on the positive steps that she had taken during the week and Dr. H would reinforce her changes. He continued on the theme of how Lucille should be seeking out new sources of companionship, challenging her notions that all her friends should be similar to herself. Dr. H brought up many possible sources of involvement, both volunteer and paid, but Lucille made only minimal attempts to follow up on these.

Several quotes that Lucille brought in summarize the themes of the final phase of treatment. In the 14th session, she quoted the voluntary action center's mottoes, which were, "Helping others is helping yourself" and "Some people make things happen and some people wonder what happened." In the next session, she quoted William James as saying, "It is only by risking our persons from one hour to another that we live at all" and Helen Keller as saying, "Security is mostly a superstition that does not exist in nature." Lucille was working through being dependent on others and compromising her own needs and was trying to figure out how to take risks and be more independent.

Dr. H felt that Lucille had achieved her major goals by the 12th session and that she was no longer suffering as much, but waited until the 15th session to suggest that termination could occur soon. During the 16th session, he set termination for the 17th session which occurred a month later because of his vacation. Although Dr. H indicated that he did not typically discuss termination, they spent a fair amount of time talking about how Lucille would feel with the termination and what she had gained from the therapy. During the 17th session, Lucille arrived with a list of what she liked about Dr. H: his attention, insight, and sense of humor, as well as a list of what she had accomplished in the past month, including losing eight pounds. Lucille was optimistic in these final sessions compared to her self-pitying style of the beginning sessions.

Client Behavior

Lucille was always well dressed and spoke with a southern accent. She was quite active in the sessions, taking a lot of responsibility for what should occur. For example, she came prepared with lists, newspaper clippings, comic strips, and books. Lucille talked quickly, changed topics, and digressed often. At the beginning of therapy, Lucille often sounded whiny, complaining, and defeated, but this behavior changed across treatment. By the end of therapy Lucille seemed more independent and in charge of her own life.

Therapist Behavior

For response modes, Dr. H used primarily information and closed question. Compared to the other therapists, he used more approval and information and less open question and paraphrase. He indicated that his style was primarily intellectual rather than emotive. Further, Dr. H was about average in his activity level. Thus, he was structured and directive, with minimal emphasis on exploration or insight.

Dr. H was always at least half an hour late, but still had sessions that lasted about 55 minutes. His lateness was never discussed. Further, Dr. H's statements were often terse or cryptic. For example, once he came into session and said, "Dogwoods." When Lucille asked, he explained that the dogwoods were beautiful outside. Sometimes he would get off into what he called "high-faluting" language, in which he would say something theoretical that was not totally comprehensible. Further, he often mumbled, was hard to understand, and played with a pipe.

Dr. H often assigned homework. For example, one time he told her to keep a list of people she idealized and what they had accomplished. Next to it she was to write what she could realistically accomplish. Although he assigned homework, he rarely checked whether Lucille had done it.

Analyses of Therapist Techniques

Lucille and Dr. H talked about their reactions to the therapist techniques in the post-therapy interviews:

R: *What did Dr. H (you) do to help those changes come about?*

C: First of all, he listened, evaluated, and advised. He was insightful and helpful in suggesting things, but most of all he insisted that I face up to looking at me and my life, my situation, and my expectations in a realistic manner rather than with self-delusion and misperception or he called it grandiosity.

T: Cognitive restructuring was useful. There was a substantial amount of work in the direction of self-acceptance, especially that she was able to let go of some of the long-held idealizations and take enough action to start getting more consistent positive feedback about being competent and independent. *How did you do the cognitive restructuring?* Interpretation of defense, especially of rationalization and idealization.

R: *What did Dr. H (or you) do best with you (Lucille)?*

C: What was most valuable is that he didn't let you fool yourself. I mean, if you started b.s.ing, he stopped you and made you look at it. He just did his job when he felt you needed to face something or see a problem as it was. He stopped and had you just look at it or face it or work on it. *What specific techniques were helpful?* I was not especially aware of techniques. It was just more of a one on one. I guess if you want to say technique, I would say he listened and was very patient. I digressed a lot and talked about a lot of extraneous stuff, but somehow he was able to correlate all that. I would bring him newspaper articles and excerpts from books. Once I brought an Ann Landers letter because I thought it related to a problem a child of mine was having and I asked him to read the letter and he said, "Why can't you tell me rather than read the letter." I always brought these articles because I felt like they expressed it better than I could. But he insisted that I speak for myself. I stumbled through all these things and he was able to sweep it up like a snowball out of all those little flakes. His ability to do that helped a lot in identifying what we needed to work on. His sense of humor helped a lot because that helps me to feel closer to a person.

T: I was smug and pleased with myself about figuring out that her idealizations were critical to the system of internalization. As long as she could compensate for inadequacy feelings by resorting to the idealized fantasies, she had no energy left to change. So by interpreting the idealism, we began to see some movement and reshaping of the defensive and coping patterns. *What was your strongest skill?* Being able to figure out what is important to work on today, despite the fact that she's not giving me a lot of help with that. By keeping herself in an intellectualizing, controlling level, she's not giving me many clues as to what emotionally might be important for her in the particular hour. I'm having to do a lot of listening with the third ear to figure out what to focus on. I'd call that interpretation.

R: *Can you remember any specific therapist interpretations, that is, feedback that helped you (Lucille) view yourself (herself) or your (her) situation in a different way?*

C: Yeah. We were discussing the years that I was married and the extremely negative view I had of it and he was able to help me see that there was a lot of positive in it too. And that I had been able to accomplish some things in that situation that I might not have in other situations. It gave me thinking time. That was particularly helpful because it covered a lot of years and I was able to evaluate it in a more realistic way. He particularly helped me look at things more realistically. I was looking at things angled, cater-cornered, or not facing them. *How did that help you?* It helped me to accept myself and life, be less critical of myself, and not kick myself as much for things I can't change.

T: The only one I remember is the attempt to interpret her performance self as compensation, but I didn't ever make that interpretation. I did interpret them as idealizing. I didn't explain that function, but right after that she began to let go of the fantasy version of those idealized figures. She still gets excited by them and can see them on stage, but she also mentioned a song or two after that again more in the way of expressing herself.

R: *Can you recall one session that was particularly satisfying?*

C: I can't say there was one. There were good things in several. *Tell me about those.* I tended to blame myself for a lot of what I regret and he helped me see that I alone was not responsible, which relieved a lot of the self-contempt. He realized what an effort it was for me to change and do certain things and he gave me credit for doing that. That increased my self-esteem, whereas I had thought it was of little value. He helped me understand that anything that you do better than before is better. Whether you take one, two, or three steps is an improvement, whereas I wanted to take eight, nine, and ten. He helped me to be more realistic and accepting of things as they really are.

T: In session 8, the self-denigration went down and the self-acceptance went up. The two crossed and the energy became self-enhancement. She was able to take a more realistic view of her interests. In session 14, the change was towards greater autonomy. She had taken a number of actions on her own behalf like having the lawn done instead of waiting on her son and she had investigated the volunteer possibilities in a musical group. Some internalizing of the interpretation of her pattern in which the inadequacy feelings and envy led to the inhibition of self-directed activity, which then led to resentment and anger but not being able to have it her way which was followed by resignation.

R: *What did Dr. H (you) do least well?*

C: I have a hard time finding one. I really can't pinpoint anything that was not accurate.

T: I missed her anticipatory anxiety of going out and meeting new people. I would presume that a combination of attitude, exploration, cognitive restructuring, and role playing would have helped her to deal with that. And in the last session, I might have produced greater change if I had used more confrontation, encounter, and exploration of resistance about her controlling herself in the hour, keeping her emotions toned down, and keeping away from dependency feelings and needs in the session.

R: *Can you recall one session that was particularly unsatisfying?*

C: I wouldn't say unsatisfying, but the one that was most painful. I don't know why but I was feeling so sad that day. I just was in tears and my voice would break and it was unpleasant to go through that way. He said that at least it shows you're feeling, that it helps to feel it and know why you're feeling it, and accept that you're feeling it, and that it isn't bad to feel that way, and that there are sad times. It's not real to expect that you're not going to feel that way sometimes. *Is there anything you wished you had allowed yourself to say to or do with your therapist?* It would have been enjoyable to know him better, but I didn't feel free to do that because I still don't know quite what to expect from a client/ therapist relationship. Maybe it's better to keep it a little impersonal because then you're freer to bring up personal things in your own life to someone you're not that emotionally involved with. I can bring up with him whatever I need to without feeling threatened outside the relationship. But he would have been a very nice, good, pleasant, enjoyable friend. *Did you have any feelings about starting at least half an hour late each week?* It didn't inconvenience me. I hope it didn't inconvenience anyone else. It might have extended the time for all of you to get through the procedures, but I was free. My time is not bound.

T: In Session 10, she was going backwards or regressing or just pissing me off by doing nothing, complaining or groping, or something like that. We went in a big circle, going nowhere. Themes that had been worked on seemed unavailable. I had to take responsibility to get things going. We did some history stuff, which I usually do when I'm feeling frustrated and like I'm not going anywhere. She was becoming more aware of being stuck on the fence and being unwilling to commit herself to change. And I was futilely trying to push on getting more relationships going and getting more support from others. She wasn't buying it or even hearing it. *Is there anything you wish you had pursued further?* A lot of stuff was left unexplored. We did not explore the relationship with Daddy much. I let her keep me away from her anxiety in developing new relationships. We didn't get into how deeply entangled she was in her children's lives. We left the husband as a sort of a shadowy figure. I agreed with her to ignore the dependency bonding in our relationship. *Were those things important?* They weren't as important as what else we were doing. I do wish I had stuck with my original behavioral approach to anxieties about getting new relationships going. I got distracted by the driving phobia. I misread her persona. It looked to me like anybody who had herself put together that well to come see me and was in that much charge would be able to use those skills in introducing herself to new associations. Now I know that was silly. It's easy to put on a mask to avoid one's anxieties. I should have used my own self to know that. Maybe that's some kind of transference. I don't want to look at that part of me either. I like being a recluse, thank you.

Quantitative Analyses

Table 5.1 shows the results of analyses for therapist response modes on the immediate outcome measures. Table 5.2 shows the codings of the post-session reviews. Most of the events mentioned were helpful. Lucille attributed most of the helpful events to the therapist manner, whereas Dr. H attributed most of the helpful events to his techniques.

Combining the results of the post-therapy interviews with the quantitative analyses shows that the most helpful techniques were interpretation, approval, paraphrase, and disclosure, whereas confrontation and direct guidance were less helpful.

Discussion of Helpful Techniques

Interpretation. Dr. H's interpretations were oriented towards cognitive restructuring rather than towards understanding past history. He interpreted the effects of Lucille's irrational cognitions of self-

TABLE 5.1 Proportion of Occurrence, Client Helpfulness Ratings, Therapist Helpfulness Ratings, Client Experiencing, and Client Reactions for Therapist Response Modes in Case 3

Response Modes	%	Client Help Rating		Therapist Help Rating		Client Experiencing		Most Likely Reactions
		M	SD	M	SD	M	SD	
Approval	.10	7.02	.61 A	5.41	.75 A	2.29	.61 BC	Supported
Information	.35	6.81	.73 ABC	5.32	.86 A	2.21	.54 BC	Supported No Reaction
Direct Guidance	.05	6.82	.70 ABC	5.50	.94 A	2.14	.42 C	
Closed Question	.17	6.75	.67 BC	5.36	.87 A	2.19	.49 BC	Challenged No Reaction
Open Question	.06	6.63	.69 C	5.52	1.03 A	2.25	.58 BC	Challenged
Paraphrase	.11	6.86	.65 ABC	5.40	.78 A	2.23	.55 BC	Supported
Interpretation	.08	6.74	.89 BC	5.43	.99 A	2.35	.72 AB	Ther. Work
Confrontation	.06	6.66	.78 C	5.48	.88 A	2.11	.36 C	Challenged Negative
Disclosure	.02	6.95	.58 AB	5.33	.71 A	2.47	.77 A	
TOTAL		6.80	.71	5.38	.86	2.22	.54	

NOTE: Helpfulness was rated on 9-point scales (9 = extremely helpful); experiencing was rated on a 7-point scale (7 = high). ANOVAs indicated significant differences between therapist response modes for client helpfulness, $F (8, 2326) = 5.56, p < .0001$, therapist helpfulness, $F (8, 2326) = 1.57$, NS, and client experiencing, $F (8, 2326) = 3.95, p < .0001$. Post hoc differences are indicated, such that response modes with the same letter (A-C) were not significantly different (A = highest ratings). The overall relationship between response modes and client reactions was significant, $X^2 (28) = 340.97, p < .0001$.

pity, low self-worth, idealization, and grandiosity and offered new frameworks for looking at her situation.

Dr. H had several interpretive themes with Lucille. The first and oft-repeated theme was that her problems were related to a lack of social support. The second was that her tendency to idealize people caused her pain because she devalued herself and anything she could accomplish in relation to these overly idealized people. A third related theme was that her grandiosity got in her way of doing

TABLE 5.2 Proportions of Helpful and Hindering Events in Post-Session Reviews in Case 3

	Client		Therapist	
	Helpful	Hindering	Helpful	Hindering
Therapist Techniques	.19	.03	.37	.06
Support	.02	.00	.16	.01
Direct Guidance	.00	.00	.06	.02
Closed Question	.00	.00	.01	.00
Open Question	.00	.00	.00	.00
Paraphrase	.02	.00	.06	.01
Interpretation	.14	.03	.01	.02
Confrontation	.00	.00	.06	.00
Disclosure	.02	.00	.01	.00
Therapist Manner	.27	.00	.04	.03
Client Tasks	.15	.12	.19	.01
Focus	.00	.02	.04	.00
Experiencing	.02	.02	.04	.01
Insight	.14	.05	.05	.00
Changes	.00	.03	.06	.00
Client Manner	.07	.15	.17	.04
Relationship/Alliance	.02	.00	.05	.03
TOTAL	.70	.30	.83	.17

anything; for example, if she couldn't have a first-class seat on a trip, it wasn't worth going at all.

A fourth theme that was explored throughout the middle phase of therapy was that Lucille's current problems were related to her marriage. After growing up in a small town with an extended family and having an important job, she compromised herself to get married to a man who was secure. In the early years of the marriage, Lucille became dependent and depressed because she lost her identity. In session 7, they explored this interpretive theme:

T: What does it do for you to maintain this irrational view of yourself as incompetent to, to do organizing?

C: It doesn't do any, it doesn't have any value, except detrimental value.

T: But you hang onto it very firmly, so there must be some kind of reinforcement mentally for continuing to hold on to it.

C: I don't know if I'm afraid to uh venture out on my own, as, as an example of a fear of driving, whatever. (T: Is that . . .) I don't know if that carries through on other things.

T: So telling yourself you're, okay, unable to do it. incompetent or inadequate to do it, (C: Mmm) how does that save you from that anxiety?

C: It doesn't. The anxiety is still there. If you don't resolve an anxiety, you don't do away with it, right?

T: You can still feel it, right? (C: Yeah) So it's hard to see what that would be protecting you from.

C: Yeah, I don't, (Pause = 7 seconds) I don't, I can't see it. Either I don't, (Pause = 7 seconds) protecting me from, uh maybe lessening my opinion of myself even more you know. (T laughs) If I try it and can't do it, "oh boy, here we go again," you know, it's that old one step forward, two back.

T: I think we all do that to some extent. (C: Yeah) It protects our grandiosity, right? (C: Yeah, our ego, yeah) We know we're really perfect inside and, and uh it would oh only work if it weren't for this little problem.

C: Now isn't that egotistic to think that we're so grand that we're not going to do anything wrong (laughs) or get frustrated or stranded in your car. Yeah, I don't know why I get uh, I want things to be so smooth. (Pause = 6 seconds). I, I sometimes feel weird when that is happening.

T: In that sense wanting things to be so, so perfect, that feels weird?

C: No, no, no, not, but I, just my whole attitudes and ways of acting, being, doing (T: MmHmm) seems weird to me. I mean not really weird. But I don't know if I like other people or not. I seem to feel um, um, more uh out of tune with the times I guess. (T: MmHmm) There is that, like, (T: Well, let's . . .) I'm not at ease or comfortable in the world. (T: Lots . . .) I find it not like my world. I don't know if I'm distancing myself from it because of fear or because of. (T: Well, now you're feeling ex-...) it's not...

T: You're feeling excluded. It's like you feel the need for some companionship and support from other people, especially if you take on some new activities.

C: MmHmm. Well, I sort of, but mostly have to do things.

T: But some, but somehow that does not get expressed straightforwardly as that wish. Instead it gets twisted into, "since I don't have that, I'm not going to do it." (C: Right) And then that gets explained by way of your being so-called dependent and incompetent so-called. It's a really complex defense that prevents you from recognizing and dealing straightforwardly with a very usual interpersonal need which is to have companionship and support from others.

C: So then I'm not so weird after all then.

T: Well this, this vision (C: is not really normal...) of yourself as weird is tied in with that too. (C: MmHmm) You feel excluded from the companionship of others. (C: MmHmm) You feel like you don't know enough what goes on with other people. And that leads to a feeling of being shut out of, (C: MmHmm) not being included. And then you explain that by means of this formulation that you must have a skewed or different world view from other people. So, (C: Well...) so in both cases we're seeing feelings that express a need to be in much more intimate contact with other people being twisted and distorted into something else. And I'm not sure why you need to disown these normal needs, these feelings of wanting to be close and wanting to have some support from other people.

Later, Lucille has been talking about her marriage:

T: Do you know what I hear? (C: What?) I hear a lot of resentment and anger. And some of it is directed at yourself that you let yourself become this kind (C: Yes) of um (C: MmHmm) housebound vegetable. (C: MmHmm, right) Um it's all rather dramatized, you know, but...

C: I kick myself for doing it.

T: What's the anger coming from? What's, what's wrong with the choice you made that you're steamed about?

C: Well, I told you I felt like I've been a failure, you know. All these years I haven't done what I, I don't know if I could have done it, maybe I haven't done it because I felt like I didn't want to risk it. I don't know, but anyway...

T: You're angry at yourself for being a coward, (C: Maybe that's it partly . . .) angry at your family for insisting that that was the best role for you to stay there. You're angry at your husband for being so dependent that he insisted you stay in that role, angry at your kids for wanting you to stay in that role.

C: Now you said something that interested me, "My husband was dependent and so he wanted me to be in that role." He told me before we were married that he wanted me to stay at home with the children.

T: Yeah, a dependent male wants that. They want their mama to be there when they get home after school.

C: Lord, I would have thought he was strong and independent.

T: Men are taught to deceive themselves and others about their emotional dependency needs.

C: Well, I was not his mother, sorry, if that's what he was trying to cast me as.

T: Boy, are you angry! (C: Huh?) Boy, you are angry.

C: Am I? (both laugh) All right, that's, maybe I am. Does that make me what I am today?

T: You fell for it. You gave into it. And that (C: Yes) just eats away at you. (C: Yes, MmHmm) I don't think, I don't think you've got a chance of moving forward until you've done something with that anger, that set of resentments.

C: What do I do with it?

T: Well, right now you're sitting on it. You're, you're not feeling it (laughs) most of the time. It's coming out instead as self-criticism and inadequacy feeling and self-blame, (C: MmHmm) continued worry. So it's eating away at you. You need to own it first. And that's what you're starting to do right now. You're saying, "All right, yeah I'm angry at him for being dependent and pretending to be otherwise and needing me so much to stay at home. I'm, I haven't said about the kids yet." (laughs) "I'm angry at myself for buying into it, for letting my little anxieties just keep me from being brave enough to say, 'Look, I'm not going to stay a prisoner in this house all my life, I'm going back there into the world and enjoy myself.' " Right? (C: MmHmm) So you're angry at yourself. You're angry at him.

C: I think that all of us would have been better off had I done that.

T: Sure would. I don't know how much better. He would have been more anxious. He probably would have had (C: Oh) spells or periods of dysphoria or something. I don't know, who knows what they do. (C: Well, you . . .) Sometimes they turn to booze and throw fits and stuff.

C: No, he didn't drink. He didn't throw fits. He, he, uh he went to church. (both laugh) Uh you know, I still feel guilty saying things like that.

Approval. The approval was in the form of reinforcement for the changes that Lucille was making. She would come in with lists of things that she had tried and Dr. H would praise her for her efforts and encourage her to change more. His approval was not in the form of supportiveness, such as telling her how strong she was and that she could change. He was more of a confrontive "tough father" who expected Lucille to change her maladaptive behaviors and then reinforced her when she did.

Paraphrase. Dr. H said that Lucille was grateful for his paraphrasing because it permitted a self-acceptance of true feelings without her having to take full responsibility. Indeed, her general reaction was to feel supported. The excerpt presented earlier where Dr. H focused on Lucille's feelings of resentment and anger at her family and herself was particularly powerful. Interestingly, Dr. H seldom focused on feelings.

Disclosure. Dr. H was quite open with sharing aspects about himself from outside therapy. He accepted that he was a recluse, artistic, and eccentric. Because Lucille wanted to allow herself more freedom to let go of restrictions held over from her past, Dr. H's model of a person who went against all these unwritten rules was very freeing and gave her the hope that she also could be free to find out who she wanted to be (see Chapter 11). The disclosures that Dr. H used were not about immediate feelings about the process. He indicated that Lucille was not receptive to examining their immediate relationship.

Discussion of Less Helpful Techniques

Confrontation. Dr. H was very confrontive with Lucille, telling her that she needed to change if she wanted to be happy. She could not expect others to change for her. Further, as mentioned earlier, Dr. H continually confronted Lucille's cognitions and clearly communicated that she needed to give up her maladaptive thoughts. In post-session interviews, Dr. H mentioned that these confrontations were helpful to get Lucille out of her patterns. Lucille also mentioned in the post-therapy review that confrontations were helpful, but her immediate reactions within the session were negative. Undoubtedly, these confrontations did not feel good. Instead of sympathizing with Lucille's negative definition of herself, Dr. H challenged her to change.

Direct Guidance. Similarly, both mentioned that it was helpful when Dr. H gave suggestions for Lucille for what she could do differently. Within sessions, however, when Dr. H used direct guidance, Lucille's experiencing levels were very low. Although direct guidance was helpful toward the end of therapy, the use of it at the beginning was not helpful. In the first few sessions, before he had even explored the problem, Dr. H suggested innumerable ways that Lucille could make new friends. Lucille had very negative, "yes, but" responses for why she could not make use of any of the suggestions. After Dr. H switched to a more exploratory, interpretive mode of trying to help Lucille understand more of what caused and maintained her problems, therapy became more effective. Lucille could then listen to and use more of Dr. H's suggestions. Thus, direct guidance was helpful when it was based on a solid understanding of the client.

Moderating Variables

Client Factors

Lucille was at a transitional phase of life. At 60, when she was ready to consider the job market, her peers were ready to retire. She was not sure where she fit in the world nor what she could reasonably expect to contribute given her age. Related to her transitional phase of life were the many losses that Lucille faced within a short period of time: of her religious values, her husband, her mother, her sister-in-law and her husband, and her physical invulnerability due to the mugging. In many ways, Lucille was going through a grieving period, which she was just beginning to be able to face and adjust to at the time of the therapy.

Lucille was reasonably wary of getting help. She was somewhat resistant to accepting suggestions and making changes in her life situation. After having done what she thought she "should" do all her life, Lucille was having difficulty figuring out who she was and what she wanted from life, but did not want anyone to push anything on her. Further, she was not in a great deal of immediate pain and thus had a hard time taking the necessary risks to change her life. Had she been poverty-stricken after her husband's death, she might have been forced to change her lifestyle, but she had just enough money so that she was not forced to make major changes.

Therapist Factors

In orientation, Dr. H was both psychoanalytic and behavioral. His first tactic with Lucille was behavioral, in that he sized up her problem as having too few contacts with other people and set about trying to figure out how to remedy the problem. When this strategy flopped because Lucille resisted being told what to do, Dr. H was able to modify his approach to helping Lucille understand what caused and maintained her behavior, with an emphasis on what she could do differently in the present. This flexibility enabled Dr. H to form a working relationship with Lucille.

One important aspect of Dr. H's style for this case was his self-confidence and acceptance of himself for who he was. This was precisely what Lucille was struggling to attain. Dr. H was clearly his own person, marching to the beat of his own drummer. Given Lucille's choice of a safe, secure husband, she may not have met many people who were able to accept themselves as they were.

Dr. H, who was 17 years younger than Lucille, did mention that Lucille reminded him of his mother, whom he described as somewhat overcontrolled and idealistic, although she was not self-pitying. How much this influenced his behavior is not evident, other than that he treated Lucille with some deference and respect.

The Therapeutic Relationship

Lucille rated the relationship as moderately strong on the WAI (see Chapter 2, Table 2.2). Dr. H's overall ratings, on the other hand, were low, although they increased over the course of the therapy, probably reflecting the change from the initial struggle over how the therapy should proceed to the cooperation that developed.

In the post-therapy interview, Dr. H said,

T: There was some warmth in it, but it sure was subtle. Part of that is my own difficulty in reading warmth. I generally find myself a lot colder and more aloof and distancing than my colleagues tell me I am with clients. It feels mostly like expert role stuff. The use of interpretation promotes that. I do a lot of bonding with humor in all my work, but felt it was only moderately successful with her. There were quite a few times when I was laughing at some absurdity which she wasn't quite able to see as humorously as I was. But still there was a blending of sense of humor. And she began sharing some of the same level of skeptical appreciation of a certain view that I have toward the end. We shared an ideological aversion to coerciveness and fundamentalism. Being a parent and recognizing some of the developmental changes that could be expected from how I was treated when I was a kid probably helped the bonding. There were a number of fortuitous similarities, such as small town and religious backgrounds, an interest in the arts, and a sense of humor. So the sharing of these values probably helped some.

External Factors

Extratherapy involvement. Comments in the post-therapy interviews indicated that both Dr. H and Lucille believed that she had tried to apply what she learned in therapy to her outside life:

R: *How did you (Lucille) use therapy between sessions?*

C: He would make specific suggestions as to things I could do. I tried to do those, such as looking for something good. It was a beautiful time to do that because it was spring and I appreciate nature. Even small things gave you pleasure. When a negative thought occurred, to try to not dwell on it, to try to turn it around to something positive. *Did you talk about your sessions to anyone?* Yes, to a couple of friends. *Were you aware of trying new behaviors as a result of the sessions?* Yes, maybe not as much as I should have, but every journey starts with one step.

T: Whenever we reached some agreement on courses of action, she would do that within the week. She'd try out one or more behaviors along the lines that we had talked about. She seemed to pick up on some emotional themes that we were dealing with and find occasion for reexperiencing these. So it felt like a lot of hard work between sessions.

Support network. Lucille was very involved with her three children, although they were not much of a source of support. Her oldest daughter, an attorney aged 32, was quite critical of Lucille. Her second daughter, a nurse aged 25, was the most supportive. Her son, aged 22, lived with her while attending college, but was removed from her emotionally. Lucille knew she needed to let go of her children, but this was difficult for her.

She had one close female friend with whom she could share her deepest feelings. This woman was quite similar to Lucille in that both had made many compromises throughout life so that they could "survive." Because this friend was married, however, their amount of time together was limited. Lucille was also friendly with a younger, homosexual male who shared her interest in the arts and would drive her places. In general, Lucille felt lonely but was ambivalent about how much contact she wanted with people. She liked solitude, but she worried that she had too much.

External events. This was a relatively calm period in Lucille's life, with no major changes. She was taking some community college courses, but had not found any satisfying volunteer or paid work.

Outcome of Therapy

Session Outcome

According to ratings on the SEQ (see Chapter 2, Table 2.2), Lucille perceived the sessions as being moderately deep and very smooth, whereas Dr. H perceived them as being moderately deep and smooth.

Pre-Post Changes

Lucille was somewhat improved at the end of 17 sessions of treatment (see Table 5.3). On the MMPI, Lucille's score on Social Introversion had decreased, but her scores on the Psychopathic Deviate and Mania scales had increased. Thus, she was feeling more outgoing and energetic as well as more rebellious and non-conformist after therapy. She reported positive change in all six target complaints. The therapist rated her as improved on all complaints except self-confidence. She was also less anxious and depressed, but unchanged in both symptomatology and self-esteem.

Lucille and Dr. H discussed more specific changes in the post-therapy interviews excerpted below:

R: *How did you (or Lucille) change as a result of therapy?*

TABLE 5.3 Scores on Outcome Measures for Case 3

Measures	Pre	5th	Expect	Post	6 Mo	1 Yr
Client-Rated Measures						
MMPI						
Depression	80			76		
Social Introversion	74			55*		
Psychasthenia	70			70		
Psychopathic Deviate	64			[88**]		
Mania	43			[55*]		
SCL-90-R	47			40	36	[45]
TSCS	37			[36]	44*	[34**]
TC (1) Achievement	10	9	7	6*	4	[6]
(2) Driving Anxiety	10	10	7.5	7*	5	[8*]
(3) Religious Values	7	6	6	4*	4	[6]
(4) Negative Feelings		10	6	5*	5	[7]
(5) Self-Confidence		10	7	6*	5	[8*]
(6) Discipline		10	6	5*	5	[7]
Satisfaction					7.5	6.5
Therapist-Rated Measures						
TC (1) Achievement	8	[11*]	5	3*		
(2) Driving Anxiety	12	7*	2.5	4**		
(3) Religious Values	9	4*	2	2**		
(4) Negative Feelings		11	7	3**		
(5) Self-Confidence		6	2	6		
(6) Discipline		12	4	2***		
Researcher-Rated Measures						
Hamilton Anxiety	19			9**		
Hamilton Depression	22			10***		

NOTE: High *T* scores indicate high symptomatology on the SCL-90-R GSI, high self-esteem on the TSCS; worst functioning on the TC, higher satisfaction, and greater disturbance on the Hamilton scales. Expect = level expected after treatment. * = significant change at $p < .05$; ** = $p < .01$; *** = $p < .001$. Negative changes are in brackets.

C: I didn't know what I wanted to do and I didn't have anybody to do it with. I had this feeling of loneliness. One of the reasons I wasn't able to do what I wanted to do was because I didn't drive at night. That's still a problem. There are so many things that I would like to do that involve driving to places at night where I don't feel right going as an older woman alone. And that revealed the lack of a support system. I have to be more aggressive in seeking that support system. One problem was feeling that I hadn't achieved what I would like to have done. I still feel that to some degree, but it doesn't bother me to the degree that it did. Then there was the problem of self-confidence. He was able to help me to some degree. I'm not saying that I've overcome all these problems and suddenly I'm on top of the world and everything's fine. I still have the problems, but not to the degree I had. I've been able to accept those problems and myself with a little more equanimity and realization of the fact that I must get off my duff and move. We had some questions about my values too. We hashed it out pretty well. I'm pretty at ease with the way I view things at the moment. They have changed and they may change again, but I'm comfortable with them. Also, I've been able to get a little more motivated and active in many areas and less critical of myself. It enabled me to look on family relationships with more equanimity. They still bother me, but to a lesser extent in that I'm able to let go of it quicker and not let it eat at me as long. *Give me an example of something that you can do differently now than before.* I look to myself to fulfill my wants, rather than expecting someone else to do something for me. I've become more responsible for getting things done in general. Specifically, I had been expecting my son to mow the yard and he was feeling put upon. So I got someone to take care of mowing the yard. I'm less disappointed when others let me down, or what I perceive as letting me down, which may be a misperception on my part. But everything goes back to that bad things don't bother me as much. *Anything else?* I felt it was a good match of client and therapist. I'm sadder, but wiser and tougher as a result of therapy. I'm sadder, but it's a realistic sadness in that I have had to give up some dreams and it's sad to give up dreams. But it's a realistic way of looking at it. I'm wiser because I understand more why I do the things I do and why I don't do the things I don't do. And I'm tougher in that I'm more like a duck that's able to let things that I can't control roll off without eating at me. We expect some sadness, that everything is not going to be 100% hunky-dory all the time and you have to not let it eat at your innards all the time.

T: Her main problems were unhappiness, loneliness, and inhibition and her mood lifted quite a bit as a result of therapy. She was not unhappy much more. She was doing something about her loneliness, not necessarily seeing more of other people but just not feeling that way as much, feeling more in charge of herself. She seemed to be a bit more assertive and was taking more action on her own behalf. So even though she still felt some anxiety about driving alone and meeting people, I think she was less inhibited by the time we stopped. *Anything else?* She gradually abandoned much of her self-critical thinking, more rapidly after we uncovered the function of her idealizing views of others and self. As she became more realistic and vented some of her resentment and anger, she began to take more responsible actions which produced an increasing sense of accomplishment and autonomy. Her relationships appeared to improve as she learned to seek more realistic versions of interpersonal needs. At the time of termination, she had begun to re-evaluate her own beliefs and values, with a sense of humor. Her sense of inner security had improved considerably, especially as she accepted her need for supportive involvements with others.

R: *How satisfied do you feel with the nature and amount of change?*

C: I'd like to make a lot more, but I think this has been a good beginning. A lot of it is just up to me.

T: Moderately satisfied. Symptoms pretty much evaporated, got some new things started. That feels great. Client's pretty intact. She doesn't need her personality changed in any crucial sense. But I would have continued longer if I hadn't had a time-limited contract. If I had a longer time, and by that I mean 150 sessions, I would have focused much more on our relationship, and used that process to try and change some fairly basic balances among her fear of vulnerability and of her demandingness.

Lucille was asked to talk about what caused and maintained one of her major problems. Her answer indicated that the therapy had helped her gain some insight into her problems:

C: My major problem is motivating myself and pursuing a life that would give me more satisfaction. The fact that I am not more aggressive in doing that is a result of my having always been dependent on someone else and having decisions made by others or just accepting what came along, rather than really getting out there and putting a lot of thought and work into what I want and how to get it. I wish I had been, but I can't put spilled milk back into the bottle. I feel like I have gotten to know myself better and identified what makes me happy and identified my values. I'm working on the motivation and self-confidence so that if I have another life, I will know these things sooner and be more aggressive in seeking a more fulfilling and satisfying total life. I think that it's possible to accomplish that now in this life to some degree. That's what I want to work on. *What do you see as keeping you back from doing that in this life?* I started to say mostly externals. But it's just that I don't push myself enough to do it. I need to push myself more, that's the problem. There are externals, but they can be overcome or should be able to be. I think I can't drive at night, but I could get involved in some group where there would be group transportation. There are possibilities if I were to pursue them. I need to work at it.

Six-Month Follow-Up

Lucille maintained the gains that she made during therapy on all six target complaints. Further, she continued changing gradually on symptomatology and self-esteem, so that she was significantly improved in both compared to pre-treatment levels.

In the interview, Lucille sounded like she was functioning very well. She had been busy with dental and medical appointments, a class on metaphysics, her younger daughter's wedding plans, and getting in touch with former college friends. She felt stresses from her children, her house, and her financial situation, but felt that she was making good choices regarding these. She reported that Dr. H had helped her face reality and deal with things as they are rather than as she wished they were. Further, she felt that the class in metaphysics was reinforcing and confirming the changes that she made in therapy, particularly as to values.

One-Year Follow-Up

Lucille relapsed to pre-therapy levels in everything except three target complaints (achievement, dwelling on negative feelings, and discipline). She had been busy with her daughter's wedding, a trip to places that she had lived previously, extensive periodontal surgery, and an automobile accident (no one was hurt). With her income dropping, she was concerned about her long-range ability to remain independent. She sounded depressed and self-pitying again.

The best explanation for why Lucille relapsed was the end of a metaphysics course that had reinforced some of the attitudinal changes she made in therapy. Further, Lucille had not yet made any moves to get a volunteer or paid position, nor had she made any new friends. I hypothesize that Lucille was not able to make these changes because she was not willing to risk much discomfort in order to change. After having gone through several traumatic events, Lucille was now relatively stable and entrenched in her way of life. She did not have enough immediate pain to make it worthwhile to change.

In the therapy, Dr. H focused primarily on Lucille's need to get out and get more support, but focused less on why it was that she had a hard time allowing herself to go out. Thus, Lucille was not able to understand her choices from the past and come to a resolution for how she could be different now. Dr. H was on the right track exploring the issues related to her compromises about getting married and becoming depressed and dependent. Unfortunately, he did not pursue this interpretive theme fully. After discussing it in the seventh session, he let it drop. Further, although Dr. H discussed Lucille's need for support, he never dealt with her romantic relationships with men, which also may have been a source of her ambivalence.

Another factor that may have influenced Lucille's emotions at the one-year follow-up was the discovery a year or so later of physical problems that had been chronic but undetected.

Long-Term Follow-Up

Four years after the termination of therapy, Lucille reported feeling content. She was more resolved about her achievement issues, having decided to accept her lifestyle rather than getting volunteer or paid positions. Since she was more confident now about driving, the driving anxiety was no longer a problem. Further, she had straightened out many of her questions of values and was much clearer about her philosophy of life. Given that most of life is unknowable, she felt that whatever she chose to believe was okay as long as it worked for her. She was no longer as negative as she used to be, had more self-confidence, more discipline, and was more motivated to get things done that she wanted to do. She still was concerned about her finances and her children, and that she had not accomplished much in her life, but was not as hard on herself as she had been previously. She had not sought out further therapy.

Summary

The therapist techniques of interpretation, approval, paraphrase, and self-disclosure were helpful in this case, whereas confrontation and direct guidance were less helpful.

Client variables, therapist variables, and the therapeutic relationship all moderated the effects of the techniques. The client was somewhat resistant to change and did not want to be told what to do. She had gone through several major life transitions and was having difficulty coping and figuring out who she was at this point in her life, but was not necessarily ready to make major changes. The therapist was able to modify his style to meet what the client wanted from therapy. Further, the therapeutic relationship was strong and enabled the client to hear what the therapist had to say. External factors, on the other hand, did not play a major helpful or hindering role in the process or outcome of this case. Thus, all these moderating factors enabled the client to make use of the therapist techniques. Through the therapy, the client was able to understand the major transitions she had gone through and adjust to her current life situation.

6

Case 4: Tell Me What to Do

This chapter will focus on the therapist techniques in the 12-session case conducted by Dr. M, a 37-year old, Black, female psychologist with Marie, a 44-year old, Chinese woman.

Client

Marie (a pseudonym) came from a disturbed family. Her mother had divorced her first husband because of cruelty and then married a disabled man who was a gambler and never worked. Marie was the first of two children of the second marriage. Because the family was very poor, the daughter born after Marie was given away. A daughter from the mother's first marriage ran away when she was a teenager because she could not tolerate the blended family. Marie felt guilty that she had experienced a better family life than her other siblings.

Marie was very close to her mother, even though her mother was critical of her and had no confidence in her. When Marie was in high school, her mother threatened suicide. Marie begged her not to do it because she would never be able to finish school. Her mother did not commit suicide, but was bitter and unhappy for the rest of her life. At about the same time, Marie attempted suicide because her fiancé broke their engagement.

At age 23, Marie married a man who worked for the federal government. The first four years of the marriage, before children and when Marie was working as a secretary, were relatively harmonious. When Marie was pregnant with her first child, her father died and

Marie asked her husband to let her mother move in with them. From that point on, the marital relationship disintegrated. Marie complained that her husband was critical and belittling, as well as loud and embarrassing in public. He was nice to everyone else, but mean to his own family. He frequently said cruel things to the children, especially the son, whom he felt was too feminine. To avoid the inevitable fights, Marie simply withdrew and said nothing of her feelings to her husband. Additionally, Marie was worried that with his traditional Chinese beliefs that devalued women when they were past childrearing years, her husband was getting ready to leave her for a younger woman.

They had two children. The daughter, aged 17, was very intelligent but had few friends because she was withdrawn. The friends she did have she never brought home because Marie was too embarrassed by her bad housekeeping to allow anyone into the house. The son, aged 14, was also withdrawn and spent most of his time playing fantasy games such as *Dungeons and Dragons.* The son had gotten quite sick when he was four, going into convulsions and having to be hospitalized. Because she worried that he would not breathe, Marie moved into his room and slept there until he was 10, which undermined sexual relations with her husband. In fact, Marie mentioned that they had sex about once a month out of obligation and that this was a source of her husband's discontent.

Relations between Marie's husband and mother had also been tense. When the fights between them got too bad, her mother would leave and go to the sister's house for a few months. When things got intolerable at the sister's, she would return to Marie's house. In the 10 months prior to Marie's coming to therapy, however, her mother had deteriorated physically and was emotionally ready to die. She stayed in bed most of the time and did not communicate.

Physical Functioning

Marie was healthy with no history of serious illnesses. In the past, her appendix and tonsils had been removed. Marie had a fear of dying of cancer, which her father had died from. Marie reported that she did not have a well-balanced diet, in that she ate too many sweets and too much junk food, but she did do calisthenics three times a week and did not appear overweight.

Pre-Therapy Expectations

Marie had never had any previous therapy. She thought that therapy was for helping people understand and overcome their problems. She wanted a therapist to be understanding and helpful.

Pre-Therapy Assessment

Scores on the pre-therapy assessment measures are shown in Table 6.3. On the MMPI, Marie had normal validity scores and high scores on the Psychopathic Deviate, Depression, and Psychasthenia scales. This MMPI profile indicates that Marie was fearful and a worrier, nervous, overanxious about minor things, prone to crying easily, unable to express emotions, depressed, impulsive, argumentative, and insecure. It also indicates that she had a need for attention and affection, but had an inner conflict over dependency.

Compared to an outpatient population, Marie was average on symptomatology, but below average on self-concept. She was functioning worse than average on her target complaints. The clinician judged her to be mildly depressed and anxious.

She was diagnosed by the research team as dysthymic with a dependent personality disorder.

Target Complaints

Marie's first complaint was a lack of self-confidence. She avoided being around people because she did not feel educated enough or equal to others. Her second complaint was her relationships with her family. She felt that there was too much arguing and bickering with her husband and children. Her third complaint was coping with her mother's dying. During the fifth session, Marie added the complaint of her marriage, which she felt was very unsatisfactory. Marie considered adding the complaint that she needed to find a job to help support her children through college, but decided not to focus on it in therapy. She had not worked since she had children and doubted her ability to return to the work force. Her self-confidence was eroded because her husband devalued her previous secretarial work as "poverty-level work."

Summary of Client Pre-Therapy Characteristics

Marie was a tense, fearful, anxious, and depressed housewife. Her major concerns were the imminent losses of her dying mother and her daughter, who was planning on going away to college. The researcher who conducted the clinical interview expressed some concerns about accepting Marie as a client because she was not insight-oriented and seemed somewhat unwilling to change.

Therapist

Dr. M had a PhD in counseling psychology and had worked as a counselor at a university counseling center for 11 years. She was licensed and listed in the National Register of Health Service Providers in Psychology. Dr. M was well-regarded by the counseling center staff and was sought out by students for counseling. She maintained an active private practice in individual, conjoint, and group psychotherapy and did consulting for several organizations.

Using three 5-point (5 = high) scales for how much she believed in and adhered to each of three major orientations, Dr. M rated herself: psychoanalytic = 4, humanistic = 2, and behavioral = 3. Dr. M viewed herself as an ego psychologist. Specifically, she believed that people's natures are basically negative until shaped by the social group and family in which they find themselves. She believed in the unconscious, which serves to protect people from thoughts and feelings that are painful or unacceptable. Although many things in life are determined, she believed that people have the free will to shape how they respond and deal with these givens. Further, although she believed that heredity plays a key role in development, she also thought that environment plays a critical role in how one's physical, social, and psychological reality unfolds. Early childhood experiences play an important role in shaping who people are and how they perceive life, while experiences at critical choice points continue to shape whom they become.

People come to therapy, Dr. M believed, when the stress in their lives is greater than their defense mechanisms can tolerate or when there is a sudden change in their support system. The therapist offers clients a safe, loving object with whom to bond while learning more effective ways of dealing with their lives. Change occurs when clients feel safe enough to face risky issues and are willing to try new behaviors, thoughts, and beliefs. They must believe, though, that the price of change is less costly than the price of remaining the same.

The Treatment Process

The verbatim excerpt from the first few minutes of the first session illustrates the process between Marie and Dr. M.

T: Why don't you tell me a little bit about what's going on?

C: Um well, I just have a lot of commotion in my household and con-, well, a lot of arguing and I guess tension. My mother um lives with me. My father is deceased. (T: MmHmm) And she's in ill health, so I'm really worried about that part of it. I don't think I can handle it. That's um, my children don't give me too much problem, except that, you know, they, you know, have basic, uh well my daughter doesn't feel she does that well socially. (T: MmHmm) so I kind of feel for her there. And uh I mean they're not too much, you know I'm not worried about them (T: MmHmm) other than maybe they could fit in more socially with others than they are now.

T: How long has your mom been sick?

C: Uh she's always been you know, uh frail-like. (T: MmHmm) I mean, she's had arthritis for many, many years and it's gotten worse and since then emphysema has developed. And she's weak, very weak and thin. (T: MmHmm) She's always talking about, "It's time," you know, (T: MmHmm) "It's a matter of a short time now." And uh I, she's really depressed because she's lost a lot of her friends, uh probably, yeah, all of her friends. (T: MmHmm) She's not, well she had several close ones. And they're not, you know, ali-, around now. And so she's pretty much lonely. (T: MmHmm) She's lonely. And I don't know how to fill that gap for her. Um I guess that she's just not going to, as far as emphysema, she's not going to get better. (T: MmHmm) And she has very much difficulty breathing. I'm taking her to breathing therapy now. (T: Mm-Hmm) And uh that's about what, you know, worries me.

T: Was your concern about your mom the primary reason that you decided you wanted to be in the study?

C: Uh n-, partly. And then the other part is to maybe improve family life and relations (T: MmHmm) and kind of help my daughter through her period of um she's not very happy as a, I mean she does well academically, but she feels she's out of it socially. (T: MmHmm) She's not, she doesn't feel accepted because maybe they think she's a brain. And they kind of hurt her, you know, you're not one of them (T: MmHmm) And she doesn't feel very happy about that. (T: MmHmm) (C sighs; pause = 7 seconds) And then my husband I guess is very jealous of my mom and the kids cause I, you know, maybe he feels I pay, you know, m-, a lot more attention. And so there is some, one other thing that really kind of bothers me about the way he, he says things about h-, his son. You know my son is kind of, well he's not outgoing, that m-, you know s-, he makes friends easily (T: MmHmm) I think and, but he just has one close friend. (T: MmHmm) So uh he doesn't really get together, you know, he's pretty much at home. (T: MmHmm) He doesn't, you know, he doesn't really see much more than this one friend, so, and my husband says these things about him and, you know, right in front of him. And I think it might ruin him.

T: What kind of things?

C: Like he's gay (T: MmHmm) or you know he's a queer, (T: MmHmm) that kind of remarks. (T: MmHmm) And he brings it up, you know, often. And I've talked to the pediatrician about that because it really upset me a lot. And, and he says that, you know, that he should never do that. (T: MmHmm) That's very damaging. But I don't, you know, he hasn't stopped doing that. (T: MmHmm) So I was wondering what I could do about that. (C laughs)

Marie's speech dysfluency in this segment was typical of her behavior in therapy and probably was a sign of her anxiety. The segment also shows her tendency to focus her concerns on others in her family, rather than on herself. Dr. M's style was to allow Marie to explore her concerns in a relatively unstructured manner.

Summary of Process

Initial sessions. The first four sessions were spent exploring Marie's past and current concerns. The sessions were marked by a great deal of catharsis, with Marie spilling a lot of her hopeless feelings about her immediate family. Although Marie seemed to be very involved in the sessions, she consistently mentioned in her post-session questionnaires that she was not getting enough advice or answers for how to deal with her problems.

At the end of session 3, Marie "tested" whether Dr. M would give her the kind of advice that she wanted. The following segment started when Dr. M asked Marie why she sought out this therapy:

C: The opportunity, you know, (T: the opportunity . . .) was there and I always felt I needed help. (T: MmHmm) You know, I said, "I bet you my life would be different if I could only get the direction to do things right or get some advice on how to go about straightening things that are so disorganized or whatever it is that's causing me to be like I am (T: MmHmm) or s-, whatever obstacles in the way. Maybe someone can tell me what it is so I can try to get around it." I've always felt that I had to have some kind of direction, (T: MmHmm) but it was just the expense of it (T:MmHmm) that, you know, made, made it just say well it would be nice to have, (T: MmHmm) to talk with, and, and straighten you out. But there are other things that are, come first, (T: MmHmm) you know, before I, you know, can even consider it.

T: So you're saying, what you're saying is that you have hope of finding some ways to make this better, this kind of heaviness and the problems that now feel very weighty, of dealing with them better.

C: MmHmm. I hope to get some direction (T: MmHmm) and some advice you know on what to do for all the things that I, you know, have been bothering me and stood in the way (T: MmHmm) and, you know, the problems that I have, I hope that someone can tell me, "This is why it is and this is what you have to do to overcome it."

T: You know, as, as we have talked, we've just really begun. We've had our initial sessions. And then we had the break and did not meet. But as we've talked, you know, the first impression is that s-, several things, first of all it seems that you've got some ideas of where the hurts are. And you're not sure what kinds of things to do differently to handle things better. And that's part of what I hope will come out of our working together and getting some direction. But the other part of that that I want to say is that I think that, I know that that direction will come out of our talking, but more important that out of you, out of your getting confidence and deciding which step you want to take, which thing feels like the next thing to do. And step by step, things will get lighter. But you'll find that some of those things, if not all of them will come from your beginning to feel better about making the next step. Does that make any sense?

C: Well, I never had any confidence in myself. So I'm not sure if I'm going to come up with all this. You know, (T: MmHmm) I don't really have any confidence that's coming, going to come out of, from me, (T:

MmHmm) because if it would, it would have happened already. (C laughs)

T: You know, some, I can hear how it would feel like that. "If I had known all these things, I would g-, already have gone and done them." I think sometimes it's a matter of um seeing things more clearly. It's hard to make the step. Like your planning to go back to work and you've known that if you're going to help with your children's education, that you'd probably have to do that, yet taking the step is very scary. So you have the information inside of you, but making the actual step is sometimes the hardest part. Now also there will be sometimes that you don't have the information. It's kind of hidden from you. You haven't thought of it yet. Or you haven't looked at it carefully enough to see what those next steps are. So it's a combination of things.

C: Will you be telling me what to do?

T: I hope not. Not like, "Marie, I think you should go get a job now" or "Marie, I think you should say this to your husband" or "Marie, I think you should do this with your mom." But what I do want to do with you is as you raise things you're concerned about, like today you talked about mom's seeming to have given up and you talked about your feeling like you don't know what to do when she says I'm just going to die. What I hope to do, and you said also that I feel so overwhelmed when she says that. And what I want to do and what I think I did was to say, "Hey, that's understandable, that's normal, that's okay to feel overwhelmed, anybody in that situation will feel overwhelmed," to help you understand and believe that at that point in time there's probably not much more you could have done. Now we can look at the situation and think about what other things you might do now. But when a mother comes to a child and says, "I'm dying," that's overwhelming, that's scary. So I think it's my job to help you believe that and help you see that. There may be some other things you want to say to your mom, you want to do yourself around your feelings about her dying, and we can certainly talk about that and about her life that she has left before she dies. So my role is to help you look at what happened, what you felt, give you permission to feel those things, and help you look at what you want to do, these things have happened now, what do you want to do next, to plan a road map for how to deal with these things that have already ongoing and how to accept the things that have already happened. But I don't want to take the, the road of saying, "Now, do this now, do that" because I don't want first of all, I might make a mistake if I don't have all the information that you have about you.

C: That's what, I'm always afraid of making a mistake. That's why it's so hard for me to make any decisions. I don't care if they're probably small as big, as, as well as large, I have the hardest time making a decision. (T: MmHmm) I'm so afraid of making that wrong decision that I just keep on letting it ride and letting it ride until the time comes where you can't.

In this segment, Marie explicitly told Dr. M that she wanted advice. Dr. M deflected this demand and indicated that the advice would come from the process of their discussions and Marie deciding what she wanted to do. Marie was not pleased with this response because she felt she would make mistakes if she made her own decisions. Thus, in a sense, Dr. M failed the "test."

There were two missed sessions in between the second and third and between the third and fourth sessions, with Marie calling either the secretary or researcher at about midnight to cancel because of sickness, trips, and concerns about leaving her mother.

Middle sessions. During the fifth through seventh sessions, Dr. M switched to working on helping Marie solve specific problems. For example, in the fifth session, they talked about how Marie could tell a friend not to smoke around her. Dr. M modeled how Marie could be direct in making her request. In the sixth session, Dr. M began by asking Marie if she had tried being direct with her friend. Marie responded that she had decided not to say anything because she did not want to wreck her friendship. They then dealt with problems the daughter was having at work, with Dr. M advising that the daughter be direct in stating her needs. At the end of these sessions, Marie told Dr. M that her advice was very helpful and she rated the sessions higher in depth (quality) than the initial or final sessions.

Final sessions. In the eighth to tenth sessions, they discussed problems the daughter was having at work and in choosing where to go to college and what to major in. They also talked about how to deal with Marie's sister and brother who visited to see their mother as she became increasingly ill. As would be expected, Marie had a lot of feelings about dealing with her mother. On the one hand, she was very sad that her mother was dying. On the other hand, she felt angry and overwhelmed with the additional responsibility of caring for her constant needs and she felt unsure of how to deal with her mother's withdrawal and noncommunicativeness. In all of these issues, Marie asked Dr. M to tell her exactly what she should do and how she should phrase her communications to people. Although she occasionally gave specific advice on how to handle a situation, Dr. M most often took the strategy of probing Marie for what she thought she should do, and then reassuring Marie that her ideas for what to do in these situations were very good. Thus, Dr. M tried to build on Marie's strengths and encourage her to trust herself.

Following the tenth session, the dyad did not meet for eight weeks due to planned vacations and because Marie's mother became more ill. Marie hardly even left the house during this time, but called Dr. M several times for support and bereavement counseling. In a separate conversation, Marie told the research assistant that she did not want to continue therapy. As the project director, I called Marie and asked her to complete the contracted 12 sessions for the research project. Because of her commitment to the research project, Marie did attend the final two sessions.

The final two sessions were difficult for Marie. Talking about her feelings about losing her mother made her very upset, so she would switch to talking about her worry that her daughter was not adjusting well socially to the university or her anger that her brother would not visit even though that was her mother's last wish. To deal with Marie's anxiety, Dr. M used an educational strategy, providing Marie with information about university services for her daughter and hospice programs for her mother, as well as explaining the stages of death and dying for both the person and the family members.

Client Behavior

Marie was very tentative in presenting herself, always wanting to make sure she was doing and saying the right things. For example, before she came for the clinical interview, she wanted to know exactly what she should wear. She was also somewhat forgetful. Even though the research had been fully explained to her, Marie forgot that she had to do the videotape review and had only planned to come for an hour for the first meeting.

In the sessions, Marie was quite willing to talk and explore her feelings, often crying. Marie revealed a lot about herself. In fact, she worried that she was sometimes too impulsive in what she said. For example, she regretted having mentioned about her husband's attitudes towards her son.

Marie told Dr. M on several occasions that she wanted more advice and that it was helpful when Dr. M told her exactly what to do. Because she did not trust her own ideas on anything, Marie wanted advice about very basic things. For example, she wanted to know how to tell her brother without offending him that she did not want him to stay for two weeks. Or since her mother was spending most of her time with her eyes closed, she wanted to know whether she should wake her mother up if she wanted to be with her.

Throughout the entire therapy, Marie would begin talking with Dr. M in the hall on the way to the therapy room and would continue after the session talking with Dr. M in the hall and bathroom during the break before the videotape replay. Additionally, as mentioned above, Marie had numerous telephone contacts with both Dr. M and the research staff between sessions.

Therapist Behavior

For response modes, Dr. M used primarily information, paraphrase, and closed question. Compared to the other therapists, she used more information and direct guidance and less interpretation and confrontation, indicating that this was a directive rather than insight-oriented therapy. Although on the average Dr. M was moderate in her activity level, in some sessions she was relatively quiet whereas in others she spoke a lot.

Dr. M was very gentle and supportive with Marie. She tried to accommodate Marie's desires for more direct guidance. Her preferred approach was exploratory and insight-oriented, but when Marie asked for specific advice Dr. M shifted to suggesting some things that Marie could do differently.

Analyses of Therapist Techniques

Marie and Dr. M talked about their reactions to the therapist techniques in the post-therapy interviews:

R: *What did Dr. M (or you) do to help changes come about?*

C: She was great for just releasing your feelings, but as far as reaching a definite solution, she wasn't so good. She was best at just talking and letting it all out.

T: Dealing with relationships, specifically how she was different from her mother. Also, helping her to strategize and cognitively structure her life. Labelling her feelings and clarifying the process. Encouraging structure.

R: *What did Dr. M (or you) do best with you (Marie)?*

C: Understanding the way I felt. *Can you think of any specific techniques that Dr. M used that were helpful?* There were some good things that came out of the problems that I brought to her, which were not related to the reasons I first went with. She did present some good ways to deal with things. I remember one thing clearly that she said, that you cannot control what people say or think, so there's no use to worry because it won't change things. That's what I remember most, that you can't let things eat you up. Like different things people say, because if they want to say it, they're going to say it and there's nothing you can do about it. But it makes you depressed to realize that you just have to live with it as best you can. But you don't blame yourself as much. *Has that helped you deal better with things that bother you?* No, because it still bothers you. *How about with your daughter?* Dr. M said to just be direct and that is the most helpful information or advice she gave me, "just come out with it." She made me realize that people will be people and you cannot change them no matter what you do. You have no control over their actions or words.

T: Helping her relax and feel safe while dealing with her pain. Also setting limits at the beginning and end of therapy over doing therapy in the bathroom and making so much telephone contact. It was also helpful to reflect feeling and clarify. The modeling, role plays, and imagery were helpful. I was generally supportive and asked her to set goals and clarify her feelings and thoughts.

R: *Can you remember any specific therapist interpretations or feedback that helped you (Marie) view yourself (herself) and your (her) situation in a different way?*

C: I just remember when I walked out that I looked at it in a different light and felt better about it. But it's hard for me to come up with a specific thing. *Did it have to do with family stuff?* Yeah, it normally has to do with family. It made me feel less bad about it.

T: I told her that her ideas and plans were good. She was impatient and angry about her mother and I normalized that and gave her permission for her feelings. When we talked about her mom, she had relief on her face, kind of an "aha" and said she had never thought of that. During the last session, she said "maybe I do have some good ideas."

R: *Do you recall any session as being particularly satisfying?*

C: There were some more satisfying than others, but I can't think of one in particular. I don't know if my mind is not, I just feel so foggy now. *Is there anything about the whole therapy that stands out as satisfying?* Just that I looked at things in a different light.

T: The 11th session because given the stress she was under, she was able to put that aside and deal with the issues. We worked well together. It was hard for her to come in, but we used the time productively.

R: *What did Dr. M (or you) do least well?*

C: She didn't give me definite solutions and advice or tell me what to do. It wasn't exactly what I expected. I thought the person would tell you what to do and give more concrete advice. This was just talking about my problems, but not actually reaching that much of an advice as to, "Okay, this is what you should do to help clear what's wrong." I was mostly talking and letting it out more than anything else. I was releasing but not solving anything. But, I can't say nothing. There were times when I felt that I did reach a solution, but this was on minor things. As far as my insecurity, my lack of confidence, I didn't feel there was a great change in that. *Anything else?* In the beginning, if you felt that you may not be compatible with one another, do you think that something should have been requested, a different. . . ? *You felt a barrier between you and wonder if you should have said something?* Yes. *Why was it difficult for you to say something about that?* Because I didn't think it would make a difference. It would still not have been any change. *What would you have liked in a therapist?* Feeling more open. *Why do you think you didn't feel open with Dr. M?* I don't know, it was just a feeling that you either click together and if you didn't feel that there was a click, then that was what it is. I don't think she liked me from the beginning. *What makes you think that?* I don't know, just the feeling you get, how a person looks at you or talks to you or reacts to you. You have a feeling that they have a distance about them. *Can you put your finger on where that came from?* There was one time she said something about, "You wouldn't lie to me, would you?" or something like that. We were talking about something and it made me kind of uncomfortable since she said that. I didn't think she thought much of me if she thought that. It made me think that her confidence in me was affected in some way. And sometimes she would look at me, I don't know, you got a sense that she didn't like me. *Did that affect the way you approached therapy and how much you expected to get out of it?* Well, I didn't give up or anything. I thought that as things went along, maybe things would start changing and getting better. But they pretty much stayed on the even.

T: She was easy to work with. I should have planned more time for summarizing at the end of each session and done a termination summary to pull together more what she had done and talk about the next steps. More role playing would also have been helpful. *Is there anything you wish you had pursued further with her?* I wish we had had more time to look at the issue of her working. That was not finished. Also, her relationship with her husband needed attention. If her mother had not been dying, we would have focused on that relationship.

R: *Do you recall any session as being particularly unsatisfying?*

C: When I didn't get any advice. I just kind of felt still up in the air about things that were brought up. *Is there anything you wished Dr. M had pursued further with you?* How to develop more self-confidence. I feel insecure about being with people and how to act with people without saying the wrong things.

T: The last session because there were so many things to deal with. It was too short. I was more cognitive than is true of my general style, although Marie was okay with the cognitive style.

Quantitative Analyses

Table 6.1 shows the results of analyses for therapist response modes on the immediate outcome measures. The codings of the post-session reviews are shown in Table 6.2, which reveals a discrepancy between Marie's and Dr. M's perceptions of the sessions. For Marie, only 59% of the events were helpful, whereas 97% of the events mentioned by Dr. M were helpful. Both felt that therapist techniques accounted for most of the helpful events. Additionally, for Marie the hindering events were also due to Dr. M's techniques, notably the absence of enough direct guidance.

Combining the results of the post-therapy interviews with the quantitative analyses indicates that the most helpful techniques were direct guidance, paraphrase, approval, and interpretation. The only unhelpful technique was the lack of enough direct guidance.

Discussion of Helpful Techniques

Direct guidance.   Marie was very explicit in her desire to be told what to do. In line with this, those sessions in which Dr. M used more direct guidance were rated as more helpful and Marie profusely thanked Dr. M for her advice. The major piece of advice that Dr. M gave Marie was the need to be direct in stating her wishes. This

TABLE 6.1 Proportion of Occurrence, Client Helpfulness Ratings, Therapist Helpfulness Ratings, Client Experiencing, and Client Reactions for Therapist Response Modes in Case 4

Response Modes	%	Client Help Rating M	SD	Therapist Help Rating M	SD	Client Experiencing M	SD	Most Likely Reactions
Approval	.07	6.21	1.55 B	8.19	1.00 A	2.22	.50 A	Supported
Information	.31	6.11	1.54 B	8.00	1.10 A	2.14	.42 A	Supported Negative
Direct Guidance	.09	6.48	1.65 AB	7.81	1.17 A	2.07	.26 A	
Closed Question	.18	5.73	1.11 B	7.73	1.22 A	2.23	.52 A	Ther. Work
Open Question	.10	5.89	1.05 B	8.02	1.01 A	2.32	.60 A	Challenged
Paraphrase	.21	5.99	1.22 B	7.99	1.10 A	2.27	.55 A	
Interpretation	.02	5.96	1.51 B	8.37	1.01 A	2.22	.51 A	
Confrontation	.01	5.96	1.19 B	8.30	1.11 A	2.09	.29 A	
Disclosure	.00	7.00	1.77 A	7.12	1.25 B	2.12	.35 A	
TOTAL		6.03	1.34	7.95	1.11	2.20	.48	

NOTE: Helpfulness was rated on 9-point scales (9 = extremely helpful); experiencing was rated on a 7-point scale (7 = high). ANOVAs indicated significant differences between therapist response modes for client helpfulness, $F_{(8, 1784)} = 5.40$, $p < .0001$, therapist helpfulness, $F_{(8, 1784)} = 4.24$, $p < .0001$, and client experiencing, $F_{(8, 1784)} = 5.27$, $p < .0001$. Post hoc differences are indicated, such that response modes with the same letter (A-B) were not significantly different (A = highest ratings). The overall relationship between response modes and client reactions was significant, $X^2_{(28)} = 152.79$, $p < .0001$.

advice was repeated over a number of instances, with Dr. M modeling examples of how Marie could be more direct. It should be noted, however, that Dr. M never actually had Marie role play to obtain examples of her behavior or to provide feedback about how she could be more effective in being direct.

Often Marie asked for advice not for herself, but for her daughter. She would present a situation that her daughter was facing at work and ask Dr. M how to handle it. Although typically therapists feel that when clients present situations for other people they are avoid-

TABLE 6.2 Proportions of Helpful and Hindering Events Reported by Client and Therapist in Post-Session Reviews in Case 4

	Client		Therapist	
	Helpful	*Hindering*	*Helpful*	*Hindering*
Therapist Techniques	.31	.22	.44	.01
Support	.06	.00	.04	.00
Direct Guidance	.16	.18	.11	.01
Closed Question	.00	.00	.02	.00
Open Question	.00	.00	.01	.00
Paraphrase	.02	.04	.16	.00
Interpretation	.08	.00	.01	.00
Confrontation	.00	.00	.08	.00
Disclosure	.00	.00	.00	.00
Therapist Manner	.14	.02	.05	.00
Client Tasks	.10	.08	.22	.00
Focus	.00	.02	.05	.00
Experiencing	.06	.04	.06	.00
Insight	.02	.00	.04	.00
Changes	.02	.02	.06	.00
Client Manner	.04	.08	.22	.01
Relationship/Alliance	.00	.02	.04	.01
TOTAL	.59	.42	.97	.03

ing working on their own problems, Dr. M allowed Marie to focus on the daughter, perhaps because it was a safe area and because the daughter's issues were so similar to Marie's issues. Focusing on the daughter's problems was an indirect way to deal with Marie's problems. To have challenged Marie to focus only on herself might well have alienated her.

Another piece of advice that Dr. M gave Marie was that because she could not control everything and would inevitably make mistakes, she should be easier on herself and not worry as much. She tried to emphasize that nobody was perfect and that Marie should accept herself as she was. This helped Marie normalize some of her experiences and not be so hard on herself.

While Marie told Dr. M that the advice was good, she mentioned to the researchers that it was too trivial. She felt that the guidance was in areas that were more tangential to her real problems in self-confidence and insecurity. It should be noted that Marie did not present specific problems in these areas nor did Dr. M probe to force Marie to be more specific about her goals for these areas. Marie's presentations of her problems with self-confidence and insecurity were vague and diffuse without specific examples of what she meant. Further, they seemed chronic, with Marie indicating that she felt hopeless about solving them.

Dr. M indicated that she did not give Marie more advice because she was afraid of Marie's becoming too dependent on her, which she felt was especially inappropriate in brief therapy. Further, she felt that Marie had a strong passive-aggressive streak that would have caused her to reject more advice. Thus, especially in the second half of therapy, Dr. M tried to shape her advice to encourage Marie to believe that she had the answers within herself.

Paraphrase. Perhaps the technique that Dr. M was best at was helping Marie express her feelings. Several sessions were quite cathartic, with Marie sharing some moving and sad experiences related to her family and present situation. Marie, however, did not value this catharsis for its own sake. She seemed to be expressing herself just so that Dr. M would have enough information to fix her, rather than as an end in itself.

Approval. Both Marie and Dr. M felt that it was helpful when Dr. M supported Marie, particularly in letting her know that her feelings were normal. Dr. M was especially supportive regarding Marie's mother, who was dying during the therapy. When Marie talked about the loss of her mother, Dr. M was very gentle and reassuring, letting Marie know that it was normal to feel sad about her mother's impending death, yet also angry and overwhelmed at the amount of work and lack of response from her mother's withdrawal.

Especially in the second half of therapy, Dr. M focused on Marie's strengths, pointing out that Marie was capable and had good ideas about how to handle situations. Marie would typically deny that her ideas were good. Perhaps Marie's background of a critical family and a husband who denigrated her at every opportunity made it difficult for her to accept any positive comments.

Interpretation. Although Dr. M only infrequently used interpretation, interpretations were sometimes helpful. Both mentioned that talking about the family was useful. Dr. M tried to give Marie some understanding of why her mother and sister acted the way they did. For example, she suggested that perhaps her sister acted more friendly with outsiders than with the family because of her anger at the family. Further, she interpreted her mother's wish to die as stemming from a difficult life. These interpretations were very mild and close to the data that Marie presented. Dr. M probably did not use more interpretations because Marie was not insight-oriented and did not value gaining understanding into her behavior.

An example of an interpretation that Marie did not hear regarded the function of her keeping a messy household. Marie claimed she could not have friends come over because her house was too messy and disorganized. Dr. M suggested that perhaps Marie did not want friends and used the house as an excuse for not making more contacts. Marie did not respond to this interpretation.

Moderating Variables

Client Factors

Marie's cultural background is relevant to understanding her behavior within the therapy. Sue and Zane (1987) indicated that therapist credibility is crucial in therapy with Asian-Americans. From this cultural perspective, Dr. M did not have ascribed credibility since she was both a woman and younger than Marie. In support of this perspective, Marie talked extensively in early sessions about how her Chinese relatives thought women were of little value. Further, Sue and Zane (1987) felt that depressed or anxious Asian-American clients need to feel a direct benefit from treatment, often in the form of a gift of reduction or alleviation of negative emotional states as early as possible in the treatment. As shown in the excerpt from session 3, Dr. M failed to provide this expected gratification, which may have been why Marie was so dissatisfied.

Further, Asian Americans generally seek advice from authority figures and expect to be told what to do (Shon & Davis, 1982). In wanting specific advice about these communication issues, Marie was clear that how she interacted with people had to fit her cultural restrictions of not offending anyone and not being direct. For example, if her brother wanted to visit, it was not culturally acceptable for Marie to be direct and even ask how long he planned to stay. Or if her brother wanted to bring his wife who acted in strange and inappropriate ways, it was not acceptable for Marie to say that she did not want her to come.

Marie's desire not to offend others extended to her not wanting Dr. M to know about her dissatisfaction with therapy, either in the sessions or by reading this chapter. She probably only told us (the researchers) about her feelings because we directly asked her about them and not to tell us would be offending us. However, she did not want to hurt Dr. M's feelings by telling her of her discontent with the process. She did tell Dr. M quite often that she wanted more advice, but not that she was not happy with what she was getting. She told us later that she felt grateful to Dr. M for giving her so much time and that she kept hoping that Dr. M would change and give more advice.

Another perspective is that Marie may have had difficulty becoming attached to Dr. M because she was facing the losses of her mother and daughter. To become attached to another woman who would be leaving soon might just have been too difficult. Additionally, Dr. M's gentleness and supportiveness may have been too unfamiliar and threatening for Marie, whose mother had been very critical.

Marie seemed to want a magical cure. She thought that she could present herself and her problems to a therapist and the therapist would make it all better. This would fit with how one would approach a medical doctor by telling all the symptoms and waiting for the diagnosis and appropriate medication. On some of the minor problems Marie presented, a more explicit behavioral approach might have worked well. However, the major issues that Marie was facing, including the loss of her mother and daughter, were not issues that had specific "cures." To resolve these issues, Marie needed to accept her grief over her losses and figure out who she was and what she wanted to be. Unfortunately, although Marie could express her feelings quite openly, she did not value expression of feelings or insight into her problems as an end in themselves.

Therapist Factors

Dr. M's personal and theoretical background was mixed in terms of enabling her to relate to Marie. On the one hand, Dr. M's mother had died recently, which helped her identify with Marie's feelings about her mother's death. Dr. M was very aware of information on death and dying and was comfortable talking about Marie's fears about her mother's death and her ambivalence about being with her as she was dying. On the other hand, the two came from different cultures. Dr. M suggested that their experiences of the therapy may have been discrepant because her Black culture, unlike the Asian culture, valued the expression of feelings.

Dr. M was not able to use her preferred exploratory, psychodynamic approach with Marie, who preferred a problem-solving therapy. Dr. M was able to modify her approach somewhat and do some problem solving with Marie, but it was not enough of a modification to satisfy Marie. One could speculate that it would have been more helpful if Dr. M had been able to adopt a more explicit behavioral approach, with a careful behavioral assessment of specific problems, followed by interventions and homework, with reinforcement contingent on behavioral change. For example, since most of the problems that Marie presented involved assertive communication, Dr. M could have engaged in more role-playing, with role reversal and perhaps even videotape feedback to give Marie the opportunity to practice the new behaviors and get feedback on how she came across (Alberti and Emmons, 1974).

On the other hand, it can be argued from an objective point of view that there was no reason for Dr. M to modify her strategy further. In the sessions, Marie repeatedly told Dr. M how much she appreciated all the advice she was giving her. In bringing up a new problem, Marie would say that she was bringing it up because Dr. M had been so helpful with other problems. At the end of sessions, Marie profusely thanked Dr. M. Given these behaviors, it is not surprising that Dr. M thought that the sessions were going very well. In fact, Dr. M felt that Marie was not at all resistant and seemed very open to whatever they were doing in the sessions. Dr. M was aware that Marie wanted more advice, but felt that they were making progress in having Marie believe that she had strengths and could make her own decisions. Dr. M told us that Marie seemed to "worship" her, making her feel uncomfortable with how much respect and authority Marie granted her. Thus, Marie's lack of directness in the sessions and desire not to offend anybody led her to act ingratiating and positive in the sessions, so that Dr. M was not aware of the extent of Marie's dissatisfaction. Further mitigating against Dr. M's awareness of Marie's dissatisfaction was Dr. M's diagnosis of Marie as "hysterical." Dr. M viewed Marie's behavior as understandable within that diagnostic framework.

The Therapeutic Relationship

According to scores on the Working Alliance Inventory (see Chapter 2, Table 2.2), Marie evaluated the relationship as poor. She indicated in the interview that she did not "click" with Dr. M from the very beginning. She felt as though they were talking two different languages and Dr. M would not give her what she wanted. In contrast, Dr. M rated the alliance as exceptionally good. Further, her ratings indicated that she thought the relationship became progressively more positive as treatment continued. Thus, the data on the alliance was conflicting based on whose perspective was measured.

External Factors

Extratherapy involvement. Comments in the post-therapy interviews indicated that Marie applied what she learned in therapy to situations outside of therapy:

> R: *How did you (or Marie) use the therapy between sessions?*
>
> C: I'm more direct in my communication with people and with family. *Did you think about the therapy between sessions?* Yeah, in those instances where it made my viewpoint change. Other than that, no.
>
> T: She worked very hard between sessions. She reported that she tried doing the things that we had talked about. For example, she told her husband how she felt about their vacation.

Support network. At first, Marie told us that she had a few close friends with whom she could talk. She said that people sought her out to tell her about their problems. In therapy, however, Marie mentioned only one friend, who she said was very supportive even though she was the opposite of Marie in almost every way. Because her friend worked the night shift and her smoking aggravated her mother's emphysema, Marie seldom saw her. Because she did not work and spent most of her time caring for her mother, Marie had limited contact with the outside world.

Marie's relationship with her husband was strained to the point that she was concerned that he would leave her. Marie felt that she never knew what to expect from her husband if, for example, she were to ask his advice. He would sometimes be helpful, but just as often would be scathingly critical.

Marie's relationships with her mother and daughter were undoubtedly her closest connections. But her mother was dying and her daughter was leaving to go to college. Not only was her daughter leaving, but she was quite anxious to get away from home because she felt very confined and did not like it that Marie was "nosy" with her continual probing questions.

External events. The impending losses of Marie's mother and daughter contributed to Marie's distress during therapy.

Outcome of Therapy

Session Outcome

Marie's and Dr. M's evaluations of the sessions were discrepant (see Chapter 2, Table 2.2 for SEQ ratings). Marie perceived the sessions as being low in depth but moderate in smoothness. In contrast, Dr. M perceived the sessions as very deep and smooth.

Pre-Post Changes

Table 6.3 indicates that Marie was improved on some measures (Target Complaints), unchanged on other measures (MMPI Psychopathic Deviate and Psychasthenia scales, SCL-90-R, TSCS), and worse on other measures (MMPI Depression and Hysteria scales, Hamilton Anxiety and Depression). (Marie's rating on the target complaint about her mother may be inaccurate since she probably did not understand how to rate the item since her mother was dying.) Overall, Marie could be classified as unchanged after her 12 sessions of treatment.

TABLE 6.3 Scores on Outcome Measures for Case 4

Measures	Pre	5th	Expect	Post	6 Mo	1 Yr
Client-Rated Measures						
MMPI						
Psychopathic Deviate	79			79		
Depression	76			[86*]		
Psychasthenia	71			75		
Hysteria	64			[79*]		
SCL-90-R	46			[54]	47	46
TSCS	35			[35]	40	42
TC (1) Self-Confidence	13	11	4.5	7**	7	6
(2) Relate to Family	10	[13*]	4.5	10	4**	4
(3) Aging Mother	13	13	5	1***	[9**]	1**
(4) Marriage		13	5	8*	7	5
Satisfaction					5	5
Therapist-Rated Measures						
TC (1) Self-Confidence	12	12	5.5	7*		
(2) Relate to Family	11	[13]	6	7**		
(3) Aging Mother	13	13	6	10*		
(4) Marriage		13	6	—		
Researcher-Rated Measures						
Hamilton Anxiety	15			[25**]		
Hamilton Depression	14			[27***]		

NOTE: High T scores indicate high symptomatology on the SCL-90-R GSI, high self-esteem on the TSCS; worst functioning on the TC, higher satisfaction, and greater disturbance on the Hamilton scales. Expect = level expected after treatment. * = significant change at $p < .05$; ** = $p < .01$; *** = $p < .001$. Negative changes are in brackets.

Subjective perceptions of the changes were discussed in the post-therapy interviews excerpted below:

R: *How have you (or has Marie) changed as a result of therapy?*

C: I haven't changed that much because I didn't get specific advice. So I kind of let things ride, as they always have. *Did you have any symptom relief?* I was better off before, because with my mother's illness I have more symptoms. But I don't think that has anything to do with Dr. M. *Did any of your behaviors change as a result of therapy?* I'm more direct now with my daughter and with everyone. *How about self-concept changes?* Maybe a little better. Maybe not everything is so impossible now. Just do your best and that's all you can expect from a person. That's all I can do and that's all I'm going to expect of myself. *Have your interpersonal relationships changed?* No. *Has your mother becoming ill affected the change that you were making?* Yeah, everything came to a standstill. Everything doesn't look that optimistic. Everything's kind of going downhill, not advancing.

T: She's begun to get clearer on her issues. The one that probably she's least clear on is her mother because of the grieving and the dying. I think she's a little clearer with her daughter. Her whole task is separating and individuating, so she sometimes is aware of it concretely and emotionally. Other times she's just totally defended against it. There were a couple of sessions when she brought in her daughter's concerns. We worked on that and as we moved back to how she felt about her daughter's struggle, Marie began to talk about how much she was going to miss her and how hard that was for her for her daughter to be away and how she worried about things she hadn't taught her. So she began to look at it. It's still not as clear as it needs to be for her to really be able to separate emotionally but she's working on it. I think that by moving out of the house, her daughter was modeling a separation that Marie was not able to do. Issues with her daughter got put on the back burner with the mother's malignancy and the conflict of her mother's care at the moment. Once the mother is dead, in addition to the depression and anger, she will be ready to struggle again with who she is and where she is. Further, she has learned that she can use therapy as a way to deal with some of the stress and pain. The process of talking with someone else helps her clarify and identify what her issues are and helps her vent and let go of whatever is blocking her feelings. She has begun to gain some self-confidence but there's a lot more work to do with that. *Give specific examples of how she used the therapy to deal with stress and self-confidence?* When she sought advice for her daughter, she was beginning to use me as a resource for the informational part of that. She stood up to her sister-in-law in terms of what she wanted. And not that it was all worked through, but she talked about her sister coming down a second time when her mother was dying and she was clearer about what she did not want from her. That had been very hard for her to do earlier. She called an old friend the last session so she was reaching out and using her environment more. I think our talking about the importance of seeking out support systems was a part of that, but it was also because she felt stronger in herself. Very often in the last third of our therapy she would come in and would have already thought about what her strategy might be for a situation. She'd present the strategy to me and we'd talk about it. She continued to be surprised that I thought that her ideas were good. For example, in the last session, I mentioned the hospice program as an option to her. She had already checked it out on her own. That was real counter to her dependent stance. I think she does a good job of identifying what's hurting her the most. I tried to point out that she is really good at prioritizing things that are going on. Even in the last month when we were working on how things were going to be with her mother, she made some wise decisions about when she could leave her mother and how she could arrange the care of her mother when she was not there. She took good care of herself in trying to work out some meaning to our work and work out her commitment to the research and to her mother. That was not easy for her to do. She did not try to avoid sorting out what she was going to do in this situation. *Any other examples of self-concept changes, how she sees herself differently because of therapy?* She has a lot of guilt because of her mom. That softened as we talked about what she could and couldn't do. We talked about her mom wanting to go shopping all the time and whether she needed to go and how guilty she felt saying no and setting limits. She did some grieving and struggling with that issue. She did some comparing of herself with her siblings, that she had a more privileged life. So she had some guilt about how she grew up versus how her siblings grew up. She began to look at the issues with her mom. She asked whether she should go on living while her mother was dying. She walked by her door and was not able to face her.

R: *How satisfied are you with the nature and amount of change?*

C: Not a great deal. A little.

T: Generally pleased. There's significantly more work to be done. She wanted answers and was frustrated to learn that answers must come from within her.

Marie was also asked to talk about what caused and maintained one of her major problems. Her answer indicated that the therapy had helped her gain some insight into the origin of her problems:

C: I know that my lack of self-confidence started with my parents that would always say they didn't feel that I could do this or I can't do this as well as the child of this family down the block that was a perfect example, a perfect child, or whatever, and why can't I be like them. I know that's how it started, because it seemed that I was being compared with some child of another family and I can't measure up. "Why can't you be like them?" And then they did a lot of things for me that they didn't want me to attempt, like cooking. They didn't feel I should get near the stove because I might burn myself. So I never learned to really cook. So I started to try something and didn't think it turned out so badly but then they didn't think it turned out so good. I thought it was really good until they said it wasn't and after that I said, "I guess I didn't do it so good." Then I just lost more confidence because they would always say, "Why can't you be like so and so? They do this and that and you should be that way too." I never felt like I measured up to people they felt were more capable. *How does it get maintained now in your life?* I don't know, it's just ingrained, kind of brain-washed. You feel like you don't meet up to people you come across and then you see that they do things better than you do and that kind of reinforces it when you see them do things much faster or more efficiently.

Six-Month Follow-Up

Marie's mother had died shortly after the termination of therapy, leaving Marie feeling very depressed. On the outcome measures, Marie was about the same as she had been at termination, with the exception that she had continued improving in her relationships with her family. She had obtained four sessions of bereavement counseling which were not satisfactory because the therapist had told her that her feelings were normal but had not given her any advice. She had begun a support group, which she thought would be more helpful because they gave more advice and made her feel less alone.

One-Year Follow-Up

Marie was about the same as she had been at termination and at the six-month follow-up. She still felt a big void and was depressed because of her mother's death. She had started a new job as a temporary employee doing secretarial work and felt relieved to be occupied. Marie had not sought additional therapy.

Long-Term Follow-Up

About four years after the termination of therapy, Marie reported that she was doing all right, although she still got depressed. She missed her mother, although not as intensely as before. Her children were both in college, but maintained close contact. She was working full time at a secretarial job. Her self-confidence had increased, which she attributed to being able to get a job. She still felt a deep-down insecurity and reported that her marriage was at a stalemate.

Summary

The therapist techniques of direct guidance, paraphrase, approval, and interpretation were the most helpful change agents in this case, although the client wanted more direct guidance.

External factors moderated the effects of techniques. Marie's mother was dying and her daughter was going to college, leaving Marie without her major support system. Client factors, particularly cultural variables, played a role in Marie's expectations of therapy. Further, Marie was anxious, depressed, had low self-esteem, and was indirect in her communication, all of which probably originated in her early childhood experiences and then were reinforced in her marriage. Therapist factors were operative, in that Dr. M preferred an exploratory psychodynamic treatment, which did not work with Marie. Dr. M modified her approach to meet Marie's desire for problem-solving therapy, but was not able to modify her approach enough to satisfy the client. Further, the therapeutic relationship was not "good enough," at least from the client's perspective. Marie mentioned that she felt she did not "click" with Dr. M from the first session and only stayed for the research and because she thought it might get better. Thus, therapist techniques helped Marie become more direct in her communication, but these techniques were "too little, too late" in that they did not deal with her major presenting problems.

7

Case 5: Rescue Me

This chapter will focus on the therapist techniques in the 17-session
case conducted by Dr. S, a 34 year-old, White, male psychologist
with Diane, an attractive, 42 year-old White woman.

Client

Diane (a pseudonym) was the oldest of three girls. Having tried
for seven years to conceive, her parents were ecstatic when Diane
was born. They thought that she was a perfect child.

Diane initially described her childhood as happy and normal. She
was particularly close to her father, whom she described as loving,
concerned, and always there to help her. She was more ambivalent
towards her mother, whom she described as more worried about what
others thought than about her children's feelings. Her mother was
cold, dominant, and controlling, demanding that Diane do things
exactly her way. She started to toilet-train Diane at six months of age
and continued pressuring her to achieve from then on. Diane needed
to get her mother's approval and live up to her definition of her as a
perfect child. She washed the dishes without being told to and got
up early to redo reports, but never felt like what she did was quite
good enough.

Diane's mother was also quite caustic about men, an attitude she
conveyed freely to Diane. Men were supposed to take care of women,
but they were not to be trusted, particularly if they were alcoholic
like her father.

The family was well-off financially. Her father owned a gas station, a taxi service, and a bus company. Her mother, although educated to be a teacher, stayed home to raise children and did not resume her career until the father's businesses all collapsed when Diane was in college. Her father died of cancer shortly thereafter when Diane was 27 years old.

In high school, Diane described herself as a very good student. She was the editor of the yearbook, chairman (sic) of the prom, in the all-county choir, on student council, and played volleyball and basketball. She remembered that boys teased her unmercifully about her nose. Her parents would not let her get a nose job because her nose was like her father's and she was told that she was beautiful just as she was, which she perceived as a negation of her feelings.

Diane received a BS degree in microbiology. She had wanted to go to medical school, but became pregnant shortly before graduation from college. Her future husband insisted that they get married rather than have an abortion. She began working following graduation and continued until her second child was born.

After five years of being a suburban housewife, Diane got fed up with pleasing everyone else. She started talking back to her husband and demanding more from their relationship, which he labeled as "women's lib." She went back to work in microbiology, proclaiming that the money she earned was hers to use as she wanted. Diane reported that her relationship with her husband started deteriorating at that point.

Diane had been married for 21 years. Her husband was 45 and worked in insurance sales. She described him as authoritarian, controlling, and obsessive, much like her mother. Just prior to the therapy, her husband had moved out of the house, but both were ambivalent about what to do about their relationship. He still spent weekends at the house and was quite involved with the family.

She had two daughters, aged 20 and 14, both of whom were living with her. Diane felt that she had finally let go of the oldest daughter and was getting along with her better. But she thought she was too involved with the youngest daughter, suffering too much over everything that happened to her.

Physical Functioning

Diane had no history of serious illnesses and reported no current health concerns. She was quite concerned about her physical appearance and fitness. For example, Diane had just finished a three-year stint wearing braces to correct an overbite. She took no medications other than aspirin, although she frequently drank coffee and alcohol. She ate three balanced meals a day and did aerobic exercises several times a week, but also overate and was slightly overweight.

Previous Therapy Experience

Diane had been in therapy previously, once for two sessions and another time for four or five sessions, but she did not feel that she had benefited from either therapy. Two years before therapy, she had been in an assertiveness training group. The trainer recommended that Diane join a weekly women's support group, which she was still in and found to be helpful. She had also had hotline training and had worked on a hotline for some time.

Pre-Therapy Expectations

Diane expected that therapy was for self-discovery, growth, and developing self-reliance. Accordingly, she felt it should last until the client was no longer dependent on the therapist. She thought a therapist should be compassionate, respectful of others, introspective, patient, and supportive, but not manipulative.

Pre-Therapy Assessment

Scores on the pre-therapy assessment measures are shown in Table 7.3. On the MMPI, Diane had normal validity scores and high scores on the Depression, Psychasthenia, Schizophrenia, Psychopathic Deviate, and Social Introversion scales. This profile revealed serious depression and anxiety, as well as low energy level, lack of self-confidence, and lack of optimism. It further revealed that she had blunted or inappropriate affect, difficulty in concentration, fearfulness, inadequacy and inferiority feelings, loss of interest, schizoid characteristics, fatigue, withdrawal, and introversion. Additionally, she was ambivalent, unable to love, withdrawn, ruminative, and sensitive.

Diane's scores on the other measures showed evidence of average symptomatology, but below average self-esteem compared to an outpatient population. She was functioning at an average level on her target complaints. The clinician judged her to be moderately depressed but not anxious.

Diane was diagnosed by the research team as dysthymic with obsessive-compulsive and dependent personality disorders.

Target Complaints

Diane's first complaint was self-image, which she attributed to not having been given enough responsibility for her life.

Her second complaint was sexual hangups. Diane said that she had many inferiority feelings and hangups about sex. She never fully relaxed and enjoyed the process because she became distracted about her performance. Marijuana helped for awhile but soon lost its potency, after which she had infrequent sexual relations.

Her third issue was indecisiveness. She obsessed endlessly over making even a small decision, feeling it was right, and then carrying it out. As examples of this problem, Diane related her previous ambivalent attempts to get therapy and her uncertain relationship with her husband.

Summary of Client Pre-Therapy Characteristics

Diane was an attractive, articulate, likable woman, whose primary difficulties were in the areas of depression and self-concept. She seemed to be motivated for therapy, willing to change, and able to form and profit from a relationship. Her pre-therapy assessment measures indicated more pathology than was immediately apparent in the clinical interview, suggesting that she was depressed, anxious, withdrawn, obsessive, dependent, and unable to form intimate relationships.

Therapist

Dr. S had received his PhD in counseling psychology three years prior to the start of the therapy. Because he had done his graduate work in our program, I was very familiar with him and had high regard for his clinical skills. Dr. S was licensed in the state of

Maryland and listed in the National Register of Health Service Providers in Psychology. Dr. S had three research publications and was active in professional organizations.

After graduation, Dr. S worked for two years at the university counseling center with an emphasis on time-limited counseling. At the time of the study, he worked part-time at an in-patient facility doing psychotherapy, supervision, and testing and also worked part-time at a private practice, providing therapy for drug and alcohol dependent professionals as well as career and educational evaluation and counseling for adolescents and adults.

Using three 5-point (5 = high) scales for how much he believed in and adhered to three major orientations, Dr. S rated himself: psychoanalytic = 3, humanistic = 3, and behavioral = 2, describing himself as integrating psychodynamic/developmental and cognitive/behavioral approaches. He believed that change in therapy occurs through the relationship with therapist, whose trust and support allows the client to reflect on his/her feelings, thoughts, behaviors (in and out of therapy session) and to try new ways of behaving. He encouraged clients to take responsibility for setting goals in therapy. In specific instances (e.g., chemical dependency cases, severely disturbed clients, clients at risk), he also emphasized active behavioral and attitude change.

The Treatment Process

The verbatim excerpt from the first few minutes of the first session illustrates the process between Dr. S and Diane:

T: I've read a little bit of some of the forms that you have filled out. And why don't, why don't we start with what brings you in here. What are you here for?

C: What brings me here? (T: Yeah) Well, the advertisement, first of all, in the newspaper (T: MmHmm) that there would be a ther-, free therapy and also the explanation that it was um geared at self-improvement, as far as self-image, or if you have a low self-image (T: MmHmm) it would be good to come, and then also uh in relationships. Well, it uh, it looked very interesting. And also um University of Maryland has a good um reputation, um (T: MmHmm, well . . .) so I looked into it.

T: What, what are you hoping to get out of it? What are you looking for?

C: I'd like to improve my self-image, be more d-, ah decisive, um and also work on improving personal relationships.

T: Any particular relationships?

C: Just in general, I think (laughs). (T: How, how . . .) I'm just not relaxed ah at any kind of relationship at all.

T: MmHmm. You'd like to work on that? You're not relaxed? (C: Yes.) You'd like to feel calm? Why do you think ah you're not as relaxed as you'd like?

C: (points to her crossed arms) I think it's body language. (laughs) What do you mean, why do I think I'm not relaxed? Ah, (laughs) (T: I guess I was wondering what, what . . .) I'm just not myself, I think that, well, totally not myself. I'm always putting on a show (T: MmHmm) of, of sorts, (T: MmHmm) sometimes more than others. I think I'm more myself with my family, but totally not with, at, not always with my husband, for example. (T: MmHmm) And ah it just would be nice to just be myself and not worry about what other people were thinking or how I look or . . .

T: So you can be pretty self-conscious when you're with other people. You worry about how you're coming across.

In this initial segment, Dr. S asked Diane to start talking immediately about what brought her to therapy. He did not talk about himself or about what Diane could expect from the therapy.

Summary of Process

The main theme that was discussed in the whole treatment was a struggle over control in the relationship. Diane wanted Dr. S to tell her what to do and offer her lots of encouragement and support. Whenever Dr. S gave any advice, however, she felt angry that he was controlling her as she had been controlled by her mother and husband. Additionally, Diane wanted Dr. S to be warmer and more personal, but at the same time was worried about becoming dependent and/or sexually attracted to Dr. S.

Initial sessions. In the first session, Diane presented an insightful overview of her history, with Dr. S taking a passive role using probing questions and paraphrases. Being concerned about wanting structure, Diane asked at the end of the hour,

C: Do you let my own agenda take over or do you have a game plan in mind as to how you approach the therapy?

T: I think right now what I'd like to do is I'll, I'll leave it up to you, let you come into it. We do have, we have some broad . . .

C: Okay, just make sure I don't go off into limbo again, you know, and just float along, I mean because I have, that's a big tendency.

T: MmHmm. Well, that's one of the things I think that we'll both be watching for, floating along and the uh intellectualizing or avoiding some of the hurtful feelings. Those are things that go. And yes, we'll be working together and developing a game plan. It will become clear as to just what, what it is we want to focus on.

Thus, she made her bid to have Dr. S take over and tell her what to do now that he had all of this information about her. In the second session, she first demanded to know Dr. S's background. He told her and then suggested that she begin with what she wanted to talk about. She brought up a topic about veterinarian bills for a stray cat, which on the surface at least, was unrelated to her presenting problems. Dr. S listened patiently, reflecting her feelings. At the first pause, Diane quickly said that she was stuck and wanted some direction about where to go. Dr. S tried to get Diane to get into her feelings, to which she responded that she was overwhelmed at having to make decisions. She soon returned to the theme of wanting him to give her a game plan for what they should work on. After the session, Diane reported feeling frustrated and unfocused because Dr. S made her feel responsible for the dialogue.

In the third session, Diane began by talking about how her mother and husband both took control and criticized her, not giving her enough responsibility for her decisions. She avoided conflicts with them by going along with their wishes. Since both had her best interests at heart, she had difficulty feeling angry at them. Dr. S asked Diane if she wanted him as another male to tell her what to do. She replied that she did not want to think of him as a male at all, but she did want him to tell her what to do. At the end of the session, Diane said that she thought Dr. S felt sorry for her because she had such trivial problems. Dr. S replied that he did not feel sorry for her but felt empathic with her struggles.

Diane came into the fourth session saying that she felt better about herself and should not waste any more of Dr. S's time. Dr. S tried to get Diane to state specifically whether she wanted to terminate therapy, to which she responded that she wanted to know if she was doing okay in therapy. After they processed her feelings for the whole hour, she decided to stay in therapy.

Middle sessions. Sessions 5-7 were very productive. They explored Diane's ambivalence about her marriage, her desire to take more risks in meeting new men, her inability to relax in a sexual situation, her inability to give affection or even allow herself to hug her daughters because of some possible homosexual fears, and her unresolved feelings over not having hugged her father on his deathbed and not having grieved his death.

In the eighth session, Dr. S raised the issue of how many sessions they should have. He proposed 18 sessions, but Diane felt that 12 sessions would be easier since she was having to work on weekends to make up her time off from work. She complained about not having made much progress and feeling stuck. During the next session, Dr. S came back to the issues regarding the ultimate number of sessions, saying that he needed to stop by a certain date because his wife was having a baby. Diane acquiesced with the proposed time limit, which led into a discussion of Diane's fear of becoming dependent on Dr. S and wanting his approval. These two sessions were disorganized and confusing, with Diane getting angry that Dr. S did not take control.

The next sessions were very productive, with Diane reporting that she had gone out on the singles scene and enjoyed herself. These experiences led to Diane's talking about seeking other's approval and control, which robbed her of self-reliance and made her unable to make choices.

Final sessions. Termination issues became a central focus beginning in the 12th session when Diane mentioned that she had not wanted to talk in her group because she should not depend on her group to help her change. Dr. S insightfully made the connection between her withdrawal in the group and her anticipatory fear about terminating the therapy. Her initial reaction was that she would be happy that therapy was over because she could go back to denying her feelings. When she questioned why he was making such a big deal over termination, Dr. S said that she had difficulty in endings with her father and her marriage and that it would be important to terminate the therapy adequately.

In the last sessions, Diane had a hard time getting started talking. She complained about having "slid backwards" and wasting the sessions. Her feelings of being stuck seemed to increase geometrically over the final weeks.

Diane redoubled her efforts to "suck" Dr. S into taking care of her in the 14th session. She told about a divorced friend whose therapist had told her exactly what to do to change her life. All of her friends agreed that a therapist should give you advice. Then she said that she knew that Dr. S would not give her advice and that she needed to rely on her own strength and convictions.

In the 15th session, Diane brought in the following dream: In the middle of a swimming lesson that she was teaching, her daughter had to be taken to the bathroom. She left the pool in a rented car and promptly got lost. She asked directions of a man who left, so she ran after him dragging her daughter behind her. Dr. S interpreted that he was the man she was chasing for an answer, with panicky feelings about the impending termination and his leaving. Diane agreed and added that she needed to quit looking to others for directions and stop long enough to figure them out for herself.

The culmination of the control theme came in the 16th session when Dr. S confronted Diane with his observation that she was very controlling in terms of trying to get people, including him, to do what she wanted them to do. Diane returned to the control theme in the final session, but was more guarded in her need to wrap up the therapy and not delve into anything too heavy.

Client Behavior

Diane alternated between being a very responsible client, bringing in issues to discuss and willingly exploring her feelings, to being very demanding and critical of Dr. S for being silent and not giving her more direction.

Additionally, Diane was very worried about her appearance on the tapes, although she always dressed nicely and looked attractive. She felt conscious about her profile and her nose.

At the beginning of therapy, Diane was late several times. As soon as the therapist, who was quite punctual, mentioned her tardiness, she apologized and was never late again.

Therapist Behavior

For response modes, Dr. S used primarily paraphrase, open question, and information. Compared to the other therapists, he used

more open question and paraphrase and less approval, direct guidance, and closed question. Further, Dr. S was about average in his
activity level.

Dr. S had two major modes of behavior. In the first mode, which
occurred primarily at the beginnings of sessions, he intervened
mostly with open question and paraphrase, seeming somewhat distant and removed from the process. Once he understood the problem
or was comfortable that he had something to contribute, Dr. S shifted
to a more interpretive, confrontive, interactive stance, in which he
processed the relationship and what Diane wanted from therapy.

During the first few sessions, Dr. S was quite anxious. He typically
sat in a rigid position with his hands clasped behind his head. He
attributed his performance anxiety to feeling competitive with the
other therapists in the project, several of whom had been his super-
visors. I would add that his anxiety probably was due in part to
Diane's constant demands or pulls on him to perform as she perceived that he "should" as a therapist.

Analyses of Therapist Techniques

Diane and Dr. S talked about their reactions to the therapist techniques in the post-therapy interviews:

R: *What did Dr. S (or you) do to help changes come about?*

C: Just making me say things out loud that I'd never really said out loud
helped me change. I became more aware of everything rather than
ignoring it and having it in my subconscious.

T: Some of her self-concept change came about through her being able
to bring up things that she thought were really awful about herself and
have them turn out not to be so awful. There was also a change in
self-efficacy, in her presentation of herself as unable to do a lot of things
and make decisions, which came about because I wouldn't make the
decisions for her in the sessions. She came into therapy and tried to do
things in the way that she had been doing them for most of her life.
When I didn't go along with that, she was faced with a choice of either
leaving therapy or doing things differently. She had enough guts to do
things differently. Also, she didn't want to come into conflict with me.
She wanted to do what she was supposed to do to get my approval, so
she made these changes, some of which transferred to other situations

in her life. It was a setting where I had unconditional acceptance of her and wasn't offering her ultimatums. I was very neutral in terms of what she needed to do. What created change was when I focused on her feelings, helping her to acknowledge and experience them as opposed to allowing her to explain or minimize them. So the overall atmosphere of coming back to feelings and neutrality on my part left her knowing that she couldn't avoid her feelings.

R: *What did Dr. S (or you) do best with you (Diane)?*

C: He was excellent at reflecting my feelings. I didn't get into my feelings a lot, so he had to keep pressuring me. He would always redirect my conversation and thoughts to my feelings, "How do you feel about that?" or "What are your feelings?" He was always challenging me with those types of questions, which I need because I don't talk about my feelings. That was good and it was a total challenge actually. I'm not sure it was good or not, but he kept the ball in my court and I always had to make the plays. That was a real challenge for me because I was on the line and had to say something. I told him a couple of times that I was planning to do something a certain way and I knew he wouldn't let me get away with it. He was also very good at drawing parallels between my behavior in therapy and things that I've done in my life. He opened a lot of doors as far as making me realize some of the things that were going on and looking at them in a different way. He was very good at pulling everything together and telling me what I had said, which is good in itself because it helps you see a lot of things. He was an excellent listener. I just wish that I had been more comfortable talking to him.

T: I think I was best at not gratifying her, but doing it in a way that was not too frustrating or painful. I did gratify her in ways that didn't feed into her pathology. I think I made her pretty uncomfortable, but it was helpful because she didn't avoid those feelings. Also, talking about our relationship was important. Another technique that was helpful was pointing out in a non-accusing way how she was avoiding feelings. It wasn't, "Aha, you're doing it again," but "Isn't it interesting what you're doing." It was most helpful, though, to focus on her immediate feelings, which helped her find what it was that she wanted. It wasn't just focusing on feelings for feelings sake, although that was somewhat helpful because that was an area that was closed off, but I focused on feelings because she subordinated her own wishes to other people and no longer knew what she wanted. Helping her focus on her feelings made it clear to her what it was that she wanted. *How did you focus on feelings?* I would just very straightforwardly say, "When we were talking about such and such, how were you feeling?" Or, "We've drifted off the topic. We were talking about X. How are you feeling?" Occasionally, I would say, "You look sad" or "You sound angry." But I didn't get terribly emotional myself. I didn't model the feelings because that would have scared her. *Do you think she wanted you to be more emotional?* I think she was ambivalent about that. Her description of real therapy was being stripped bare, which she thought needed to be done for her to change, but I don't think she really wanted it. She said I was too neutral, but at the same time she would say she didn't think of me as a computer or part of this vast clinic that she was dealing with. So she had mixed feelings, wanting more emotionality but distancing me at the same time.

R: *Can you recall one session that was particularly satisfying?*

C: There was one session where we talked about my family and how I tried to repeat the same pattern in the rest of my life, finding a man who was much like my mother, not being able to say goodbye to my father or express my feelings to him. That whole session was really good. I left the session feeling much better about myself and that I could really change. The session just seemed to flow for some reason. I wasn't aware of time at all. It was over so quickly, because there wasn't any stopping or pausing or thinking about what to consider next.

T: There were a couple that just seemed to click. In the third session, my behavior changed and so did hers. She acknowledged how sad and depressed she could be. Also, the dream during the 15th session was really important. It was a rich dream that brought out a lot of the issues in therapy that we were working on.

R: *Can you remember any specific interpretations?*

C: The fact that he told me that because of certain behavior I was controlling other people, when what I was complaining about is that other people were controlling me. I had never looked at it that way. It made me aware of what was going on because I agreed with it. I can see that it was a very valid observation. Now I can stop what I'm doing and change my behavior, so it was positive.

T: There was one time when I said I viewed her as a controlling person. She said that she hadn't thought of herself that way.

R: *What did Dr. S (or you) do least well?*

C: It was a combination of the taping and the therapist's style, but I wasn't comfortable talking deeply about sexual matters. When he asked me questions about masturbation, that was real hard to deal with. I might have talked deeper about it if I wasn't on tape. The other things was I felt that he didn't reveal any of himself to me and in that respect I felt a distance. I couldn't get into his personality or mind. He was too technical or scientific. I need to get a feeling for somebody before I can relax and let go. Although based on my hotline training, I know that he was doing everything right, I didn't feel at ease as far as reading him. He seemed very controlled to me, in total control of that he was doing. At points I felt like he just wanted to say something personal or nice, but instead it would always be, "It sounds like . . ." or "I hear you saying this," throwing it back. So I never got a feeling of how he felt about me. I guess I wanted his approval as a person. I wanted him to say, "You're a good person." He did a couple of times and I liked it. But I think he made up his mind that was not what I needed. I felt like I didn't know him as a person, only as a therapist. Almost like a robot could have been sitting there. Sometimes I felt like he was just being nice to me and spending the hour with me because he had to. I felt like I was just another client, not someone special. I never had an interchange with him below the level of therapy. Even when I tried to get close to him as far as talking about his family, I wasn't sure of my own motives. I was just trying to get something to hold to in a personal way. I would have liked him to be more friendly, but not to the point were I would start analyzing him. Maybe it's my problem that I need somebody to be less distant. I can relate to people better if I feel that I know them a little deeper. *Did you ever try to change his behavior?* I tried a couple of times. I felt real silly when I was doing it. Maybe it's just a technique of mine to draw someone else out instead of dealing with my own problems. The other negative thing is that although he was good at repeating back what I said, I felt there was something missing. I felt like I was running the whole session. I felt very uncomfortable with the silence because I felt that I was screwing up and should come up with something quickly. I guess I needed more support that I was doing okay. *Are there things you wished your therapist had pursued further with you?* The sexual area and the sad feelings I have about my family and self, but I didn't feel comfortable letting myself go all the way to gut level with him. He started and we got a little bit into it, but I didn't feel comfortable crying in front of him or the camera.

T: What was least helpful was going back over history when it just encouraged her intellectualizing. When it stimulated feelings though, like when she was talking about her father and getting sad, that was useful. I felt least comfortable with the termination part. That's something I have trouble with in general. Maybe I could have modelled feelings more too. *Were there other therapeutic techniques that would have benefited this client?* She was a well functioning person and a good therapy client. She would have benefited from a lot of different kinds of therapy. *Is there anything you wish you had pursued further with*

Diane? It would have been useful to pursue her sexual feelings and sexuality. Also, at the beginning she dropped a couple of hints about using alcohol to cope with things. Since her father was an alcoholic, I wish I had checked that out more.

R: *Can you recall a session that was particularly unsatisfying?*

C: In one of the first few, I felt stuck and felt like I had regressed and was going over the same thing. I also wasn't real satisfied with the last one either because I didn't feel that he wrapped things up. I rambled most of the beginning of the session trying to summarize and get some perspective on what we'd been through and where I was. That's what I expected from him, but he didn't do it. He just let me go, so it was very disoriented. And he didn't really say goodbye. He just said, "Well time's up, good luck." He didn't have to say that he enjoyed it, but it was nothing, just like a normal session. It wasn't like it was the final one and I'll never see him again. I would have liked a little encouragement that you've come a long way and can handle it in the future. But maybe he didn't feel that way and so he couldn't say it. I would have liked a hug or a handshake or a pat on the shoulder, a touch I guess, because I felt like I had been very intimate with him in some respect and I just didn't want to be shoveled out and then the next one brought in.

T: The first session because I was feeling pressured to do well, felt competitive with the other people of the research team, and was not sure of my own talent. I didn't feel as free to do things my way. Also I was aware that this was time-limited therapy and I haven't been doing that for awhile, so I felt more pressure.

Quantitative Analyses

Table 7.1 shows the results of analyses for therapist response modes on the immediate outcome measures. Table 7.2 shows the codings of the post-session reviews. For Diane, only 58% of the events were helpful, whereas 76% of the events mentioned by Dr. S were helpful. For both, the helpful events were primarily attributed to therapist techniques. For Diane, the hindering events were attributed equally to therapist techniques as well as to client tasks. For Dr. S, the hindering events were attributed primarily to therapist techniques.

Combining the results of the post-therapy interviews with the quantitative analyses, the most helpful techniques were paraphrase, interpretation, and approval. The least helpful techniques were closed question and the lack of enough approval, disclosure, and direct guidance.

TABLE 7.1 Proportion of Occurrence, Client Helpfulness Ratings, Therapist Helpfulness Ratings, Client Experiencing, and Client Reactions for Therapist Response Modes in Case 5

Response Modes	%	Client Help Rating		Therapist Help Rating		Client Experiencing		Most Likely Reactions
		M	SD	M	SD	M	SD	
Approval	.02	7.80	1.42 A	7.34	1.20 A	2.29	.56 A	Supported
Information	.19	7.39	1.25 A	7.13	1.31 A	2.26	.56 A	No Reaction
Direct Guidance	.01	7.41	1.15 A	7.00	1.54 A	2.52	.87 A	
Closed Question	.10	7.17	1.17 A	6.78	1.21 A	2.22	.51 A	Negative No Reaction
Open Question	.21	7.22	1.06 A	7.17	1.11 A	2.44	.66 A	Challenged Negative
Paraphrase	.32	7.53	1.08 A	7.19	1.12 A	2.30	.59 A	Supported
Interpretation	.09	8.00	1.02 A	7.81	.91 A	2.29	.61 A	Supported Ther. Work
Confrontation	.06	7.78	1.01 A	7.54	1.10 A	2.17	.40 A	
Disclosure	.00	7.67	.58 A	6.00	1.73 B	2.33	.58 A	
TOTAL		7.46	1.11	7.20	1.15	2.31	.59	

NOTE: Helpfulness was rated on 9-point scales (9 = extremely helpful); experiencing was rated on a 7-point scale (7 = high). ANOVAs indicated significant differences between therapist response modes for client helpfulness, $F_{(8, 2094)} = 11.83$, $p < .0001$, therapist helpfulness, $F_{(8, 2094)} = 12.00$, $p < .0001$, and client experiencing, $F_{(8, 2094)} = 5.06$, $p < .0001$. Post hoc differences are indicated, such that response modes with the same letter (A-B) were not significantly different (A = highest ratings). The overall relationship between response modes and client reactions was significant, $X^2_{(28)} = 339.56$, $p < .0001$.

Discussion of Helpful Techniques

Paraphrase. Both Diane and Dr. S noted the value of focusing on Diane's feelings. In her life, Diane had carefully warded off her feelings since they had not met with approval from others. Diane had a difficult time believing that she had a right to her feelings and preferred to accept "shoulds." When Dr. S encouraged Diane through reflections of her feelings (e.g., "You feel stuck and overwhelmed," "You looked sad a minute ago"), she felt supported and was able to

TABLE 7.2 Proportions of Helpful and Hindering Events Reported by the Client and Therapist in Post-Session Reviews in Case 5

	Client		Therapist	
	Helpful	Hindering	Helpful	Hindering
Therapist Techniques	.24	.17	.43	.09
Support	.02	.00	.05	.00
Direct Guidance	.01	.06	.05	.04
Closed Question	.00	.02	.00	.01
Open Question	.00	.00	.00	.00
Paraphrase	.06	.05	.21	.03
Interpretation	.11	.00	.04	.00
Confrontation	.04	.02	.07	.01
Disclosure	.00	.00	.00	.00
Therapist Manner	.15	.01	.04	.02
Client Tasks	.16	.16	.18	.02
Focus	.00	.07	.03	.01
Experiencing	.06	.09	.07	.00
Insight	.10	.00	.07	.01
Changes	.00	.00	.02	.00
Client Manner	.02	.08	.09	.11
Relationship/Alliance	.00	.00	.02	.03
TOTAL	.57	.42	.76	.27

begin to identify and accept her own experiencing. When Diane focused on her feelings, she was able to decide what she wanted to do in a given situation. Thus, the feelings were not used as a vehicle for greater experiencing as an experiential therapist (e.g., Mahrer, 1983) would use them, but more as a vehicle for examining for cognitive assumptions and making decisions (e.g., Beck, Rush, Shaw, & Emery, 1983).

Dr. S also made extensive use of open question (e.g., "How do you feel about that?" "How are you feeling right now?") to help Diane get in touch with her feelings. Although sometimes helpful, open questions made Diane feel challenged and worse about herself, perhaps because they placed a demand on her to respond, which she interpreted as pressuring her. Paraphrase, on the other hand, required the therapist to take a more active role in trying to understand the client, thus making the client feel more equal.

Interpretation. Both Dr. S and Diane indicated that the interpretation regarding Diane's controlling behavior was one of the most powerful interventions in the therapy. When presented in the 16th session, this intervention consisted of a confrontation regarding Diane's controlling behavior followed by an interpretation regarding the reason for her controlling behavior:

> T: When you talk about your sister as being the one in control, what makes me think that, I was thinking that you're also very much in control and can be very controlling.
>
> C: Uh in what situation? (Well, in, in . . .) I don't like to think of myself as a controlling, or you mean of, of my own psyche, or . . .
>
> T: No, in terms of getting other people to tell you what to do. (C: Oh.) And, and in fact you get, (C: That's a switch.) you get ticked off (C: That's the way you look at it.) if they don't do it. That's what happens, I think that's what happens in the group a lot. They don't go along with the scenario (C: MmHmm) and say what they're supposed to do and supposed to say and you get angry. And I think in here it has probably happened too.
>
> A minute later C: I never looked at it as control as far as, I looked at it as more dependent.
>
> T: In a way you're very dependent on people's approval. And so you're going to do the best to control things so that you can get it. And one way to be in control is to sometimes be helpless and people will take care of you.
>
> C: I'm so self-pitying, then people come and uh help you take care.

The confrontation apparently focused Diane's attention on her behavior. Although she initially resisted the confrontation, she was later able to accept it and then hear the interpretation about why she was controlling and give a further example of her controlling behavior. Undoubtedly, this interpretive sequence was helpful because it followed an entire therapy spent dealing with control issues in the therapeutic relationship.

Diane also mentioned that Dr. S was particularly good at drawing parallels between her life and therapy. This seemed especially helpful regarding Diane's feelings about termination. Diane would talk about her feelings about something outside therapy, for example feeling angry that her support group was not giving her enough advice, feeling angry that her husband was too controlling, wanting to quit the support group because she was ready to be on her own. When Dr. S drew the parallels and invited Diane to discuss directly her feelings about him, this typically resulted in a productive discussion about their relationship. In this way, Dr. S helped Diane to be more direct in her communication.

Approval. Dr. S used approval extremely infrequently. Diane's major problem was in seeking other's approval to the detriment of looking within herself for what she felt. Thus, she "pulled" dramatically for Dr. S to give her approval and tell her that what she was doing both inside and outside of therapy was right. He typically resisted her "pulls," insisting that Diane needed to look within herself for her own approval.

Dr. S's stance of neutrality by not giving much approval made him appear somewhat reserved, although he was never hostile. Since Diane was so desperate to get his approval, Dr. S's withholding might have been damaging had he not discussed the issue thoroughly. In other words, if he had simply withheld his approval without ever having told her why he was doing so, Diane may have felt so anxious that she would not have been able to continue therapy. But because Dr. S explained his reasons for withholding the approval as being for her benefit, Diane was able to tolerate the anxiety and examine her need for approval. Of course, Diane was still unhappy about not receiving more approval and warmth.

Discussion of Less Helpful Techniques

Closed question. Diane particularly mentioned that some of Dr. S's direct questions about her sexuality were hindering. For example, in the first session, he asked if she had ever masturbated. Since the question was somewhat abrupt and perhaps mistimed, she felt put off. Such questions seemed intrusive.

Disclosure. Both felt that it would have been helpful if Dr. S had disclosed more. Dr. S said he would have liked to have expressed his feelings more. Diane said that Dr. S seemed like a robot whom she could not get to know personally. She was particularly upset that Dr. S had not disclosed during the final session about enjoying their working together. Interestingly, Dr. S was the only therapist in the study who did not disclose to his client during the termination that he enjoyed the therapy process. I speculate that Dr. S tried so hard not to get "sucked" into gratifying Diane that he also withheld the "normal" socializing behavior that might have made him seem more human and approachable.

Direct guidance. Diane felt strongly that Dr. S did not focus and structure the therapy enough. She was angry that she had to take too much responsibility for what to talk about and to fill silences. On the other hand, Dr. S felt just as strongly that what he did best was remaining neutral and not gratifying Diane's needs to be taken care of in the session. He would start the session by asking her what she would like to talk about, but remained silent and let Diane take control of determining the topic. It is clear that overtly Diane wanted Dr. S to be more directive and that this would have made her feel more safe. It is less clear that this would have ultimately been good for her, as she may have felt that Dr. S was simply repeating her mother's and husband's roles. Perhaps had Dr. S provided somewhat more approval and disclosure, Diane could have tolerated the lack of direction more.

Moderating Variables

Client Factors

Diane presented the image of a confident, attractive, articulate woman who was "together." Yet underneath that facade, Diane felt very incompetent and disturbed and was suffering from tremendous inner conflict. Further, while she overtly demanded that others take over for her because she was incompetent, she covertly refused to go along with what anyone wanted her to do because she wanted to be self-reliant. Her feelings had been negated all her life, so that she had no sense of her inner core of her personality outside her reaction to others.

Not surprisingly, these issues became the major theme of therapy. Based on her overt demands, Diane wanted approval and direct guidance from Dr. S, which would have put her back into the little girl position she had been in with her mother and husband. From a theoretical perspective (Weiss et al., 1986), Diane was testing Dr. S to see if he would react the same way as others in her life had. If he had, she would not have been able to change. By not falling into the trap of responding as others had, he helped Diane to disconfirm her beliefs and change. Rather than giving her approval and direct guidance, he used reflection of feelings and interpretation to talk about her controlling behavior in their relationship, which Kiesler (1988) has labeled metacommunication. Dr. S was thus able to side-step the demands and help Diane change.

Therapist Factors

Dr. S described himself as naturally reserved and not controlling in relationships, which probably helped him resist the pull to take care of Diane. He was also somewhat anxious about being evaluated, which forced him into more of his natural reticence. Further, based on his theoretical approach, Dr. S strongly believed that it was important for him to withhold gratification and be as neutral as possible, so that Diane would quit looking to him for approval and advice and begin to turn to her own inner resources. Thus, both personal and theoretical reasons contributed to Dr. S's stance within the therapy.

The Therapeutic Relationship

Based on the Working Alliance Inventory scores (see Chapter 2, Table 2.2), both Diane and Dr. S perceived the relationship as moderately strong, with scores increasing over time for Dr. S.

In his post-therapy interview, Dr. S said,

> I think the relationship was positive. I respected Diane and think that she trusted me. I believed that she could change and was capable of doing the things that she was working on, so I didn't buy into her negative feelings about herself.

Diane, in contrast, felt like she did not get as close to Dr. S as she would have liked. She wished he had been warmer and more personally revealing, although she was also afraid of becoming sexually attracted to or dependent on him.

In summary, the picture of the therapeutic relationship is mixed. On the one hand, the therapist felt that the relationship was good. In fact, the dyad worked well together discussing issues in the relationship. On the other hand, Diane was disappointed that Dr. S was not warmer and that the relationship was not more intimate, even though she was conflicted about intimacy and may not have been able to handle it.

External Factors

Extratherapy involvement. Comments in the post-therapy interviews indicated that Diane did a lot of work on her problems in between sessions:

R: *How did you (or Diane) use the therapy between sessions?*

C: I committed myself to dealing with my issues and decided that I was going to deal with them in the best way I could. I used what I learned quite a bit in between sessions. It seemed like almost after every session, I would have a good conversation and bring up things that I'd found out about myself either with my group, my sisters, my children, or a friend. I might make a general statement about humanity or women, but it would be based on what I'd found out in therapy or what I considered when I left therapy. I was trying to get a handle on life and how I felt about it.

T: She did a fair amount of work between sessions. She would try things even though they were difficult, like going out alone on the singles scene. She brought up issues in the women's group that she had talked about in our sessions. She also complained in the women's group about how I wasn't offering her enough direction. In that way, she kept the issues alive for herself instead of avoiding them. She brought in a dream that she had, talked with her sister about her family, and noticed that her husband was acting like a therapist. Those are the things I look for to see if someone is working between sessions.

Support network. Diane's main source of support during the therapy was her weekly support group. When Diane complained to her group that Dr. S was not giving her more direction, her group responded that she was up to her old tricks again of trying to get someone to take care of her. This confirmation undoubtedly speeded up the process of Diane's being able examine her controlling behavior. On the other hand, her support group gave a lot of advice and often pressured Diane to start making some decisions, which caused Diane to rebel and feel bad about herself.

Although they did not live nearby, Diane was close to her two sisters and had some good conversations with them throughout the therapy regarding their perceptions of their childhood. Her two daughters also gave her encouragement and support. Although Diane mentioned doing things with friends, she never discussed specific friends to whom she turned for support. The impression Diane gave was that although she appeared sociable and friendly, she was actually pretty much of a loner.

External events. The lack of resolution over her marriage was perhaps the biggest external event affecting Diane's progress in therapy. Neither she nor her husband could make a decision about whether to divorce or reconcile. On one hand, this "limbo" was okay with Diane because it protected her from having to get involved in any new relationships. But on the other hand, she felt trapped and not able to investigate new possibilities. In the middle of therapy, Diane forced herself out of her ambivalence and went to some singles bars and had a very good time, getting a lot of attention from men. Immediately afterwards, her husband became very attentive and less controlling, asking for a reconciliation. She was soon back in the old familiar quagmire and could not decide what to do.

Although Diane mentioned the need for marital counseling in the beginning of treatment, she chose individual therapy both because her husband refused to go for counseling and because she needed to resolve some of her own issues first to be able to decide what she wanted from a relationship with any man.

Outcome of Therapy

Session Outcome

Based on the SEQ scores (see Chapter 2, Table 2.2), Diane perceived the sessions as being moderately deep but rough, whereas Dr. S perceived them as being moderately deep and smooth.

Pre-Post Changes

Diane was greatly improved as a result of therapy (see Table 7.3). Diane's MMPI scale scores were now all below 70. Her highest scores were still on the Depression, Psychopathic Deviate, Psychasthenia, and Schizophrenia scales, but the scores were all at least 15 points lower. Further, she had significantly higher self-esteem, less depression, was lower on all of her target complaints, and had slightly though not significantly less symptomatology.

More specific changes were mentioned in the post-therapy interviews excerpted below:

R: *How did you (or Diane) change as a result of therapy?*

C: I really feel better about myself. I like myself more. I'm not totally to the point where I'd like to be, but I'm at least halfway there. Another thing is that I don't mind talking about myself. Therapy has really helped me get to the point where I can talk about my problems. Another thing it's done is that it's opened my mind to the fact that I have feelings. Before I started therapy, I just ignored my feelings. Therapy opened a whole realm of things I hadn't even thought of before and helped to direct my energies to myself and go in a more positive direction with my life. I was in a limbo, just wallowing around and doing a few things, taking a few courses, reading a few books, but not really focusing on where I was going and what I wanted for the rest of my life. It's also given me a lot of courage or impetus to handle some of the things I've been avoiding. *Have you seen specific behavioral changes?* My relationship with my husband has definitely changed. We've gotten on a much more communicative level. I never dealt with feelings or telling him how I felt about things. That has changed. With other people, too, I'm a lot better. Because I feel better about myself, I'm different with them. I'm less self-conscious. I'm working on my personal image and taking better care of myself. I'm really working on exercise and diet. For about a year, I was letting myself go down the tube because I was not motivated and was depressed and feeling sorry for myself.

T: She feels better about herself and is more accepting of herself. She also has more insight into her dependent nature. The insight was not necessarily into what caused her to be that way, which was something she was looking for. The insight was into how it operates with her, how she looks to other people to give her direction and ignores her own feelings and desires. She seems to have an understanding that she does that and how it gets her into trouble. For example, it gets her into trouble with her off-again, on-again relationship with her husband. But even

TABLE 7.3 Scores on Outcome Measures for Case 5

Measures	Pre	5th	Expect	Post	6 Mo	1 Yr
Client-Rated Measures						
MMPI						
Depression	84			67*		
Psychasthenia	81			60**		
Schizophrenia	77			60*		
Psychopathic Deviate	74			60*		
Social Introversion	71			53*		
SCL-90-R	44			37	[41]	38
TSCS	34			53***	[41**]	47
TC (1) Self Image	10	10	4	7*	[8]	8
(2) Sexuality	8	[9]	5	5*	[10*]	9
(3) Indecisive	10	[12]	5	7*	[10*]	8
Satisfaction					6	3
Therapist-Rated Measures						
TC (1) Self Image	11	11	8	6*		
(2) Sexuality	12	12	8	9*		
(3) Indecisive	10	10	6	8		
Researcher-Rated Measures						
Hamilton Anxiety	8			4		
Hamilton Depression	18			6***		

NOTE: High T scores indicate high symptomatology on the SCL-90-R GSI, high self-esteem on the TSCS; worst functioning on the TC, higher satisfaction, and greater disturbance on the Hamilton scales. Expect = level expected after treatment. Change was determined from pre to post, post to six-month follow-up, and six-month to one-year follow-up. * = significant change at $p < .05$; ** = $p < .01$; *** = $p < .001$. Negative changes are in brackets.

more, it creates this general sense of being unhappy and ineffective. One example was that in her women's group she brought up the issue of whether she should go to Disneyworld with her husband. She knew it wasn't a good idea and that's what the people were going to tell her and that she had to stick with that. Another time she ordered charter tickets for Europe with a group of friends and went off and did it. She didn't do her usual route of investigating and finding a cheaper airline. She ordered the tickets and then went into a panic and anxiety about what people are going to think, the plane is going to crash, and all this crazy stuff. But then she seemed to go a step back and observe herself doing it. So she was able to make some decisions herself and follow through on them despite the discomfort and then to see what she was doing instead of pulling in other people. She was also getting out more and doing things that she wanted to do. Her interpersonal skills were always very good, but what would hang her up was when she would get into a dependent mode. She would deny a lot of the conflicts and work to please people, which probably helped her interpersonal relationships at least on the surface.

R: *How satisfied are you with the nature and amount of change?*

C: I'm satisfied. For the amount of time, I came a long way.

T: I'm very satisfied. It would have been nice to work with her on an open-ended basis. There were a lot of other issues that came up that were important but I never had a chance to get a handle on. *Like what?* This idea of saying goodbye to her father. We worked on that, but I think there's still more going on there. Her father was a shadowy figure and there was probably more going on with her and her father. Some of her concerns about sexuality were probably tied to some Oedipal concerns about her attraction to her father. Probably the concerns she feels in terms of hugging her daughters are related to that. *Why didn't you deal with those things?* I didn't push her because of the time limit. There was just so much we could cover in 17 sessions. Also, the sexual area was difficult because she had some attraction to me and that felt too risky to deal with.

Diane was also asked to talk about what caused and maintained one of her major problems. Her answer indicated that the therapy had helped her gain some insight that her current problems were a result of problems in her family of origin.

C: My main problem is low self-image. The origin is not clear. I had a foggy theory about it, but I'm not real happy with it so I'm still working on it. I was the first child. My parents were married about seven years before I was conceived so they were very happy that I was there and everything was perfect. I was the perfect child and daughter. Everything I did was right and okay. Even if something wasn't up to their standards, I'd still get, "Oh it's good. Why are you doing it over?" It was a discounting of my feelings and it just perpetuated itself all through my childhood and college days. I was trying to live up to the image that I could do no wrong and that everything I did was good. And even though my mother thought that everything I did was okay and good, there was always just one thing that wasn't quite right. That's hard to explain. It happened more to my sisters than me. But it was not always perfect, "Well, that's excellent, but . . ." Then I perpetuated it by marrying a compulsive person who couldn't be pleased no matter what. It was a self-fulfilling thing that I couldn't always get to the point where it was just right. After so much of that, I finally started thinking I really can't do anything right. Or even if I did something, I didn't give myself credit for it. I'd always find one flaw or reason why it was negative.

Six-Month Follow-Up

At the six-month follow-up, Diane had relapsed to pre-therapy levels. Compared to post-therapy, her self-esteem was significantly lower and she felt worse about her functioning on her complaints of sexuality and indecisiveness, probably because she had still not resolved the issue of her marriage. Her support group had pressured her to make some decision about her marital situation, so she had decided that she would soon file for divorce. But she had not done anything about it. She was also thinking about going back to school so that she could get a job earning more money, but again had taken no steps towards that goal. On the other hand, Diane was proud of herself for taking the initiative to do some traveling that she had been wanting to do.

One-Year Follow-Up

Diane's self-concept had increased, but she was about the same on the other measures as she had been at the six-month follow-up. Diane had not filed for a divorce nor had she gone back for further schooling during this six-month period. She did indicate that she was finding it easier to make decisions involving money and major changes, but that she was having trouble focusing her energy and completing tasks at work and home.

Long-Term Follow-Up

When I contacted her three years after therapy was over, Diane reported that she had been to the Lifespring program, had undergone plastic surgery on her nose, had been through several relationships with men, and was moving up in her career, all of which made her feel better about herself. After the Lifespring program, her husband came back wanting a reconciliation. They attended five sessions of marital therapy, which ended in a stalemate. So Diane was still separated from her husband, but was planning to begin divorce proceedings soon. In general, Diane was taking more responsibility for herself and seemed more self-confident.

Summary

The most helpful aspects of the treatment were the therapist techniques of paraphrase, interpretation, and approval. Closed questions were less helpful and the client would have liked more approval, disclosure, and direct guidance.

Client factors played a large role in which techniques were helpful in this case. The client had conflicting needs to control and be controlled, as well as to be loved but not to get intimate. Thus, therapist approval and direct guidance would have played directly into Diane's pathology, even though she wanted them. Reflections of feelings and interpretation were particularly useful with Diane, probably because of her ability to handle feelings and insight. Unfortunately, the brevity of the therapy may have prevented Diane from being able to assimilate this new understanding or perhaps it would have been necessary to bring the husband in so that Diane could generalize her understandings to a relationship outside therapy.

The other factors also moderated the effects of the techniques. The therapist's stance of neutrality, which he adopted because of his personality and theoretical orientation affected which techniques he was willing to offer. The effects of the therapeutic relationship were not clear, in that it was adequate to allow the work to progress but the client was not happy with it. The external factor that probably hindered the progress of the therapy was the relationship with the husband. As Diane began to change and move away from the husband, he reacted strongly to draw her back. With Diane's problem with indecisiveness and fear of making the wrong decision, she was paralyzed over the magnitude of a decision about her marriage. The lack of resolution over the marriage left her unable to take on decisions over other issues.

Thus, the therapist techniques seemed adequate for helping Diane make changes while therapy was in progress. But the lack of a decision over her marriage prevented her from maintaining changes in the other areas of her life.

8

Case 6: Daddy's Girl

This chapter will focus on the therapist techniques in the 20-session case conducted by Dr. C, a 44-year old, White, male psychologist with Gloria, a 32-year old, White woman.

Client

Gloria (a pseudonym) was the middle child out of five children, the second of whom died when she was one year of age. Gloria, who was born shortly afterwards, was also sickly. Twice before she was five years old, Gloria was hospitalized for extended periods for life-threatening illnesses. Since this was before hospitals allowed parents to room in with children, she undoubtedly felt abandoned by her parents during these hospital stays. After she recovered, she had to go to the doctor for weekly visits for several years for blood disorders and severe asthma. Because he was afraid that she was going to die, Gloria's father overindulged her and gave her special attention.

Right before she was to start school, the family moved to a new house, which was a traumatic change for Gloria. Additionally, her mother missed Gloria's first day of school because she was in the hospital giving birth to Gloria's younger brother. Gloria again felt abandoned and still resented her mother's absence and her brother's birth. Subsequently, Gloria developed school phobia and her father had to bribe her to go to school by buying her junk food. Dating from that time, Gloria had recurrent dreams of coming home from school and discovering that the house had disappeared. These events set the stage for Gloria's view of the world as a dangerous place and established the pattern of her father's overindulgence and pampering of her.

Gloria said that she had a generally good family, although her mother was frequently mad at her father. She described her mother as a quiet person with a good moral character, who was more concerned about other's opinions than about her children's feelings and who was uninvolved with the family. Her father was described as a fun-loving person, who "worshipped" her and gave her whatever she wanted. He was also irresponsible with finances and "ran around with other women."

Gloria's father died suddenly of a blood clot when she was nine years old. She had begged him to go to the doctor the night before his death, but he had refused. Gloria found him in the morning, but did not go to his funeral or admit for some years that he was actually dead. As she had before he died, Gloria waited up for her father to come home from work for months after he died. She believed that he visited her several times after his death.

Right after high school, Gloria got married (when she was pregnant) and had two children. Her husband, a policeman, was violent and unpredictable. He frequently battered her and upon several occasions held a gun to her head for hours threatening to kill her. Gloria finally left him, although he kept harassing her for several years. When they separated, she took one of the children and he took the other, refusing to let Gloria even talk to her daughter for some time.

Gloria then got a job as a bank teller, bought a car for herself, and became more independent. During this time, she dated a couple of different men, but as soon as they got close she pushed them away. She met her current husband, a truck driver, after his second wife had abandoned him, leaving him with two children. Gloria felt that she married (again when pregnant) primarily to take care of the oldest child who subsequently died of cancer. The second child, who may not have been the father's biological child, was psychologically disturbed. He urinated and defecated all over the house and was a behavior problem in school. Gloria and her second husband had two more children together, both of whom were toddlers at the time of therapy. Gloria was a full-time homemaker, but felt somewhat worried about not working because she felt too dependent on her husband. Her husband was an easygoing man, who had a need to be the boss. She felt that she needed more love, respect, and consideration than he gave her. She felt that she had gotten along with her husband relatively well while her stepson was dying, but the marriage began deteriorating after his death.

During the five years prior to therapy, Gloria had befriended two persons with terminal illnesses and had taken them to doctors daily. She obviously had filled her life with dying people.

Physical Functioning

Gloria was 25 pounds overweight, which she attributed to over-eating and no regular physical exercise. Further, she had asthma, sinus trouble, and recurrent colds, and was always worried about her health.

Pre-Therapy Expectations

Gloria had had some therapy with her mother when she was in high school because of continual conflicts. Currently, she was taking her stepson to child therapy which involved some parent and marital consultation. She had no previous individual therapy. She expected that therapy was to help people understand themselves, but had no idea how long therapy should last. She thought that a therapist should be able to help her realize problems and give alternatives on how to change or deal with these things.

Pre-Therapy Assessment

Gloria's scores on all the pre-therapy assessment measures are shown in Table 8.3. On the MMPI, Gloria had normal validity scores and high scores on the Social Introversion, Psychopathic Deviate, and Depression scales. This profile suggests that she was withdrawn, shy and sensitive, hesitant to be involved in social situations, impulsive, resentful, immature, passive-aggressive, and depressed and pessimistic.

Gloria's scores on the other measures showed evidence of average symptomatology, but an extremely low self-concept compared to an outpatient population. She was functioning at an average level on her target complaints. The clinician judged her to be moderately anxious and depressed.

Gloria was diagnosed by the research team as dysthymic with a secondary diagnosis of cyclothymia because of her mood swings.

Target Complaints

Her first complaint was depression and not feeling good about herself without looking to others for approval.

Gloria's second complaint was a fear of abandonment. Her early illnesses, the family moving, and her father's death made her very frightened about losing anyone to whom she might get close.

Her third complaint was that she felt unhappy and moody. Gloria said that her husband often called before he came home to find out what mood she was in so that he could prepare himself.

Summary of Client Pre-Therapy Characteristics

The things that stand out in Gloria's history are her bouts with physical illness, her father's death, and her poor relationships with men. Her main current complaints were her depression and fear of abandonment. Diagnostically, she was depressed with some tendency towards mania. Personally, she was articulate and likable.

Therapist

Dr. C was a Jesuit priest prior to and throughout his graduate training in clinical psychology. After completing his PhD, he joined the faculty of a psychology department and was presently an associate professor. His program of research was in biological factors in schizophrenia and the affective disorders and he had published 39 journal articles and one book. Additionally, Dr. C was active in state and national professional organizations.

Dr. C was licensed and listed in the National Register of Health Service Providers in Psychology. He maintained a small private practice of 5-6 hours per week of individual psychotherapy with anxious and depressed adult clients.

Using three 5-point (5 = high) scales for how much he believed in and adhered to each of three major orientations, Dr. C rated himself: psychoanalytic = 4, humanistic = 3, and behavioral = 2. In a written presentation of his theory, Dr. C stated,

People learn from experience. Much of this personal learning (as opposed to school learning) is automatic and not cognitively explicit. Some of it is through modeling; for example, I learn how to parent from watching my parents. Some of it is non-explicit generalizations from strong experiences; for example, my mother dies when I am young and I learn not to depend on anyone again because I have lost the person I love. Some of it is through operant conditioning; for example, my exuberance is contained, punished, and extinguished by my depressed household. Some of it occurs in situations of high emotions and therefore may not be recalled except under similar emotional cues. Some of it was learned before we had much speech and therefore is closer to nonverbal motor skills than an abstract concept. This understanding of the nature of personal learning has a number of implications:

(a) The first task of the therapist is to grasp these learnings in their specific form and help the client become aware of them first as a pattern, then in the very act of performing them. Once the client is aware of the pattern as it happens and what it does for the client (its reinforcing properties), there are innumerable ways to set about changing that pattern.

(b) An optimal way of grasping these learnings is to have the client enact these neurotic learnings in the therapy session so that the therapist and client can see, hear, and verbalize them. This can be done in many forms: a real interaction, a fantasy, a role play, a psychodrama, etc.

(c) Furthermore, the most powerful and personally transforming new learnings as an adult are not usually new verbal concepts, but new corrective full-bodied experiences. Thus, whereas I range from cognitive therapy to Rogerian support to arranging the environment, my preference and the most powerful interventions are experiential.

Treatment Process

In the beginning of the first session, Dr. C structured the treatment very carefully, letting Gloria know what he knew about her from examining her testing data and what to expect from treatment. He then asked her several questions that were raised for him based on the material he had read prior to therapy. One of the questions towards the end of the session regarded Gloria's writing that her mother was like a "cold fish." She responded:

C: It's like from way back from when I could remember, first of all I was Daddy's girl. (T: MmHmm) And that's all I cared about was my father. I mean, I got up every morning and looked for him. I waited for him to come home at night and that's, that was my life. I remember very few things about my mother. I remember my mother folding the clothes and ironing. I remember my mother used to have some arguments with my father about me, like . . .

T: What, like what was that about?

C: Like we would go for a ride and I would decide that I was tired. I was probably about 4 or 5 years old. And I would want to lay my head on his leg (T: MmHmm) in the car and sleep. We used to go for rides on Sundays. And she used to get mad and say, "How can you drive and have her lying there at the same time?" You could tell that she really resented it. And it's those kinds of (T: All right) things I remember about my mother.

T: Right. What do you make of that now as an adult?

C: I don't know. I've been thinking about those things in particular a lot lately. I don't know, at first I thought she resented me and then I'm beginning to wonder if maybe it was the other way around.

T: Other way around of?

C: You know, I wanted my father's attention so much that I didn't even want her to pay attention to her. (T: Yeah) I mean, I used to get up in the middle of the night scared to death and I was really scared of noises and stuff and I'd want to go in there and get in bed with them, (T: MmHmm) but I had to be between them. I wasn't satisfied being on my father's side and I for sure was not going to be on my mother's side. (T: Yeah) There, there has always been bad feelings with my mother. (T: Yeah) And I don't know why.

This excerpt provides an initial glimpse of Gloria's relationship with her parents.

Summary of Process

The major theme of therapy was dealing with the death of Gloria's father. Dr. C gradually helped Gloria to express what had happened at the death scene and to talk about her feelings about her father. Gloria often said she was a spoiled brat because her father had given her everything she wanted. She missed her father terribly and compared every man she met to her father. Dr. C encouraged Gloria to visit her father's grave and say goodbye to him. The anniversary of her father's death came close to the end of therapy, providing a marker event to focus on his death. Toward the end of therapy, Gloria was able to recognize some of her father's faults and limitations, rather than just idealize him as she had previously.

Another issue that was dealt with during the therapy was Gloria's relationship with her current husband. Prior to marriage, they had agreed that in finances everything would be equal. Because of this, Gloria had felt comfortable quitting her job to take care of her husband's dying child and the other children. Just before the first session of therapy, Gloria discovered that her husband kept a secret savings account while telling her that she had to scrimp on all their family needs. She also discovered a box of condoms amongst his possessions even though he had had a vasectomy. Additionally, he kept all of his ex-wife's possessions and pictures of her naked and refused to let Gloria change anything in the house that belonged to his former wife. These events eroded Gloria's fragile sense of trust in her husband. Dr. C suggested that Gloria bring her husband in to give him an explanation of Gloria's behaviors and some hints for how to deal with her when she became anxious. At first, Gloria thought bringing her husband in was a great idea, but later rejected the idea and never did bring her husband in to see Dr. C.

They also spent a fair amount of time discussing Gloria's previous relationships, including her tumultuous first marriage and the intervening dating relationships. Gloria seemed to establish relationships in which she would get close, but then would destroy the relationship when she started feeling too intimate. Further, she selected men who were abusive and unacceptable once she got to know them better.

Another major topic was Gloria's fears of danger. Given her severe illnesses as a young child and her father's death as well as the violence in her first marriage, her fears of danger were clearly based in reality. Gloria slept with a knife or gun and had a Doberman dog to protect the house. She worried about her children's safety, often not sleeping at night because of her need to keep checking them to make sure that they were breathing. She would never let her children go out with anyone else for fear that they would get in an accident. Although Gloria had kept a teddy bear since childhood that she relied on as her only trustworthy object, she had given that away to her daughter.

Another theme that persisted across treatment regarded Gloria's defenses. In an early session, Gloria used the metaphor of her "walls" to describe her defenses. Her walls protected her but also isolated

her and made her lonely and confused. If her walls were down, Gloria
felt freer to express some of her pain. But if her walls were down too
far, she felt vulnerable and afraid. One could observe her walls in
operation, in that she shielded her face so that others could not see
how she felt. When she was near tears, she kept a tight grip so that
she would not cry overtly. After they explored the idea of her walls,
Dr. C often used this term to calibrate how she was feeling that day.

Termination. The final three sessions were spent discussing the
termination. These sessions were marked by a withdrawal on
Gloria's part, undoubtedly because of her fears of the impending
separation. For her, it was a step just to attend these final sessions,
since she typically avoided good-byes. During the final session, the
therapist used a number of metaphors, of therapy as a journey and of
the client's similarity to a little bird (excerpted later), to help her deal
with the loss of the relationship.

Client Behavior

Gloria's personal style was to talk in a glib, entertaining, but
offhand manner without much personal involvement. She was interesting to listen to, but one often had the feeling that she was describing events that happened to someone else rather than to herself.
Gloria mentioned that this was her way of dissociating herself from
painful affect. She also held tight control over herself in the sessions,
not allowing herself to cry. She often resisted experiencing her
immediate emotions. Sometimes she would cooperate with the
therapist's experiential exercises, but just as often she would shift
the topic to avoid the exercises.

In her talk, Gloria was full of contradictions, and it was often
difficult to get a clear sense of the facts in her case. She also often
acted the opposite of what she felt. Her cognitive style was to
characterize everything in black and white terms; for example, her
father was God's gift to the world or he was a rat. Gloria rarely
initiated topics, but waited for the therapist to tell her what to talk
about.

The most striking aspect of the client's behavior was her change
across therapy. Initially, she seemed surprisingly articulate and psychologically aware, especially given that she had only a high school
education. As the therapy became more intense, she became more
hesitant and withdrawn. In session 13, she said,

C: One thing I noticed about coming here, (T: Yeah) I don't look at people anymore. You make me nervous, being here makes me nervous. I, I used to have eye contact with people all the time when I talked to them, but now I look away a lot of times and I haven't figured out why. I, it's not always when I feel bad about something or it's not always something I'm feeling emotional about. It can be anything.

T: You do, you don't, you seem to look at me all right.

C: Well, I, I do it a lot here. I always, my eyes go that way, I don't know why, but I never did that before.

T: Hmm. Do you have any hypotheses? I mean, what do you think that's about?

C: MmHmm. I just feel nervous.

Thus, the uncovering process of the therapy seemed to make her anxieties emerge. A pattern emerged, where she would have a good session in which she was very engaged and active, followed by a session in which she talked rapidly and jumped all over the place, refusing to let the therapist pin her down to any one topic. She wanted to understand herself, but became very frightened and vulnerable when she made progress.

Therapist Behavior

For response modes, Dr. C used primarily information, paraphrase, and closed question. He was very active, which he attributed to feeling pressured to keep tight control on the process since there was a lot to accomplish in 20 sessions. He also felt he had to be active to restrain Gloria from running away and to give her instructions for how to do the experiential tasks.

Dr. C's approach was aimed at pushing Gloria to experience her feelings about her past and current situations. He often tried to get Gloria to engage in exercises in which she would express her feelings to her father or to some part of herself. Although Gloria would sometimes comply, she was generally afraid of her feelings and would often change the topic to avoid talking about her feelings. When Gloria wanted to run away from what they were discussing, Dr. C took the strategy of trying to make her aware that she was running away rather than making her discuss the topic.

Additionally, Dr. C was very supportive and encouraging of Gloria's efforts to change. On the other hand, Dr. C did minimal problem-solving or confrontation in the treatment.

Analyses of Therapist Techniques

Gloria and Dr. C talked about their reactions to the therapist techniques in the post-therapy interviews:

R: *How did change come about?*

C: He picked up on things that I didn't. He persisted about some of those things that I had hoped he would, like with my father. I had thought that I had gotten over all that and he kept after me and made me realize that I didn't. *What part did therapy play in changing your attitudes?* Part of it was coming in and watching the video when I realized that I wasn't such a bad person after all. I realized that I needed to do more things that I wanted to do, like go out and get a part-time job.

T: Change came primarily through just telling her story and my making sure that she told all the gruesome details rather than just the superficial ones, and my not being a critical mother around that to counteract the critical mother that's in her, to interject my good parenting. We began that process and it made her life a little less harsh. I was an attractive alternative to her mother in terms of being non-judgmental and calling a spade a spade. Unlike her father, I was firm in limit setting and not letting her run away. It was an informal systematic desensitization in that it kept going back to these things that she was really phobic and fearful about talking and dealing with. I kept bringing her back to these points even when there wasn't a lot of energy. I heightened the terror as much as she would allow, by looking at the most awful aspect I could get her to look at. So now she is not particularly overwhelmed, frightened, or even anxious thinking about her father. My deliberate aim was to get her to see that I relished the richness of life, whether it was fearful or not, and that her craziness and fear and running away were very engaging and human, and therefore brought me pleasure.

R: *What did Dr. C (or you) do best with you (Gloria)?*

C: He had ways of getting things out of me. He would say, "Well what do you think?" or "What do you think that could mean?" Fortunately sometimes when I turned the tables and said, "What do you think?", he would give me a little bit of feedback, which was really helpful. It was nice to hear him evaluate things besides just what I think all the time.

Also, he had a knack of knowing how far he could push me. Like in making me feel emotional, he knew what my limit was and would back off some. That was a big help. I trusted him because he didn't make me feel uncomfortable feelings for longer than I could stand.

T: One, I kept her on target. Two, my general enjoyment of human nature. I really enjoyed her and her struggles and the interaction. Third, I did a good job at keeping it focused on her emotional experiencing, as well as anyone could have. It was a good balance between keeping her focused and enjoying her efforts to run. I felt attuned about my attitudes and feelings about her and about how that came off. I was generally pleased with how my theoretical reflection guided where I was going and what I was doing in therapy. *What specific techniques did you use?* A lot of reframing. A lot of stopping her deflection, just verbally bringing her back. I tried to heighten her experience of whatever she was talking about and move it away from thinking about it to an actual experience. Whenever I tried to do a fantasy or a more formal type of enactment, Gloria undermined it and would run away.

R: *Can you remember any specific therapist interpretations or feedback that helped you (Gloria) see yourself (herself) or your (her) situation in a different way?*

C: At one point, I was having a problem and felt peculiar after we'd been talking about things like my father that I hadn't realized. I was beginning to realize that there is some truth in this and I don't want to realize it. I had this little battle going on inside of me. During this time, I started feeling odd, like I'd be driving down the street and I'd feel like, "Gosh, where am I?" I was telling him about it and he said it was called dissociation and told me that it was when you open up a lid on something that's really traumatic to you and you seem disoriented and it's only temporary. That was a great help and made me feel a lot better. Right after that, it all stopped.

T: The one I liked most was the *Are you my mother?* translated to *Are you my father?* story at the end. The notion of losing her father and then going around looking everywhere for him, and being angry at her father and the world for this terrible thing. Also, it was useful when I told her about the fright and the grieving being joined and helped her see that they were really separate. It was also useful to her that I made lots of interventions around how actually unhelpful her father was in setting up these tremendously high expectations for all subsequent relationships that nobody could live up to and how some of that carried over in present expectations. *How did she demonstrate that she heard your interpretations?* She would be quiet and frequently tear up. She has very little emotional expressiveness and is fairly awkward at anything except being angry. But what struck me is that she would tear up. Once we talked about it and she said she had a cold, which I think is absolutely bullshit. She would get up and blow her nose, but she was actually crying. You couldn't see it on the film very well, but there were a number of stretches where she was really quite touched.

R: *Try to recall one session that was particularly satisfying?*

C: A couple back when we started talking about what I had gotten out of therapy and he started talking about his views of it too. All the way through I had these different ideas going through my head, like a puzzle with the pieces everywhere. Little by little they went together and then at the end to sit down and talk about it was really nice. Just sitting and talking about how things are seeming to fall into place and how they didn't before. I didn't know about these different pieces before.

T: Around the 16th or 17th session, when we finally got past the fright and she was very quietly, gently grieving, it was a very moving session. The other was the last session, even though it was somewhat chaotic and we jumped around, I was extremely pleased that it brought together a lot of issues and there were a lot of memorable experiences.

R: *What did your therapist (you) do least well with you (client)?*

C: There's really nothing I don't like about him. I think he did a very good job.

T: I didn't do much with our interpersonal interaction. Also, I was pretty controlling in taking too much responsibility for the content, so that she didn't really learn to offer what was most pressing for her but waited to find out what I wanted to deal with. Also, by excluding talking about her relationship with her husband and divorce thoughts, I lost a lot of really good information. I gained something by it, but I lost good information in terms of working on the current relationships.

R: *Try to recall one session that was particularly unsatisfying?*

C: A lot of the times we talked about my father, at the time I thought it was awful. When I was here I knew it was things that we needed to talk about, but they were like, man I want to go home. I mean I was depressed a lot of times after spending time talking about my father. He even sent me over to visit the cemetery a couple of times and for somebody who's denied that somebody died for 27 years, that was hard. I guess those were the hardest or worst, but they were also the best because of what I accomplished. *Do you feel anything left over that you wanted to get to?* After I left here last time, I thought that one of my problems is not so much that I'm afraid to get involved with other people, it's that it scares me when they care about me. *What triggered that in the last session?* When I sit and talk through these things, I feel truly sincere. Then I get in the other room and watch these videos and think, "How could I say that? I don't feel that way." Maybe by the time I got in there, my walls were so down that I felt differently. I'm not sure, but a lot of times, like at the end of the last one, he said something like, "Is there something we should do to say goodbye?" I said, "Sure, how about a handshake?" He wanted a hug. I said it was okay, but that blew my mind and scared me. It wasn't him, it's something to do with somebody else caring about me. *Were there any areas you wish had been pursued further?* He said we should have, not here but somewhere else, maybe I should have been talking with a marriage counselor about my husband. That might be true. But as far as this therapy, I didn't want to talk about it. I mean I did on occasion, but that wasn't why I was here.

T: There were a number of sessions where I was not very emotionally in tune with myself or her and we ended up fairly cognitive and advice-giving and I was off-target a bit. *Is there anything you wish you had pursued further with her?* It seemed too remote to deal with in 20 sessions, but the hospitalization when she was 2 seemed to be very key. I conceptualized her as having unfinished business about grieving over her father, whereas a better way to conceptualize her might have been her fear of abandonment starting with that hospitalization, her father's fear of her dying and therefore overindulgence. This was tremendously reinforced by her father dying. So I would have liked to have conceptualized it more as an abandonment, of being drawn to relationships because of her ideal father image, and hoping to get from other people in her life this unconditional love, continuous attention, and indulgence, as being sort of a narcotic drainer. At the same time she was really frightened about being out of control and abandoned. All the things we talked about really fit, with ways of controlling that, ways of manipulating the relationship, ways of preventing it and not getting engaged, the walls and the emotional insulation and withdrawal. I think I was correct in thinking that I could not do much with that, but I could have done more at a cognitive level which would have at least given her a metaphor.

Quantitative Analyses

Table 8.1 shows the results of analyses on therapist response modes on the immediate outcome measures. Table 8.2 shows the codings of the post-session reviews. Both Dr. C and Gloria were quite positive in their comments, attributing most of the helpful events to therapist techniques.

TABLE 8.1 Proportion of Occurrence, Client Helpfulness Ratings, Therapist Helpfulness Ratings, Client Experiencing, and Client Reactions for Therapist Response Modes in Case 6

Response Modes	%	Client Help Rating		Therapist Help Rating		Client Experiencing		Most Likely Reactions
		M	SD	M	SD	M	SD	
Approval	.06	5.49	1.14 B	6.05	.90 AB	2.27	.51 B	Supported
Information	.22	5.34	1.14 BC	5.82	.91 BCD	2.30	.52 B	Supported
Direct Guidance	.06	5.03	1.25 C	5.97	.84 ABC	2.30	.50 B	Negative
Closed Question	.18	5.09	.90 BC	5.52	.80 D	2.25	.47 B	No Reaction
Open Question	.14	5.00	.96 C	5.70	.84 CD	2.38	.54 AB	Negative No Reaction
Paraphrase	.20	5.16	.99 BC	5.76	.85 BCD	2.26	.50 B	
Interpretation	.10	5.17	1.19 BC	6.06	.93 AB	2.28	.55 B	Supported Ther. Work
Confrontation	.04	5.03	1.03 C	5.99	.92 ABC	2.20	.46 B	
Disclosure	.01	6.06	1.63 A	6.17	.71 A	2.50	.51 A	
TOTAL		5.18	1.05	5.79	.86	2.29	.51	

NOTE: Helpfulness was rated on 9-point scales (9 = extremely helpful); experiencing was rated on a 7-point scale (7 = high). ANOVAs indicated significant differences between therapist response modes for client helpfulness, $F(8, 3049) = 8.21$, $p < .0001$, therapist helpfulness, $F(8, 3049) = 15.47$, $p < .0001$, and client experiencing, $F(8, 3049) = 3.47$, $p < .001$. Post hoc differences are indicated, such that response modes with the same letter (A-D) were not significantly different (A = highest ratings). The overall relationship between response modes and client reactions was significant, $X2 (28) = 397.38$, $p < .0001$.

Combining the results of the post-therapy interviews with the quantitative analyses shows that the most consistently helpful techniques were interpretation, support, disclosure, and paraphrase. Direct guidance and open question were both rated as less helpful.

Discussion of the Helpful Techniques

Approval. Dr. C was very supportive and gentle with Gloria, allowing her to run away from painful affect when she needed to.

TABLE 8.2 Proportions of Helpful and Hindering Events Reported by the Client and Therapist in Post-Session Reviews in Case 6

| | Client | | Therapist | |
	Helpful	Hindering	Helpful	Hindering
Therapist Techniques	.25	.09	.33	.04
Support	.08	.00	.07	.00
Direct Guidance	.07	.03	.06	.02
Closed Question	.00	.00	.02	.00
Open Question	.00	.00	.01	.00
Paraphrase	.05	.03	.14	.01
Interpretation	.04	.02	.04	.01
Confrontation	.00	.00	.01	.00
Disclosure	.00	.00	.00	.01
Therapist Manner	.21	.01	.16	.05
Client Tasks	.21	.11	.18	.02
Focus	.00	.00	.01	.00
Experiencing	.10	.11	.10	.02
Insight	.04	.00	.03	.00
Changes	.06	.00	.04	.00
Client Manner	.06	.04	.12	.06
Relationship/Alliance	.00	.00	.04	.00
TOTAL	.74	.26	.84	.16

Gloria mentioned that Dr. C was kind, sensitive, and understanding. He was quite accepting when Gloria discussed seeing ghosts and having strange dreams, thus allowing her to express herself freely. Examples of approval are that Dr. C told Gloria that she was brave and courageous and that he was delighted with her playfulness.

Paraphrase. Using reflection of feelings, Dr. C would get Gloria to slow down from her fast pace of talking and focus on what she was feeling, for example scared or angry. He would get Gloria to fantasize about whom the feelings were targeted at and what she would like to say to these persons, trying to get Gloria to speak to them as if they were present. They worked particularly on Gloria's emotions about her father's death. By raising her level of feelings of grief and anger and abandonment as much as she could handle, Dr. C helped Gloria deal with her fears and thus desensitized her to her anxiety. Talking about feelings was difficult for Gloria because she had spent years stuffing them down inside herself. Gloria wanted to understand herself, but was frightened and had a hard time letting down her walls.

Self-Disclosure. Dr. C's disclosures, which were primarily reassuring and about his immediate experience, received the highest ratings of all response modes on the objective measures. Gloria liked when Dr. C revealed his own vulnerabilities, probably because she felt less exposed and more equal. Similarly, she liked when Dr. C gave her feedback about how he reacted to her in the sessions. She would sometimes turn the table on Dr. C and ask what he thought. He would respond rather than questioning why she wanted to know. His willingness to respond made her trust him more. For example, he disclosed, "It makes me a little anxious too" in response to her nervousness about the videotaping and "I have two (children), so I can understand how you feel that" in response to her fears about anything happening to her children.

Interpretation. Although Dr. C's treatment approach was more experiential and exploratory than interpretive, interpretations were helpful. The major thematic interpretation that Dr. C offered regarded the connection between Gloria's feelings of being abandoned by her father and not being able to allow herself to get close to anyone currently. He also helped Gloria reexamine some of her idealized feelings about her father, bringing her to a more realistic perspective of his faults.

In the final session, Dr. C used a metaphor comparing Gloria to a little bird to interpret her search for her father.

T: Have you ever read the uh kid's book, uh *Are you my mother?* (C: HuhUh) Well, you might want to get it sometime for your kids. It's a wonderful book. It's about a little bird whose mother goes away to get some worm or something for birds. And the bird falls out of the nest. And it's a cozy little nest. And the bird falls out and sets out to hunt for mom. (C laughs) You know, goes up to a dog, you know, "Are you my mother?" "No." To the hen, "Are you my mother?" To the cow, goes to the automobile, airplane, you know keeps realizing that, "You're not my mother!" They keep telling, actually the bird doesn't realize, they keep telling him. Goes up to great big steam shovel and says, "Are you my mother?" And the steam shovel goes, "Snort." And he realizes the snort is not my mother. (C laughs) So he starts to turn away. And the steam shovel picks the little bird up, puts the bird back in the nest. And the mother comes. (C: Mmm) And I said, "Something about that story sounds real familiar to me." (T laughs) I was thinking of you. And I said, "Except that's not it." It's sort of like there's this nice cozy nest and the little bird falls out and is hunting for her father and goes up, "Are you my father?" "No, I'm not your father." Goes through all these different things and goes up to the steam shovel, you know, "Are you my father?" "Snort." But the way it's different is the steam shovel doesn't put you back in the nest and your father doesn't come back. So it's, I mean the other's a fairy tale you know. And the little bird stomps her foot (C laughs) you know and says, "But I want my nest and I want my father." And then every time somebody says, "I'm not your father," well, "You should be, you know, I want it." And something like that is how I sort of um experienced it. And I think it's a very sad story and a very true one. It's a sweet, you know, adorable little bird. And it's been really hurt, has lost a lot.

C: I guess I have to build my own or fly, huh? (laughs)

T: I guess so. Or you can build your own. It won't be like a nest when you were a little baby. You certainly have to build your own and make it as good as you want to.

C: Pause = 4 seconds. It seems like um through my life, I've always even thought I don't want things changed. A lot of times I go back to what I had before I made the change. And it's never the same. It's never what I really wanted. (T: MmHmm) So I know that um, you know, that would have also been true of that. (T: MmHmm) It wouldn't of been. (T: Sure) And yet people have such wild expectations, unreasonable expectations of things.

T: MmHmm, yeah, and because you're not, you're not a baby anymore, you know. You're not a 3-year old or 5-year old. And there aren't any fathers for a grown up. (C: Pause = 4 seconds) And I may be a snort. But I, even I cannot get you back in that nest, you know, because that nest was 20 years ago. It's all gone away.

C: Pause = 14 seconds. So what do people believe in, just themselves I mean?

T: The thought that comes to mind is what do people hope in? Hope, mostly hope that they can make something nice for themselves, for their family, their kids.

Although Gloria gave a high rating (7 on a 9-point scale) to the turn when the therapist described the book, she gave the lowest possible rating (1) to the next turn when he told her she needed to build her own nest and a neutral rating to the next turn (4) when he said there were no fathers for grown ups. Gloria did not like to be confronted about taking care of herself.

The interpretation that Gloria said was most helpful occurred in session 14:

C: Um (laughs) I don't know how to explain it all. I feel like a stranger.

T: Pause = 7 seconds. Do you ever catch yourself sort of withdrawing from yourself?

C: I think maybe that's what I'm doing. You know, I just, I don't even know how to explain it all. It's like I guess maybe I've decided I'm not going to be part of everything, so I'm just, I don't, I just shut everything out. I mean, I mean I go, I drive down the street and I, and places I go all the time, and it's like I don't know how to explain this, it's like, I know I've been there before, but it doesn't look like I have, (T: MmHmm) if you can understand what I mean. (laughs) (T: Yeah) And I don't know, I feel like when I'm places, I feel like somebody high, like I've never been on drugs or anything, but you know like you were drinking, (T: MmHmm) you know, like everything looks different. (T: Yeah) You know it's not, but it looks different.

T: That's right, you find yourself really distracted, I mean, like not paying attention to what's going on like when you're driving?

C: Yeah, I noticed I did that when I was driving. And then when I was, you know, paid attention, that was like, "Where am I?" And it, maybe I forgot to get off the beltway or, (T: at the right exit) and then I look around and nothing looks familiar. And then I see something that is and th-, I mean, I've been on this road a hundred million times. I mean, I ought to know all the little details of it by now, you know, but anyway I find that disturbing. (laughs) I mean, I, you know this is something that makes me nervous. I don't like it. And I . . .

T: Pause = 6 seconds. This often happens when there's sort of a fundamental shift. Something is very fundamentally going on deep down in yourself.

C: Okay, what is this called?

T: It's called dissociation. (C: Mmm) And it's as though you disassociate yourself a little bit from what's going on.

C: Yeah, it's like um, it's like in my mind maybe I've decided, "Well, shit on everybody, I don't belong here, I can be here when I want to be and otherwise I won't be." I mean that's just an idea I have about, maybe that's my attitude about it cause I, it feels like that sometimes.

T: You see, I think a part of you is very preoccupied with processing other types of stuff. That's my fantasy.

Having Dr. C affix a label to her feelings allowed Gloria to feel more normal. As a result, her "strange" feelings dissipated. Further, she felt freer to reveal other feelings to Dr. C.

Discussion of Less Helpful Techniques

Direct guidance. Both felt that it was helpful when Dr. C structured the session and kept Gloria on task when she wanted to run away. Sometimes Dr. C would allow her to escape, but then would bring the topic back in a way that she could handle it. He structured the therapy, often bringing up the topics for them to discuss and breaking silences when they became too unbearable for Gloria. Thus, he took care of her, which undoubtedly made her feel safer and more trusting. Dr. C, however, felt that he occasionally took too much responsibility for structuring the session and should have forced Gloria to take more initiative. Further, Gloria did not like the exercises that Dr. C suggested that she do, because they made her feel vulnerable and silly.

There were two helpful ways in which direct guidance was used for outside the session. First, Dr. C told Gloria not to make any major decisions regarding her marriage while she was in therapy because she was going through too much emotional turmoil to make a good decision. Secondly, he suggested that Gloria visit the cemetery so that she could work through her feelings about her father. Going to the cemetery helped Gloria begin to grieve and come to terms with the fact that her father had died.

Open question. Although Gloria thought that open questions were a good way for Dr. C to get things out of her, several other indicators suggested that they were not helpful and led to negative reactions. Open questions caused her experiencing levels to go up, but this seemed to make her feel out of control. In contrast, reflections of feelings seemed to be a less risky, more helpful way to get Gloria into her feelings.

Process Issues

Although Dr. C talked in the post-session reviews about the possibility of referring Gloria for medication for her swings of mood, he decided not to refer her. His rationale was that he felt that things were going well using a psychological treatment so there was no direct indication for trying medication at the present time. Further, he was not sure whether to recommend an antidepressant or a manic-depressive medication, given that she had manic swings but they did not seem pronounced, so he hesitated to recommend either medicine.

Dr. C broached the possibility of having Gloria's husband come in, but she vetoed the idea. Given her poor experiences with marital therapy, Gloria may have felt that she was better off in individual therapy where she did not have to share the therapist. However, given the contradictory information Gloria gave about her husband (easy to get along with versus verbally abusive), it would have been useful diagnostically and therapeutically to have a more accurate picture of their relationship.

As mentioned earlier, both Gloria and Dr. C used many metaphors. Because these metaphors seemed central to the outcome of this case, they will be examined further in a separate study (Hill & Regan, in preparation).

Moderating Variables

Client Factors

On the positive side, Gloria was insightful and motivated for therapy. She was also, however, skittish and scared, ready to run at the least indication that Dr. C was not supportive. She had faced a lot of abuse and abandonment in her life, had a very low self-esteem, and was wary of trusting anyone. Gloria said that she was a spoiled brat, as if she were not entitled to any caring or affection. One has to wonder whether she was ever actually spoiled or whether she had such a low self-concept that she thought she did not deserve anything that was given to her. Thus, it was important for Dr. C to be active and use a lot of support and guidance within the session, but little confrontation and silence.

Therapist Factors

Dr. C's style was experiential with an emphasis on immediate feelings and openness of communication. However, he was able to be flexible and modify his orientation to fit the client's needs. Further, Dr. C's patience, gentleness, and empathy were reassuring and important to combat Gloria's distrust. Given Gloria's past history of preferring men to women, it was probably fortunate that she was paired with a male therapist, especially one who did not treat her as badly as had all the other men in her life.

The Therapeutic Relationship

Based on scores on the WAI (see Chapter 2, Table 2.2), Gloria and Dr. C both felt that the working alliance was moderately strong. Interestingly, Dr. C rated the working alliance as increasing across treatment, whereas Gloria rated it as decreasing across treatment. The decline in Gloria's WAI scores over time reflected her growing defensiveness and withdrawal. As therapy progressed, Gloria felt progressively less safe in the relationship because her "walls" were down and she felt exposed and needy. Further, she was facing another separation from a caring man, so she probably withdrew first to prevent herself from being hurt.

In the post-therapy interview, Dr. C said, "There was mutual respect. I certainly respected her and I think she respected me. I enjoyed her. She appreciated the kindness. There was a real strong working alliance, by which I mean we both worked hard." Gloria mentioned that Dr. C knew just how far to push her.

Thus, there was a strong bond between Gloria and Dr. C. They liked each other. Dr. C was gentle and permitted Gloria to be herself. She was able to trust Dr. C in ways that she had never trusted anyone before. She could hear things from him that she might not have been able to hear from a more confrontive therapist.

External Factors

Extratherapy involvement. From the comments in the post-therapy interviews, it appears that Gloria thought a lot about what had been discussed in the therapy sessions:

> R: *How did you (or Gloria) use therapy between sessions?*
>
> C: I spent a lot of time thinking about it. For the first 5 weeks I wrote notes every time. Then we started talking about bad things, so I didn't write that down. But I would usually think about it all the way home, quite a bit that day, and over the week. That morning I would start thinking about it again because I wanted to keep running everything through my head in case I missed something that I might pick up if I kept thinking about it. *Did you try new behaviors as a result of the sessions?* I think so, but even more, I caught onto my bad behaviors. Like if I woke up in a real bad mood and I was pissed off at the world, all of a sudden I would realize why. Before maybe I wouldn't have. Then I could apply it and say, "Okay you stupid idiot, are you going to ruin the rest of your day?"
>
> T: She was thinking about a lot of the stuff at home and trying to apply some of the stuff.

Support network. At the beginning of therapy, Gloria seemed to be involved mostly with her children. She mentioned having a lot of fun with her children because she felt like a "kid" herself. Toward the end of therapy, she felt more like an adult and was able to discipline them better. Since she started work during therapy, she had made some friends outside the home.

Gloria said that she had friends with whom she felt comfortable confiding, although she rarely talked about friends in therapy. She did mention that she had good relationships with her two sisters, who were supportive of her therapy. In general, Gloria said that she got along better with men than with women. Her relationships with men, however, were fraught with conflict, so that did not leave her much of a support system. In general, because Gloria was so wary of people, she relied mostly on herself.

External events. During the course of the therapy, Gloria's marriage began falling apart. Gloria removed herself emotionally from her husband, got a job and a new car, and was prepared to leave at a moment's notice. An additional stressor was that Gloria had several young children to care for, including a stepson who was a behavior problem. Further, when she began working, Gloria got very little sleep, which added to her stress level.

In sum, the period of therapy coincided with several stressful events in Gloria's life. The press of the external events often made it difficult for her to focus in therapy and thus may have interfered with the facilitative effects of the techniques.

Outcome of Therapy

Session Outcome

Based on the SEQ scores (see Chapter 2, Table 2.2), Gloria and Dr. C both perceived the sessions as moderately deep and smooth.

Pre-Post Changes

Gloria was greatly improved on all measures at the end of 20 sessions of treatment (See Table 8.3). On the MMPI, Gloria improved significantly on Depression, Hysteria, Psychasthenia, and Mania scales. Further, her symptomatology decreased, her self-concept increased, she improved on all three target complaints, and her anxiety and depression were both lower.

These changes were reflected in the post-therapy interviews:

R: *How have you (or has Gloria) changed as a result of therapy?*

C: I was depressed a lot and had a lot of high periods and problems sleeping at night. They've gotten a little better. Coming here I felt for awhile like a little animal laid out on the operating table that everybody's cut open and taken pieces out of, like man I've been ripped apart. It was what I let myself do, thinking things that I didn't want to think about. Then as time went on, everything went back together. I'm beginning to see things a lot differently than I did. Depression was something I brought on myself that I didn't realize. I thought everybody else contributed to my misery. But as time goes on, I'm changing. I've realized that I'm responsible for myself, nobody else is. I'm beginning to see that the only people that can affect me are the ones that I allow to affect me. So if I want to get miserable, that's because I choose to and not because somebody did something mean to me. I don't like to admit I'm wrong, but I guess I'm changing my attitudes about all these things and I'm admitting my part in it. *How else have you changed?* I don't get as affected by things and people, like I don't pay much

TABLE 8.3 Scores on Outcome Measures for Case 6

Measures	Pre	5th	Expect	Post	6 Mo
Client-Rated Measures					
MMPI					
Social Introversion	77			68	
Psychopathic Deviate	74			71	
Depression	73			59*	
Hysteria	56			45*	
Psychasthenia	68			56**	
Mania	48			38*	
SCL-90-R	44			33*	[45*]
TSCS	28			42***	[25***]
TC (1) Depression	13	13	4	3***	[6]
(2) Fear Abandonment	10	[13*]	4	3**	[4]
(3) Unhappy/Moody	13	13	4	4***	[6]
Satisfaction				10	10
Therapist-Rated Measures					
TC (1) Depression	10	[11]	6	6*	
(2) Fear Abandonment	12	12	7	6*	
(3) Unhappy/Moody	11	11	6.5	7*	
Researcher-Rated Measures					
Hamilton Anxiety	22			6***	
Hamilton Depression	21			4***	

NOTE: High *T* scores indicate high symptomatology on the SCL-90-R GSI, high self-esteem on the TSCS; worst functioning on the TC, higher satisfaction, and greater disturbance on the Hamilton scales. Expect = level expected after treatment. * = significant change at *p* < .05; ** = *p* < .01; *** = *p* < .001. Negative changes are in brackets.

attention to what my husband says. I don't take things as personally as I used to. I used to be real concerned about what everybody thought of me and spent so much time and energy trying to please everybody and made myself miserable in the process. Not any more. I'm beginning to be more patient with other people and my kids and at work. What's the sense of getting all upset about this crap when I can't change it. I'm the one who has got to change. *Sounds like you've become more important to you.* Yeah, I guess I have. He was real good at pointing out my good points that I had overlooked. That helped me realize that I really am a good person. There is a lot of good things about me that I hadn't thought of before. I am a worthwhile person. *How about interpersonal relationships?* I've gotten close to my sisters, especially my oldest sister. Not because I've been coming here, but well actually partly it was, because they'd call up and ask how it went. They were curious about it.

T: She was a lot less phobic about the death of her father. And there's more fluidity. She's easier to move in and out and make those types of connections without as much terror for her. The exploration has concretely lowered some of her terror about abandonment, about her kids getting hurt, and some of her fear of loss. She learned a lot conceptually that will help her organize her experience some. One is that her father was not perfect, so she wore away at the edges of this idealization. Also she's beginning to understand how that relationship is affecting her relationships, so she can begin to separate out what's here and what's back there. That probably needs a lot more reinforcement, because it won't hold very strongly against the onslaught of the present tense. I see her slowly moving toward some type of independence, although I didn't have much to do with that other than in providing some support for her self-esteem. *Anything else?* She still needs to work on her relationships. She married beneath herself in terms of intellectual and emotional abilities. She is starting to confront whether this is the person she wants to live out her life with. I don't think it's a good choice, but for her children another divorce would be a real problem. She is going to have to either become reconciled to living in that state or move and become independent where she can set up a relationship that has a chance of working.

R: *How satisfied do you feel with the nature and amount of changes?*

C: I'm real satisfied. About 8 weeks ago I was wondering, "Gosh when am I going to get out of this?" That's when we were still in the middle of everything. It was very close to the end that I realized how much I had gotten out of it.

T: I'm generally satisfied. She did not change as much as I would have liked, but my hopes were probably pretty unrealistic.

Gloria was also asked to talk about what caused and maintained one of her major problems. Her answer indicated that the therapy had helped her gain the insight that her depression was related to her feelings of loss for her father.

C: When I get depressed, it's related to my father. I think it's because I feel like nobody cares for me. So then I have to make myself somebody nobody would care about. So I just get in a bad mood and act mean and hateful and hate myself because if I don't like myself, then of course nobody else will, right? So it's like I'm saying, "I really need somebody to care about me," but at the same time making damn sure nobody does. It's like I never wanted anybody to replace my father. The whole thing is like this little kid throwing a temper tantrum. If I couldn't have him or someone to care about me as much as he did, then I didn't want anybody at all. I didn't realize what I just told you until I was going through this therapy.

Six-Month Follow-Up

Gloria had relapsed to pre-therapy levels of symptomatology and self-concept, although she maintained her gains on the three target complaints. She was currently holding both a full-time and a part-time job and was becoming more independent, although she still felt depressed. In her interview, she discussed several cognitive changes, which made her more reality-oriented but more disillusioned. She realized that she was not really special as she had felt as "Daddy's girl" and was trying to adjust to feeling like a "nothing." She also felt that she had more control over herself, but that meant she had no one else to blame. Things were still tense with her husband, but she was resigned to staying with him. They were moving into a new house to get away from the memories of her husband's first wife. They had a few sessions of marital therapy with another therapist, which Gloria felt was a disaster. The therapist had told her husband to stand up to her and told her to have an affair.

One-Year Follow-Up

Gloria returned to Dr. C for 10 sessions of individual psychotherapy about a year after termination. Dr. C described Gloria as having been more passive and less willing to work during these sessions. She seemed overwhelmed with her full-time work at a bank, her deteriorating marriage, and her childrearing responsibilities, and did not have much energy for therapy. Gloria did not respond to our repeated attempts to contact her for the follow-up, so we have no empirical data on status.

Long-Term Follow-Up

Three years after treatment, Gloria reported that she no longer had as many mood swings, which she attributed to having resolved the issues with her father in the therapy. Gloria had visited the cemetery a couple of times and could now think about her father with pleasure. She was working full-time in a bank, where she had made many friends and was doing work that she enjoyed. Although still with her husband, Gloria was actively looking for an apartment so that she could move out. Because of her husband's repeated violence to Gloria's daughter from her first marriage, social services had removed the child from the home and placed her with her father and had not even given Gloria visitation rights. Gloria felt that she needed to move out, take care of her children, and learn to manage on her own. She said that she had not responded to our one-year follow-up because she had been depressed and just kept putting off the task.

Cause of Relapse

One explanation for the relapse was the deteriorating marital relationship. Although Gloria stayed in the relationship, she removed herself emotionally from her husband. She tried marital therapy, but found it to be unhelpful. Further, Gloria began working full-time, not allowing much time for herself or for her family, which caused an additional stress. While she was in therapy with Dr. C, the support she received and the energy she took to change seemed to be enough to build her self-esteem, but without the continual reinforcement and with the interfering external events, she was not able to maintain her changes. A more open-ended therapy may have been useful in this case.

Another explanation was that Gloria's fear of abandonment may have prevented her from benefiting from brief therapy. In effect, she was abandoned once again, reinforcing her belief that she was unlovable. In an open-ended therapy, she would have been able to leave the therapist when she was ready.

From another perspective, although the therapy was effective in helping Gloria grieve over her father, Dr. C did not teach Gloria coping skills to deal with problems in her everyday life or help alter Gloria's cynical, pessimistic, and negative outlook on life. In retrospect, Dr. C said that he wished he had used a more cognitive behavioral approach (Beck et al., 1983).

Summary

The evidence indicates that the therapist techniques were the most helpful change agents in this therapy. Approval, paraphrase, disclosure, and interpretation were the most helpful, with mixed results found for direct guidance and open question.

The moderating variables of client, therapist, and external factors influenced the effects of techniques in this case. Gloria was frightened and scared of intimacy and did not allow Dr. C to use confrontive or experiential techniques. Dr. C adapted his style to fit Gloria's needs, shifting from an experiential approach to a more supportive approach. Further, there was a good therapeutic relationship that allowed Gloria to trust Dr. C. Unfortunately, external events hindered the progress that Gloria was able to make in therapy. Several stressful events occurred within the therapy and there was not much of a supportive network for Gloria to turn to. Perhaps if therapy had been longer, Dr. C would have been able to overcome these obstacles.

9

Case 7: Caustic Love

The focus of this chapter is on the therapist techniques in the 12-session case conducted by Dr. E, a 44-year old, Black, female psychologist with Jane, a 35-year old, White, married woman.

Client

Jane (a pseudonym) was the oldest of three children, with a sister two years younger who was studying for a PhD in psychology and a brother seven years younger. Her father, who worked in management, was very quiet, intelligent, and reserved, somewhat similar to Jane. Jane said that he was loving to her in his own quiet way, but that it was hard to tell as he didn't really express it and neither did she. Her mother, who was a housewife, was described as very dominating, friendly, outgoing, and helpful. Regarding her home atmosphere, Jane said that her parents argued some, were not greatly compatible, and had almost divorced once. Jane mentioned that her father often got angry at her brother and that her sister was rebellious, so they apparently were more outspoken than Jane.

Jane met her husband while they were both in high school. They dated throughout college and then were married. Her husband, also 35 years old, worked in management for the federal government. She described him as selfish, immature, demanding, and self-centered. Jane tried to avoid sex with him because she did not enjoy it. She felt that if she were involved with someone whom she loved and who loved her, sex would be different. Jane had two children, an 8-year old daughter and a 5-year old son.

Jane indicated that some of her current troubles began five or six years prior to the therapy when she saw an old boyfriend, whom she described as the only person she had ever loved. This experience started her looking back over her relationship with her husband. Then, a couple of years before the therapy, when they were on their summer vacation and her only friend encouraged her, Jane started behaving more coldly towards her husband. These experiences convinced her that she wanted to leave her husband.

Jane had graduated from college with a BA in early childhood education but never got a job teaching because there were no jobs available. She had held jobs as a laboratory technician, recreation leader, and district manager. At the time of the study, she worked about eight hours a week doing inventory and decorating cakes. She described her past ambitions as wanting to be a teacher, marry, be a housewife, have children, and raise them to be good. Her current ambitions were to get a good job to support herself and her kids, to divorce and happily remarry.

Physical Functioning

Physically, Jane was healthy with no history of serious illnesses. She often overate and never exercised.

Pre-Therapy Expectations

Jane had never had any previous therapy. Her expectations were that therapy was for helping someone see or understand why he (sic) acts or feels certain ways and how to correct it. She thought that therapy should last until the person is able to change his (sic) ways or thoughts and is comfortable with the change. She wanted a therapist to ask leading questions and give helpful suggestions, insight, and persuasion.

Pre-Therapy Assessment

Jane's scores on all the pre-therapy assessment measures are shown in Table 9.3. On the MMPI, Jane had normal validity scores and high scores on the Psychopathic Deviate, Depression, Schizophrenia, Social Introversion, and Psychasthenia scales. Her profile revealed both depressive and anxiety states. Although she seemed distrustful of people and avoided close interpersonal relationships, she showed a basic insecurity and needed attention. Jane was withdrawn and alienated, shy and sensitive, constricted, anxious and tense with fears and excessive doubts, immature, with a low energy level and a lack of self-confidence. She was ambivalent, unable to love, resentful, argumentative, and sensitive to anything that could be construed as a demand. She utilized projection, rationalization, and acting-out as defense mechanisms.

Compared to an outpatient population, Jane's scores on the other measures showed average symptomatology, but a very low self-concept. She was functioning at an average level on her target complaints. The clinician judged her to be moderately depressed and mildly anxious.

Consequently, Jane was diagnosed by the research team as dysthymic with dependent and avoidant personality disorders.

Target Complaints

Jane's first complaint was a lack of self-confidence. Her second complaint was her relationships with people. Jane felt that she needed to learn how to handle people better. She tried to please others rather than being aware of what she wanted and ended up feeling like a doormat. Her third complaint was that she needed to be more assertive in expressing herself.

Summary of Client Pre-Therapy Characteristics

Jane was an introverted, passive, unassertive woman who had a lot of covert anger. She lacked self-confidence and was depressed and anxious. Her family background was calm with an undercurrent of family discord. Jane was unhappy in her marriage and was planning to get a full-time job and leave her husband. Interpersonally, she was very quiet. It was hard to establish a relationship with her because of her anxiety and withdrawal.

Therapist

After completing her PhD in clinical psychology, Dr. E had done extensive post-doctoral training, including training to practice psychoanalysis. She had held positions in a department of psychology and a community mental health center, and was currently in a department of psychiatry. She had published 10 journal articles. Further, she was very active and well-known for her contributions to local and national professional associations.

Dr. E was licensed, listed in the National Register of Health Service Providers in Psychology, and had a diploma from the American Board of Examiners in Professional Psychology in clinical psychology. She maintained an active private practice in psychotherapy, psychodiagnostics, and psychoanalysis.

Using three 5-point (5 = high) scales for how much she believed in and adhered to each of three major orientations, Dr. E rated herself: psychoanalytic = 4, humanistic = 2, and behavioral = 1. Asked to describe the way she works with clients, Dr. E stated that she places a heavy reliance on transference as the "curative" element. In a supportive therapy, she mobilizes and tries to maintain the positive transference through encouragement, suggestion, and advice. In more insight-directed cases, she promotes ego growth by clarifying and interpreting any transference that serves as a resistance. Change, she postulated, occurs through insight and ego expansion and/or through positive identification with the therapist.

Treatment Process

The verbatim excerpt of a segment a few minutes into the first session illustrates the initial process between Dr. E and Jane. Prior to this segment, Dr. E summarized the data that she had seen, indicating that Jane had problems with self-confidence, marital difficulties, and some somatic complaints. Dr. E then asked if Jane wanted to add anything. Jane responded,

> C: Uh, I need to learn to be assertive with my husband and everybody in general, you know. (T: MmHmm) I just let people walk over me, whatever. And I've gotten so that I don't like myself much anymore (laughs).

> T: MmHmm. Now this is the first time you have uh taken steps to have professional assistance with these difficulties? (C: Yeah) MmHmm. Um, what made the, this opportunity appealing enough for you to pick up the phone?

C: Well, I think uh maybe within the past year I know that I have to do something now. I've gotten, I'm ready now that I, I'm ready to start (laughs) (T: MmHmm, MmHmm) planning for the future. Like I say, I know something has to be done. And they said free therapy, so I thought it might be a good opportunity.

T: MmHmm. What if it had not been free?

C: Uh, probably just sat back.

T: MmHmm, MmHmm. It might be good to review also something of the terms of this work. One you just alluded to namely that uh it doesn't cost you any money to participate in it. But there are other elements in the contract that, that I think are important to make sure we understand mutually. (C: MmHmm) Uh, for example, that we will meet each Thursday at 12. And th-, the number of times we meet in part is determined between the two of us as between 12 and 20 sessions. And you and I, uh once we fill in more of the details of your troubles, we'll agree together on precisely how many sessions. And I, I think we'll be able to accomplish that within the first two or three sessions so that we'll have a, a clear picture of how many times we will meet for this purpose. Uh I've been informed that you know in uh some detail about the fact that this is a therapy research project. And that the uh tapes, as you know, this is being uh audio and video recorded. (C: Yeah) And that um of course the research team here will make use of these uh feedback mechanisms to learn about the process of therapy and similarly I uh may use them also in my uh teaching. (C: MmHmm) Um do you have any questions about any of those aspects of the work?

C: No.

T: MmHmm, okay. Um well there may be other um things we need to touch on in terms of the arrangements. But those are what I can think of at this time. Do you have any questions about uh any of the arrangement aspects of the work?

C: I don't think so.

T: MmHmm, okay, all right. Well now to get a fuller picture just to know what to work on and just how we're going to work on it. I have to hear in considerably more detail what brought you here. And I think it best to start with the current concerns. Now you noted that some of these problems you have had have been going on for a number of years. But what makes them most acute now?

C: I've just gotten more and more unhappy. And um then as I say, I realized a lot of things about me that I don't like anymore. And I see that affecting my children and being there with my husband.

T: Hmm. Spell that out for us, some for you and me. Um what effects on your children are you concerned about?

C: Well, he's uh well, I guess the biggest thing is he doesn't ever praise them. He's always cutting them down. And just like he does me too. And we're just, it's like we're supposed to be there to make his life good for him, you know. He just takes advantage of us. And he just cuts us down all the time, never sees any good points in us. (T: MmHmm) And . . .

T: Could you give me a specific example of that problem?

C: Well every time that we do something he doesn't like he, more with the kids I guess, he gets mad, yells at them. And if I, if we're working on a project or whatever and I give him an idea on something, he never likes my ideas or opinions. I'm just, I just feel like I'm supposed to be a robot there helping him (laughs) you know. And uh well like if he's watching, if one of the kids or watching a TV show or even myself, he'll, if he even, if he wants to watch something else, he'll just come flip the channel with no concern for anybody else. And then I feel bad too because I don't stand up for myself, but I don't stand up for the kids either when he does things like this to them. I should say something (T: MmHmm) and I just, like with everybody else I sort of sit there and keep it inside (T: MmHmm) whatever I feel.

T: It will help our work for us to know together what it is you're keeping inside. What does run through your mind at those times?

C: Well, maybe some anger mostly.

T: MmHmm. You're aware of feeling angry at those times?

C: Well you know not, not real angry but well if I feel anything, if I feel disappointment in something that he does or says or anger or anything, I just don't express my opinions about things.

In this segment, Dr. E did not track Jane well. When Jane mentioned her problem with assertiveness, Dr. E switched the topic to asking why Jane sought help at that particular time, and then again switched to informing Jane about the parameters of the therapy, and then turned the focus back to asking Jane to tell her more about her problems. Jane responded by saying that there were things about herself that she did not like, but quickly shifted to blaming her husband for his behavior.

Summary of Process

Initial sessions. In the first couple of sessions, Dr. E structured the treatment and asked Jane about her target complaints. As in the initial few minutes, Dr. E did not track well during these sessions, but often shifted topics. Dr. E indicated that she was not trying to delve intensively into any problems, but was doing a reconnaissance to find out where Jane could be engaged.

Middle sessions. During the third to seventh session, the dyad seemed to jell and work together well. Jane became progressively more relaxed and began to open up. During the seventh session, Jane talked quite freely and at length about several problems. The following is an excerpt from the middle of the fourth session, which Dr. E indicated was the first time that she felt optimistic about Jane changing:

C: I don't want to get into an argument about anything.

T: Well, how, how, how realistic is that, do you think, how workable? Has it worked for you?

C: No, no.

T: It hasn't worked.

C: I mean, it keeps me out of the arguments, but then it causes other problems.

T: You, you're talking about being kept out of more than arguments, young lady, (C: MmHmm) aren't you?

C: Yeah, it causes other problems, (T: Yeah) worse than arguments, (T: Huh?) probably worse than arguments.

T: Worse than arguments. Yeah, right, such, such as what are you thinking of?

C: Well, instead of the short term upset I would feel being in an argument, I'm just upset most of the time.

Final sessions. In these sessions, the process again seemed more disjointed. Jane was more quiet and cautious, whereas Dr. E was more confrontive and demanding. Rather than focusing on the content of the problem, Dr. E focused more on the process. For example, when Jane talked about worrying about people seeing her dirty house, Dr. E interpreted that Jane might be worried about how Dr. E felt about her. Jane did not understand these transference interpretations and felt that Dr. E did not like her.

Overall process. The focus of the treatment was only minimally on the past. In the second and third sessions, Dr. E probed for precursors to Jane's problems in childhood. Jane remembered being withdrawn in junior high school and also recalled conflicts between her parents when they had to pay the bills. These conflicts were upsetting to Jane because she felt that people should not fight openly.

More typically, the focus was on current conflicts. In the beginning of therapy, Jane would bring up a vague complaint such as her low self-esteem. As Dr. E tried to get her to be more specific about her complaint, Jane would typically shift the blame for the problem to her husband and his insensitive treatment of her. Jane felt that her husband ought to be able to read her mind and know what she wanted him to do without being told. Using specific examples, Dr. E analyzed Jane's behaviors and confronted Jane with taking more responsibility and speaking up for what she wanted.

Although Jane presented early in the treatment that she wanted to leave her husband, Dr. E spent little time exploring her thoughts about the separation. Rather, she focused on how Jane's communication with her husband could improve. Dr. E gave a lot of reinforcement when Jane brought in examples of how she tried to act differently. When Jane would complain that she had not gotten the desired response from her husband, Dr. E would explain how she had to accept her husband for his efforts. She did this through an educational approach, lecturing Jane about what she should be doing differently. In the post-session questionnaires, Jane indicated that she felt that Dr. E was taking her husband's side. Dr. E's attempt was to help Jane restructure her cognitions and to take more responsibility for her own behavior and to try to understand more about her husband's behavior.

Client Behavior

Jane dressed and looked more matronly, staid, and middle-aged than would be expected for her age. The most notable features of Jane's behavior were her fixed, rigid smile and nervous laughter, both of which decreased over the course of the therapy. She gave off few affective cues, so that one could not tell from her face what she was experiencing inside.

Jane was extraordinarily quiet and passive in the sessions, waiting for Dr. E to direct the session and tell her what to talk about. She would generally respond to questions with a "yes" or "no" or brief answer. Jane's complaints were vague rather than specific problems or situations. She blamed her problems on others or on her personality, implying that she could not change. Not being introspective, Jane had minimal insight into herself.

Therapist Behavior

For response modes, Dr. E used primarily closed question, information, and open question. Compared to the other therapists, Dr. E used more open question and confrontation and less approval. Thus, Dr. E's style was to ask a lot of questions trying to clarify Jane's statements and to confront Jane about inconsistencies to get her to be more specific and aware of what she was saying.

Dr. E's overall strategy included confrontation, education, and reinforcement. She tried to break through Jane's defenses by battering them down. She would then obtain a specific example of a problem, typically in communication, and work toward some understanding of Jane's role in the problem. She would educate Jane about her understanding of the problem and the negative consequences of her current behavior. Finally, she would make suggestions as to how Jane could behave differently, and reinforce her when she made even the slightest movement towards the goals. In the sessions, Dr. E often sounded more behavioral than psychoanalytic, especially when she analyzed specific examples and gave suggestions for how Jane could behave differently. Her conceptualizations of the case, however, were psychoanalytic.

Dr. E was average in her activity level. There were, however, long segments of silence, where Dr. E would wait for Jane to say something. These silences became more prominent toward the end of therapy, when Dr. E tried to get Jane to take more responsibility for what was happening in the sessions.

Dr. E spoke in a formal, pedantic manner and had a brisk, precise, business-like style. Observers of the sessions remarked that they felt intimidated by Dr. E's style because she seemed very direct, confrontive, and impatient.

Dr. E was also very careful regarding time. She ended sessions, which lasted about 45 minutes, promptly on time. At each session, Dr. E mentioned the number of sessions until termination.

Analyses of Therapist Techniques

Jane and Dr. E talked about their reactions to the therapist techniques in the post-therapy interviews:

R: *What did Dr. E (or you) do to help changes come about?*

C: When I'd tell her things that happened, then she questioned me as to maybe what else I could have done, what other ways could I have handled it.

T: She became more self-reflective through my use of suggestion, urging, and education, aimed largely at her ego in terms of intellectual persuasion and some at her superego in terms of easing her tendency to be overly critical of herself and others. Also through some confrontation, saying if you don't change things they're not likely to change. So change happened through the various ego, superego, and supportive techniques. There were three ingredients: support was 65%, confrontation maybe 20%, and insight 15%. *Did you have to have the support before the confrontation as some theorists say?* Oh yeah, I think so. In the beginning, I was not so much demanding her to do things or not so much the bottom line stuff, "Look lady if you don't change, it's not going to change." I held that in reserve until session 4 or 5.

R: *What did Dr. E (or you) do best with you (Jane)?*

C: I liked it when she would give her opinions or ideas on something. I wished she would have done it even more. *What did you do with her opinions?* Since she's the therapist, I would consider it to be pretty right. *You would value her opinion over your own?* Well sort of, on problems and things like that. *What if your opinion was different?* Probably I would tell myself that I was wrong. *Anything else?* She was nice to work with. She doesn't get in big arguments that are real emotional, like you see on TV with people working with therapist where they get to crying and all that stuff. She seemed to remember a lot from past sessions. Makes you feel like she's more interested in you. She was good at trying to draw stuff out of me. *How did she do that?* By questions, I guess.

T: Something called narrative persuasion. She found me believable that I had a view of what wouldn't work. She trusted that and felt she could rely on my suggestions in terms of what kind of way she'd have to set up her interactions with her husband. So there was something in the dynamics of the relationship, a good rapport where she could relate to me as a mature woman who knew about how relationships worked and could communicate with her about that. *How much do you think was due to the relationship versus your techniques?* 45% relationship, 55% technique. Maybe the other way around, they're close. *Anything else?* It was purposeful with her to be active. I did try to get to the point where she would have more responsibility. I think she needed a fairly active therapist, one who recognized that the activity was for the purpose of drawing her out, not just for the purpose of gratifying her.

R: *Recall a session that was particularly satisfying.*

C: Probably the one where I had to tell my neighbor about babysitting. I'd done some positive things in relation to the things we'd been working on and she could reinforce me.

T: The first time she showed me she could really do it, I think that was the fourth session. That was the best in the sense of showing her in all her promise. Up until then we were both groping the best we could. That was convincing to me that she would be able to use the process.

R: *Can you remember any specific interpretations?*

C: She said that maybe I was attracted to my husband when we were dating because I like a lot of security. He always thinks he knows everything and does everything right. She said maybe I feel secure in that. *How did that help you?* It sounded real logical. I've been wondering lately why I was attracted. I guess it just again brings out to me that I'm afraid to go away from anything that's secure. *Any other interpretations?* There was two or three things in the way that I treat other people. *What?* I treat them in a certain way, but then if they treat me in the same way, I don't think the same way about it. The double standard or whatever. *Others?* She told me once that if I wanted to have people over not to worry about what my house looked like, which I really do when I have people over. That's why I don't even ask them most of the time. So I tried it once, kept telling myself I'm not even going to think about the house. It seemed to work pretty well.

T: I don't remember anything. There were very clear moments where there was a good fit, but I can't remember when they were. I can't remember specific interventions that I made to her, but I know there were times when something was clicking, but I don't have a catalog of them. That may mean there's no particularly brilliant moments in terms of something shining a lot, but I don't tend to remember things like that.

R: *What did the therapist (or you) do least well?*

C: The silences. When I answered a question, she wouldn't say anything back. She'd just pause, would be waiting for me to say something. I wouldn't know what to say. I'd get all nervous. I would just be trying to think of something or wishing that she would say something. *Anything else?* I wanted her to give me more of her ideas. *From my watching of the sessions, you seemed intimidated by her. Did you feel that?* A little bit when she'd maybe cut me down about something cause that always intimidates me. *Like what things?* Things that I would do that are wrong or that I'd continue doing. At the beginning, I was always assuming things and she didn't like that.

T: Although she showed some gains, she showed the least gains in terms of her marital relationship. If I had been working with her longer or if it had been more open-ended, I might have let that alone a lot more, even though she complained of it, not made it so central so quickly. Then after she grew in confidence from these more peripheral relationships, she might have come to do work with her husband more willingly and less defensively and thereby more deeper and meaningful changes could take place. So partly it was the way the therapy was constrained in the short term effort that my aim was to try to reduce the most serious faults in their relationship. Of course at first I didn't know how intent she was on leaving. I don't think she's going anywhere actually, not any time soon. I don't know what the ultimate state of their relationship will be. She was disturbed enough that I didn't think it would be wise to give any encouragement to her leaving. What I am saying is that it's about her husband that she is most defensive clearly. In a short term effort, you want to help her in the area of her greatest trouble. I don't eliminate the countertransference possibilities in terms of my getting married. I'm high on marriage you know. My only reason for not believing in that too much is that my general orientation to couples has always been more conservative. If I lean any way, it's to work it out the best you can given what you've got. I do not advise people to break up.

R: *Recall one session that was particularly unsatisfying.*

C: In the first session that she made a lot of real long pauses, it seemed like half the time we just sat here saying nothing. I checked off a lot of low ratings on the paper afterwards. [Note: her lowest ratings were in the eighth session.] *Was there anything that you wish your therapist had pursued further with you?* Maybe we could have talked a little bit about how I feel with the kids. I feel bad if they act bad and I wonder what's wrong with me if they won't behave. I feel like I'm a no-good mother when they don't act right.

T: One time when I watched the tape, I noticed that I was very confrontational with her. I noticed it more on the tape than I had realized when

I was with her. I never saw her recoil at anything I did. That doesn't mean it was right because her character is masochistic. You could beat up on her a lot and she wouldn't protest. A few times when I watched later I thought this is really hard for her. Maybe a few times I would have said to her, "I realize this is rough for you, making these changes," or something like that to support her. Maybe from a countertransference point of view, I found myself resisting that because she comes across as a woe-begotten character, begging for that in a way. But there were 2 or 3 times in the aftermath of watching the videotape that I would have a fuller sense of her pain and rather valiant effort to do things differently.

Comment. In the post-therapy interview, Jane gave brief answers and did not explore any of the issues. Thus, she acted similarly with me as she had with Dr. E, which suggests that her passivity was a generalized behavioral pattern.

Quantitative Analyses

Table 9.1 shows the results of analyses comparing therapist response modes on client and therapist helpfulness ratings, client experiencing levels, and client reactions. Table 9.2 shows the codings of the post-session reviews. Although Dr. E was very positive about the therapy, Jane was very negative, in fact more so than any other client. Specifically, she mentioned feeling tense, anxious, and embarrassed when Dr. E was quiet and forced her to take initiative. The helpful and hindering events were attributed mostly to therapist techniques by both Dr. E and Jane.

Combining the results of the post-therapy interviews with the quantitative analyses shows that the most helpful techniques were approval, information, direct guidance, interpretation, and disclosure. In terms of less helpful techniques, Jane disliked confrontation although Dr. E thought it was helpful. Further, Dr. E felt that paraphrase was not very helpful.

Discussion of Helpful Techniques

Approval. Approval, although employed infrequently, was used primarily to reinforce Jane for making a change. When Jane spoke up for what she needed or wanted in a relationship, caught herself making assumptions about what other people thought, or made an effort to be friendly with other people, Dr. E liberally reinforced her

TABLE 9.1 Proportion of Occurrence, Client Helpfulness Ratings, Therapist Helpfulness Ratings, Client Experiencing, and Client Reactions for Therapist Response Modes in Case 7

| Response Modes | % | Client Help Rating | | Therapist Help Rating | | Client Experiencing | | Most Likely Reactions |
		M	SD	M	SD	M	SD	
Approval	.03	5.61	1.33 B	6.76	.76 A	2.08	.40 A	
Information	.20	5.53	1.21 B	6.63	.72 AB	2.11	.45 A	Ther. Work
Direct Guidance	.05	5.51	1.15 B	6.48	.73 BCD	2.19	.49 A	
Closed Question	.22	5.36	1.04 B	6.35	.66 CD	2.08	.37 A	No Reaction
Open Question	.20	5.30	1.16 B	6.29	.59 D	2.12	.38 A	Challenged
Paraphrase	.13	5.44	1.15 B	6.36	.68 CD	2.08	.41 A	Supported
Interpretation	.08	5.57	1.37 B	6.69	.76 AB	2.09	.44 A	Ther. Work Negative
Confrontation	.09	5.36	1.29 B	6.52	.59 BC	2.08	.38 A	Negative
Disclosure	.00	6.75	.50 A	6.75	.50 A	2.25	.50 A	
TOTAL		5.42	1.18	6.45	.67	2.10	.41	

NOTE: Helpfulness was rated on 9-point scales (9 = extremely helpful); experiencing was rated on a 7-point scale (7 = high). ANOVAs indicated significant differences between therapist response modes for client helpfulness, $F_{(8, 1815)} = 1.80$, $p = .08$, therapist helpfulness, $F_{(8, 1815)} = 13.03$, $p < .0001$, and client experiencing, $F_{(8, 1815)} = 1.05$, *NS*. Post hoc differences are indicated, such that response modes with the same letter (A-D) were not significantly different (A = highest ratings). No post hoc differences were found for client helpfulness or experience ratings. The overall relationship between response modes and client reactions was significant, $X^2_{(28)} = 186.56$, $p < .0001$.

and encouraged her to look at the positive results of her behavior. This approval was juxtaposed with criticism for Jane's present inappropriate behavior of blaming others for her difficulties and not asserting herself.

The following is an example of approval from the seventh session mentioned by Jane as particularly helpful:

C: We [neighbor] weren't really good friends, you know, before we were just kind of talked while the boys played. Seems like we're closer now.

TABLE 9.2 Proportions of Helpful and Hindering Events Reported by the Client and Therapist in Post-Session Reviews in Case 7

	Client		Therapist	
	Helpful	Hindering	Helpful	Hindering
Therapist Techniques	.18	.23	.45	.07
Support	.09	.05	.10	.00
Direct Guidance	.02	.04	.09	.01
Closed Question	.00	.02	.01	.00
Open Question	.00	.00	.00	.02
Paraphrase	.04	.00	.06	.02
Interpretation	.04	.04	.10	.01
Confrontation	.00	.09	.09	.00
Disclosure	.00	.00	.00	.00
Therapist Manner	.09	.07	.08	.01
Client Tasks	.15	.02	.24	.00
Focus	.00	.00	.02	.00
Experiencing	.02	.00	.01	.00
Insight	.11	.00	.10	.00
Changes	.04	.02	.10	.00
Client Manner	.07	.19	.12	.01
Relationship/Alliance	.00	.00	.03	.00
TOTAL	.49	.51	.90	.10

T: MmHmm. What's the object lesson there?

C: Hmm, discussion even though I was embarrassed about doing it.

T: Discussion can?

C: Make you closer even though it's, some things you don't like to talk about.

T: Do you believe that?

C: Yeah.

T: They say seeing is believing. It's happening to you, (C: MmHmm, pause = 4 seconds) largely as a result of your efforts.

Information and direct guidance. Jane seemed to like these interventions because Dr. E was active and in charge, taking responsibility for the direction in the session. She also liked specific instruction and advice about what to do about her problems. Dr. E suggested that Jane should be more direct in stating what she needed from other people. For example, rather than expecting her husband to read her mind, she would have to tell what she wanted from him. Of course, she later stated that she did not apply any of the advice to her husband but thought it was helpful in her interactions with other people.

In many ways, Jane seemed like a medical patient going for a prescription for her illness. Information and direct guidance fit with her image of what a doctor should do for a patient to make everything better. Jane would have preferred advice about how to leave her husband whom she felt was at the core of all her problems, but took the information and advice she got.

Interpretation. Jane remembered specific interpretations, such as how she was attracted to her husband for security and how she expected others not to treat her as she treated them. Although interpretation led Jane to positive reactions of therapeutic work, she also had negative reactions, probably because she felt threatened. She was not an insight-oriented person, preferring static explanations for her behavior rather than viewing herself as capable of understanding and changing.

Disclosure. Although used extremely infrequently, disclosures were very helpful. Perhaps they helped change the power balance in the relationship, making Dr. E seem less formidable and perfect.

Discussion of Less Helpful Techniques

Confrontation. Dr. E's major confrontative theme was that Jane had to be more assertive and take more responsibility for her own life, rather than expecting others to read her mind and do what she wanted them to do. This was especially important for Jane, who came into therapy expecting to get affirmation for her belief that her problems were all because others treated her in a "lousy" manner. An example of such a confrontation occurred in session 11:

> T: I don't think you credit uh your own style enough in terms of how the things go between you and your husband. (Pause = 5 seconds) And my uh my, my thought is uh a very absolute one. If you want him to help you more, you have to ask him. And if that hurts you too uh, too much to do that, then you're not likely to get what you want from him. I offer you no assurances beyond that and very little sympathy. If you want something from him, you have to ask him. And it, it's still a puzzle that I, I you know, we've got 22 minutes today and 50 minutes next time to figure out why it bugs you so much to be able to ask a person for what you want.

> C: I guess I'm afraid they'll say no or either that or be annoyed that I asked them.

> T: Would that be worse than what you have?

> C: Yeah. (laughs)

> T: It is your prediction that regularly uh your husband would say, "no" with your asking him to do things or he would regularly be annoyed if you asked him to pitch in and help him directly?

Dr. E thought that the confrontations were helpful, although on two occasions she mentioned that she might have been too harsh. Jane, in contrast, had negative reactions to the confrontations both on the client reactions and on the post-session questionnaires. For example, after session 3, Jane wrote, "She's putting me more at fault and I feel perhaps attacking or not recognizing a quiet personality which was what I thought I am basically and she sounds like she doesn't like that." After session 11 where Dr. E gave the confrontation excerpted above, Jane said that Dr. E cut down things she had been doing. She felt that Dr. E was right, but she didn't like to hear it because it made her feel bad.

Jane seemed to "pull" from confrontation. In her passivity, Jane demanded others to take care of her. One wanted to shake her out of it. Dr. E commented that Jane was masochistic and would not complain if she was beaten up.

Although Jane disliked confrontation, it jolted her out of her complacency and forced her to look at needed changes within herself. Underneath the confrontation, Dr. E had kind of a "tough love," in that she did not accept Jane's negative self-image but believed that she could change.

Closed question, open question, and paraphrase. These three techniques received mixed evidence of helpfulness. All three were rated low in helpfulness by Dr. E. On the other hand, Jane mentioned in the post-therapy interview that open questions were quite helpful. Further, Jane felt supported with paraphrase, and Dr. E mentioned in post-session reviews that paraphrase was helpful. Therapists generally use all three of these techniques to encourage clients to explore their problems. Since Jane seldom responded to any of the techniques by exploring herself in greater depth, Dr. E probably thought the interventions were not very helpful. In contrast, Jane visibly showed her pleasure when Dr. E used approval and disclosure. Perhaps Jane's lack of response to these exploratory techniques was why Dr. E used more confrontation, which at least got a reaction from Jane.

Process Issues

A major issue in this therapy was how Jane's marriage was dealt with. When Jane blamed all her problems on her husband, Dr. E challenged her to take responsibility for her own behavior. She spent time trying to explain how Jane's beliefs about her husband's motivations were often assumptions or projections rather than being based on direct communication with her husband. She would also point out how Jane's husband was changing in response to Jane's efforts. Dr. E's message was that Jane needed to learn how to express her needs to her husband and find out how he was feeling and thinking instead of basing her decisions on guesswork.

Thus, a major focus of the treatment was on the marriage. Dr. E thought that she had made some headway talking about the communication problems in the marriage. Jane did indeed report some changes in her communication patterns with her husband during the therapy. In the post-therapy interview, however, Jane said that she listened to whatever Dr. E told her and applied it to other relationships, but not to the marriage. Obviously, Jane was as indirect with Dr. E about her displeasure with the focus on the marriage as she was with everyone else in her life. Since Jane never mentioned this displeasure, Dr. E assumed that whatever she was saying about the marriage was accurate and being accepted.

Given Jane's presenting problem of her marriage, one could question whether the treatment should have been marital or divorce therapy rather than individual therapy. Jane was clear that she did not want marital therapy, but wanted only to work on improving herself so that she could get out of the marriage.

The corresponding question, though, is why the anticipated divorce was not at least discussed. Dr. E judged that it was inappropriate to discuss the divorce without the husband present, which was particularly salient since Jane did not even tell her husband that she was going for therapy. An alternative explanation is that Dr. E did not believe that Jane's desires for a divorce were very strong. In the post-therapy review, Dr. E indicated that she did not think that Jane would actually get divorced. Further, Dr. E believed that Jane's problems were individual rather than systemic. She asserted that if people did not work out their problems, they would simply carry them over to new relationships. On the other hand, Dr. E admitted that she might have been somewhat blinded to Jane's dissatisfaction with marriage because she valued and was "high" on marriage. Hence, Dr. E seemed to have both theoretical and personal reasons for focusing on the communication issues in the marriage rather than on the divorce possibility.

In addition to the discrepancy between Dr. E's and Jane's views of the marital issues, there were discrepancies in other portions of the treatment, as indicated in the post-session comments. Dr. E thought almost everything that happened in the therapy was positive, whereas Jane had negative reactions. Jane clearly did not let Dr. E know when she had negative reactions, which made it difficult for Dr. E to modify her behavior.

The choice of 12 sessions for this client was interesting. At the beginning of the third session, Dr. E informed Jane that they would have 12 sessions, later indicating to the researchers that Jane might have difficulty terminating if they had as many as 20 sessions. When asked if she were planning to have fewer sessions because Jane was not very gratifying, she said that she could not dismiss that factor, but felt that it was more due to not wanting Jane to get too attached. Toward the end of therapy, Dr. E revised her stance and said that Jane could have profited from more sessions, but did not want to change the contract at that point.

Moderating Variables

Client Factors

Jane was relatively disturbed, as indicated by her scores on the MMPI. Perhaps the strongest indication of her pathology was her quiet, passive, resistant behavior within sessions. She was often like a statue, having a difficult time even talking, let alone expressing any of her underlying feelings. She seemed to spend a lot of time warding off attention or danger and had little energy left for looking within herself introspectively. It was very painful for Jane to learn that she was responsible for her own behaviors and that she could not go on blaming others for making her life miserable. Given these factors, it is not surprising that Jane wanted and perhaps even craved approval and reinforcement and disliked confrontation.

Therapist Factors

Dr. E's choice of approach was probably due to theoretical reasons. Although her theoretical orientation was psychoanalytic, Dr. E modified this approach to a more directive, active approach. She tried to get Jane to understand her current behaviors, but did not probe heavily into childhood factors. Dr. E felt that the therapist should go after childhood issues only when there was some block in working with the present issues. She felt that working through the immediate relationship, via the transference, was more important than searching for antecedents of the behavior.

Dr. E's described her style as "caustic love," which meant having an empathic attitude but being intolerant of pathology. At the beginning of treatment, she said that her stance is typically one of diffidence and aloofness, which enhances the probability that the client will be in awe of the therapist. This awesomeness capitalizes on clients' tendency to respond positively to a benign authority who urges them to take steps to change. During treatment, she supports a person's strengths but not weaknesses, feeling that the therapist must confront the client with the fullest truth he or she can handle but do so without cruelty and rejection. Dr. E felt that clients could tolerate the confrontations during treatment because of the early diffidence. In Jane's case, Dr. E indicated that she might have been too forceful because she was reacting to the client's passivity, but she did not feel that she was rejecting of Jane.

The Therapeutic Relationship

According to scores on the WAI (see Chapter 2, Table 2.2), Jane and Dr. E both perceived the relationship as moderately strong.

Issues in the therapeutic relationship were not discussed. On a couple of occasions, Dr. E did say to Jane that she felt she had been too harsh with her, but Dr. E never asked Jane her feelings about their relationship. Not unexpectedly, Jane never mentioned any dissatisfactions to Dr. E, although she did write them in the post-session questionnaires.

On post-session questionnaires Jane mentioned being worried that she had not changed enough for Dr. E. In the final session, she dressed up, which Dr. E interpreted as being a sign of Jane's wanting to please her. The final interaction in the treatment was,

T: I wish you well. Good luck.

C: Thank you. I hope I changed enough for you. (laughs)

T: Uh, more importantly for you. Should I see you again, we'd start with that comment.

Dr. E indicated that Jane's change was due to a transference cure, which would imply that it was due to the relationship. Dr. E thought that Jane changed because she was very attached to her and wanted to please her. Jane did respond well to reinforcement, but no other evidence for a relationship or transference cure could be found in the data. In fact, the match between them did not seem ideal, in that Jane probably would have preferred a more supportive therapist. Of course, the question remains as to whether she would indeed have become too dependent and more resistant with a non-confrontive therapist. My view was that rather than being motivated to please Dr. E because she liked her and was attached to her, Jane was afraid of Dr. E and did not want to displease her. Underneath her acquiescence, Jane seemed angry at Dr. E's confrontations. Further, in the post-therapy and follow-up reviews, she seemed upset about Dr. E's tactics. Thus, although the positive changes may have been due to a transference cure, I do not think it was due to positive feelings. In fact, there was no evidence that Jane got too attached to Dr. E.

External Factors

Extratherapy involvement. From the comments on the post-therapy interviews, Jane seemed to work in between sessions on the issues raised in the sessions:

> R: *How did you (or Jane) use the therapy between sessions?*
>
> C: I'd think about the things in terms of how I generally feel or act in situations with people, maybe afterwards or before I would think of it in terms of the therapy, or maybe specific things I would sort of plan ahead to try things that we'd talked about. *How much did you think about it?* Quite a bit. If I did things that I wasn't supposed to be doing, I'd stop and think about why.
>
> T: In between she had this big picture of me in her head as one she has to please. She went around doing that with her husband and her neighbors. You could say then the cure was a transference cure. To the extent that I stay a live image in her she'll continue to make these gains. That's all right in the sense that hopefully what she does will become sufficiently gratifying that I'll drop out as a sort of mediating variable. She'll just be high on the fact that she can make things happen in her life.

Support network. Jane mentioned one friend, a woman who had a summer cottage near hers. This woman encouraged Jane to talk and confide in her. During the rest of the year, however, Jane had no one she felt comfortable confiding in. Because she only worked a limited amount outside the home, she had few contacts with people. Most of her time was spent cleaning the house and caring for her children. Her family lived nearby, but she did not spend much time with them, nor were they much of a source of comfort.

External events. No major events occurred during the therapy to aid or interfere with the process of treatment.

Outcome of Therapy

Session Outcome

Based on SEQ scores (see Chapter 2, Table 2.2), Jane viewed the sessions as moderately deep and smooth, whereas Dr. E perceived them as moderately deep but rough.

Pre-Post Changes

At the end of 12 sessions of treatment, Jane was somewhat improved (see Table 9.3). On the MMPI, Jane's F score, which had been high before therapy ($T = 66$), was above average ($T = 73$), suggesting that her profile be interpreted with caution because she admitted a large number of unusual experiences, feelings, or symptoms. Her L score was also higher ($T = 66$) at post-therapy than at pre-therapy ($T = 56$), indicating that she presented herself in a more favorable light regarding conformity, self-control, and moral values. These scores indicated that she was more defensive. On the five clinical scales that had been above 70 at pre-therapy, Jane was unchanged. She was, however, higher on the Mania scale, which suggested that she had more energy after therapy.

On the other measures, Jane was about the same on symptomatology and self-esteem, was functioning better on all of her target complaints, and was less anxious and depressed.

The post-therapy interviews are excerpted below:

R: *In what ways have you (or has Jane) changed as a result of therapy?*

C: Some things I don't let bother me as much anymore, like that baseball date I was worried about. I shouldn't be worried that my husband's going to be mad that he can't play tennis. I should just forget about it and let him take care of it if he wants to. I don't let it bother me like it would have. Also, the house isn't in perfect order when somebody comes in. I just don't worry what people are going to think about it. And I have been going to visit my neighbors more. *Has your feeling about yourself being a doormat changed?* Probably. I know I have to do something about it now. I'm more responsible as to how much a doormat I am. I see that it's more my fault or responsibility. I have to work more on changing than on understanding why other people are like they are. *Anything else?* I'm trying to be more direct with people instead of assuming they can read my mind. It takes a lot of work because I'm just afraid to say it. I'm doing it more though. *How have you changed in your attitude towards your marriage? At the beginning you said you wanted out because there wasn't anything there anymore.* In the therapy, we just seemed to work with my husband and my dealings with each other, which I guess I'm long past wanting to work on too much. We sort of had to focus on the marriage because I don't have any outside friends or situations to talk about. *But you wished she hadn't focused*

TABLE 9.3 Scores on Outcome Measures for Case 7

Measures	Pre	5th	Expect	Post	6 Mo	1 Yr
Client-Rated Measures						
MMPI						
Psychopathic Deviate	83			74		
Depression	82			[84]		
Schizophrenia	80			72		
Social Introversion	80			78		
Psychasthenia	74			73		
Mania	45			[55*]		
SCL-90-R	52			44	[46]	42
TSCS	28			33	[31]	36
TC (1) Self-confidence	11	10	6.5	7*	[9]	5*
(2) Relationships	12	11	4.5	7*	[8]	3*
(3) Assertiveness	13	10*	5.5	7**	[8]	7
Satisfaction					7	7
Therapist-Rated Measures						
TC (1) Self-confidence	11	10	6.5	8*		
(2) Relationships	9	[10]	6	6*		
(3) Assertiveness	8	[11*]	5.5	5*		
Researcher-Rated Measures						
Hamilton Anxiety	15			9*		
Hamilton Depression	19			14*		

NOTE: High *T* scores indicate high symptomatology on the SCL-90-R GSI, high self-esteem on the TSCS; worst functioning on the TC, higher satisfaction, and greater disturbance on the Hamilton scales. Expect = level expected after treatment. * = significant change at *p* < .05; ** = *p* < .01; *** = *p* < .001. Negative changes are in brackets.

on the marriage so much? Yeah. *So how do you feel about your marriage?* I feel more interested in changing the way that I am with other people than with my husband because I don't want to rock the boat too much until the time is right. I don't know how willing I am to try a whole lot with him because of the tension it would create. But I remember her ideas and carry it over into other areas, new people I meet or whatever. *On a post-session questionnaire you said that Dr. E was siding with your husband. Did you feel that you could be honest about your feelings about him in the therapy?* I always attributed a lot of the way I act to my personality. I'm just quiet. I'm a follower. To her, that didn't seem to make any difference. She thought everybody had to be a leader and outgoing if they want to have a good life or have fun. *Is that what you thought she wanted you to be?* That's what it seemed like, that being quiet isn't good. *So you felt that she wanted you to change your personality style to something that you couldn't or didn't want to be?* I didn't know that you could. I thought your personality was just your personality. But I find out if I want things to go a different way that I have to change it. She says that your life is your responsibility and if you want friends you have to go out and meet them.

T: She said she would like to like herself better and I think she did to some extent. Perhaps the most vivid illustration was her dressing up the last time and being able to take some pleasure in that. *Any changes in interpersonal relationships?* Her relationships improved rather significantly, more with people who are less important to her like neighbors and friends and sometimes under rather difficult circumstances. To some degree, significant though not marked, with her husband as well. I thought her approach to their relationship improved. I don't know about the quality of the relationship overall, but he was more responsive to her when she did not go into this martyred altruistic role. He would state more clearly where he was at.

R: *How satisfied are you with the nature and amount of changes?*

C: I haven't gotten near as far as I want to yet, but I feel there's hope for me as time goes on. Like I said, 35 years is a long time to change in 12 weeks.

T: Moderately satisfied. It was a good experience. I feel quite satisfied that she did make some changes. If I lack anything in terms of satisfaction, it's that I'm not sure of the robustness of the changes. I think she may indeed need more help later too. I don't know that there are any final solutions, no matter what the therapy approach. I think she got hooked enough in terms of the process and its effects that she would come back. I don't think anything happened in terms of the bond between us or to her self-esteem that would keep her away from therapy.

Jane was also asked to talk about what caused and maintained one of her major problems. Her response indicated she had achieved only minimal insight into the origins of her problems.

C: I always remember being indirect and a doormat. I guess probably my personality. I'm quiet. I don't want to rock the boat. Probably security. If you get people upset, you don't know what's going to happen. *Do you mean it's genetic or from your family or what?* I guess it's not really genetic, but along the same lines. I don't know if personality is in the genes or not. *What part does your family play in this?* Well, it's what forms your personality, real early family life. I always liked to please them. Maybe the way I act, they acted when I pleased them or something. I just didn't want to be in trouble.

Six-Month Follow-Up

Jane maintained the changes that she made during therapy. She was at about the same level on all measures.

Jane's husband had been transferred, so the family was going to move shortly. She said that things were going better with her husband. As a result of therapy, Jane realized that she was the one who would have to change. She had to take more responsibility for her behavior and could not blame others. Further, Jane felt that she expressed her opinions more than she had before therapy.

One-Year Follow-Up

Jane had changed further on two of her target complaints and had maintained her levels from the six-month follow-up on all the other measures. Compared to her scores at pre-therapy, she was functioning better on all measures, including symptomatology, self-concept, and target complaints.

Since moving to the new town, Jane had filed for divorce, obtained a full-time job to support herself and her children, and gotten a boyfriend with whom she was "experiencing things I've been dreaming of for so long—he's wonderful." Further, she said that, "Having found love, happiness, and finally feeling cared about with my boyfriend, I feel fantastic—better than I have since I remember." On the other hand, her soon-to-be ex-husband, who was completely shocked by the request for a divorce, kept her upset and depressed because he made her life miserable.

Apparently the move to a new location forced her to make some changes. She had been angry at herself for not getting divorced before moving and realized that if she did not take responsibility and get out of the marriage then, she might never leave.

Jane had not sought further therapy since the termination and was not considering it.

Long-Term Follow-Up

Three years following termination, Jane had maintained her changes. Now legally divorced from her husband, she had a good relationship with the man she had been dating at the time of the one-year follow-up. She had worked herself up from a job on an assembly line of a factory to working in the office in customer relations. She reported more assertiveness and self-esteem, which she attributed to making the break from her husband and progressing on the job. Being a single parent was hard for Jane because she had no time for herself, and her children did not understand why she had less time for them. Because of difficulties with her daughter, who would not talk and was mean to her brother, Jane and her daughter had been in brief therapy. Unfortunately, the therapy did not help much because of the daughter's resistance.

Jane still remembered and used Dr. E's confrontation that if she wanted things to change, she would have to take responsibility for making them change.

Summary

Therapist techniques were more helpful than other variables in this case. Approval, information, direct guidance, interpretation, and disclosure were all helpful. On the other hand, confrontation and paraphrase seemed to be less helpful.

Client variables, therapist variables, the relationship, and external factors all seemed to be important moderating variables in this case. The client was introverted, passive, and set in her ways, wanting support rather than confrontation. The therapist was demanding and confrontive and aimed at understanding and changing behavior. The relationship seemed to be moderately strong. Further, external factors seemed to be partially responsible for helping the client continue changing after therapy, in that moving forced her to evaluate her marriage and make changes.

This case was complicated and unusual because the client had a good outcome with clear behavioral changes, but the process was uncomfortable and somewhat negative. Observers and raters of the case had strong negative reactions to both the client and the therapist. In conclusion, we can say that what the therapist did was effective in breaking through the client's defenses and forcing her to change, but it was not a pleasant process.

10

Case 8: Admitting the Past

The focus of this chapter will be on the therapist techniques in the 12-session case conducted by Dr. R, a 78-year old, White, female psychologist with Sophia, a 39-year old, White, divorced mother of three children.

Client

Sophia (a pseudonym) was the eighth of 16 children. Her mother had been 14 when she married and was not capable of taking care of the children. The father was a self-taught electrical engineer and farmer who started having strokes when Sophia was about six years old and died when she was 10 years old. After his death, the mother started drinking heavily and neglected the remaining nine children still at home.

When the child welfare department stepped in, the older, married children divided the younger children amongst themselves and raised them. Sophia was raised by an older sister, whom she described as unloving, demanding, unforgiving, and cruel. She said that her sister tried to control her thoughts, dominate her life, and use her for free labor. Her sister was particularly harsh on Sophia because she was afraid that Sophia would turn out to be a "tramp" like her next older sister.

After Sophia graduated from high school, the sister forced her to stay for two years to help raise the sister's six children. On a trip to visit a friend, Sophia surreptitiously found a job and left her sister's house. After working as a bookkeeper for a few years, she married a man who was from near her hometown. Her husband was an intense person, whom she described as insensitive to the needs of anyone around him. He was in business for himself and had quickly become very successful. When they first married, they traveled back to their hometown every weekend to see his parents.

Although her husband did not particularly want children, Sophia wanted them very much and had three children. While she was pregnant with their second child, her husband left and did not return until the child was four months old. Sophia described herself as having gone through a nervous breakdown at that time. She slept most of the time and could remember none of the details of that period. The marital relationship further deteriorated, with her husband being "mean to her" and running around with other women, leading Sophia to divorce him five years prior to the therapy. Since the divorce, Sophia had dated and been involved with two different men. Her latest boyfriend had left suddenly without giving any explanation, which she described as a pattern that recurred with men whom she dated.

At the time of the study, Sophia was a full-time mother, taking care of her three children, a daughter aged 16, a son aged 13, and a son aged 6. The ex-husband was presently supporting the family, although Sophia knew that she would have to get a job to support the family when the child support for the oldest child and the alimony ran out in a year and a half.

Physical Functioning

Sophia said that she compulsively overate and got minimal exercise. She complained of many symptoms. During the course of therapy, she had kidney stones removed, was tested for high blood pressure, and was prescribed sleeping pills. She had been taking Elavil for about three months prior to the therapy for depression and sleep problems.

Pre-Therapy Expectations

Sophia had been in marital therapy briefly at the time of her divorce, but said that it never "took" because her ex-husband refused to go with her. Her expectations about therapy were that a professional could help her decide whether she was using rational methods to effect change in her life. She believed that therapy should last at least six months and that a therapist should be concerned for the client as a human, have a true desire to be helpful, and have a pragmatic outlook on life.

Pre-Therapy Assessment

Sophia's scores for pre-therapy assessment measures are shown in Table 10.1. On the MMPI, Sophia had normal validity scores and high scores on the Schizophrenia, Psychopathic Deviate, and Psychasthenia scales. This profile indicates immaturity with a tendency to alcoholism and sexual deviation, with some paranoid, schizoid, and obsessional trends.

Compared to an outpatient population, Sophia's scores on the other measures evinced average symptomatology and self-concept. She was functioning at an average level on her target complaints. The clinician judged her to be moderately anxious and mildly depressed. The Elavil, however, may have masked the depression on all of the measures, since Sophia revealed depressive symptoms, for example sleep problems, depressed mood, and past suicide attempts.

Sophia was diagnosed as dysthymic (mildly depressed) with a mixed personality disorder, in that she had some features of both the histrionic (self-dramatization, perceived as shallow and lacking genuineness) and borderline (she had a pattern of unstable and intense interpersonal relationships, with marked shifts of attitude, idealization, devaluation, and manipulation). Sophia also had mood swings from elation to severe depression, although these swings were not as predominant as the depression.

Target Complaints

Sophia's first complaint was that she did not have a way to express her anger. Her second complaint was that she did not understand her relationships with men. She wanted to have a long-term relationship with a man, but could not seem to maintain a relationship and was unaware of why her relationships fell apart. Her third complaint was that she was too involved with her children. She had particular difficulties dealing with her middle child, a boy who reminded her of her ex-husband.

During the fifth session, Sophia added the problem of being able to project her true self to other people. She thought that people saw her as harsh and angry, when underneath she felt warm and giving. She felt that her problems prevented her from being able to be her real self.

Researcher's evaluation. After the clinical interview, Sophia was placed on the waiting list. Although she seemed motivated for therapy, we were concerned about her ability to form a relationship given her histrionic style, relationship history, and high MMPI Schizophrenia scale score. When another client dropped out, she was accepted into treatment.

Summary of Client Pre-Therapy Characteristics

Sophia was the middle child in a large, chaotic, dysfunctional family. Her main complaints were her anger, desire to understand her relationships with men, overinvolvement with her children, and a desire to project her true self. Test scores indicated that she was depressed and somewhat out of touch with reality, and had a lot of symptomatology, but was functioning in her everyday life. Although she had only a high school education, she was quite articulate and psychologically oriented.

Therapist

Dr. R first earned a PhD in philology and then a master's degree in psychology. She had extensive training in psychotherapy, individual supervision, and Zen study, as well as A. K. Rice and Tavistock Group Relations training. Dr. R was licensed, listed in the National Register of Health Service Providers in Psychology, had a certificate in applied psychology for psychologists from the Washington School of Psychiatry, and had a diploma from the American Board of Professional Psychology in clinical psychology. Further, she was a distinguished and well-respected member of the psychological community, with a long record of achievements. To mention just a few, she had published 36 articles and a book and was well known for her research on teaching housewives to do psychotherapy. She had been a professor, on many editorial boards, and had brought the A. K. Rice Institute to America from the Tavistock Institute in London. Although past retirement age, Dr. R remained active with her private practice and also in running conferences, teaching, and giving talks.

Using three 5-point (5 = high) scales for how much she believed in and adhered to each of the three major orientations, Dr. R rated herself: psychoanalytic = 4, humanistic = 2, and behavioral = 2. About her theory, she stated,

> My orientation can best be described by mentioning my two major teachers: Dr. Frieda Fromm-Reichmann and Dr. Harry Stack Sullivan. In other words, my orientation is modified psychoanalytic theory with a large dose of interpersonal theory. I am also influenced by the systems theory orientation of the A. K. Rice Institute, always remembering that the client is a member of many groups.
>
> I tend to see that the client takes the lead, but I intervene whenever it seems to me to be useful. I often say to clients that I think there are at least four major life areas which can be talked about usefully in therapy: (a) the present life situation, (b) past history with family, (c) dreams and fantasies, and (d) the relationship with the therapist, including thoughts, attitudes, feelings, and fantasies about him or her and behavior going both ways. I emphasize discussing the relationship. On the first two areas, the current and the past, I emphasize the interplay between them because nothing can be done to change the past.
>
> Change occurs as patients, with the help and support of the therapist, acquire more courage to face the less acceptable or negative aspects of themselves. That automatically helps them to get more courage to face and deal with "reality." As they learn to relate to one real person, namely the therapist, they can also relate to others.

Treatment Process

The verbatim excerpt from the first few minutes of the first session illustrates the process between Sophia and Dr. R.

T: I uh take it that you've been told about the setup here and what's expected of you and all that? (C: Yes) May-, maybe you have some questions?

C: I think I understand it.

T: Now, it's probably been a long time since you've been told. (C: Yeah) So if you have any questions, uh I'll try to answer them.

C: Uh, I was wondering what the primary aim was and that if, if I knew the primary aim, what you were looking for, maybe I could be a little more specific in my feedback to you.

T: Well, uh my personal primary aim is to be of use to you as much as possible. The primary aim of the research team is to find out as much as they can about brief psychotherapy (C: Okay) uh and how it works and why if it doesn't, (C: Okay) and just to find things out. That's their aim and your aim, I presume, has something to do with you. (C: Right) Uh I read uh whatever you filled out in the blanks. That's all I really know about you, (C: MmHmm) which is not much, uh but a little bit. And I know what you wrote in your target complaints, (C: MmHmm) but that was some time ago.

C: That was, and at that point, I was going through two major crises. (T: MmHmm) And I was, and since then, I, I've resolved those particular things somewhat. (C laughs)

T: MmHmm. Well, maybe you'd like to change your mind about (C: But . . .) what is the chief uh thing that you want to work on?

C: Well, but those are bas-, those things were basically things that I have a problem with chronically. (T: MmHmm, MmHmm) They weren't just one little incident. They were things that (T: MmHmm) I continually have problems with.

T: So that you think that what you wrote then as the target complaints are still?

C: Pretty much, (T: MmHmm) pretty much. I would add one to them and that would be that uh I, I don't work and I feel decadent, I feel nonproductive, and I hate that. Are, it really makes me feel badly about myself, (T: Hmm) but, but I have other things that I'm sc-, I'm going, planning on going back to work in the fall, (T: Oh really? Hmm) but I'm frightened (C laughs) (T: Yeah) about that.

This segment was representative of this dyad's process. Dr. R briefly set the stage and then turned the floor over to Sophia. When Sophia presented her complaint, Dr. R probed to clarify the details. As was typical of her style, Sophia first said that she had solved everything, but when probed admitted that she still had some problems. She also described things in extremes: for example she is decadent and nonproductive.

Summary of Process

The time in therapy was spent dealing with whatever Sophia brought in to talk about during a particular session. One of her major themes was her ex-husband, with whom she was still tied both emotionally and financially although she did not see him much. She described several events in which she tried to manipulate her ex-husband. For example, when he volunteered to buy her oldest daughter a car, Sophia told him that her daughter should have to work for part of it. He then told the daughter that he would buy her a car, but she had to work for him to pay him back for it, at which the daughter got very angry at him. Sophia then got angry at her ex-husband for being so withholding with her daughter, forgetting that she was the one who interfered in the first place. On other occasions, Sophia described trying to manipulate her ex-husband to either spend more or less time with the children.

Sophia also talked a lot about her children. Sophia was overprotective with all her children and seemed to be trying to compensate for being neglected herself as a child. Regarding the middle child, she jokingly said in the first and second sessions that she would like to give him away. This was undoubtedly a reference to her being given away as a child. She talked frequently about her own parenting style, as well as her sister's and ex-husband's parenting abilities.

The most significant work took place around Sophia's past. In the first session, she discussed her chaotic family history only briefly. This issue was not discussed again until the next to last session when Sophia "told all" in a powerful, emotional catharsis of the effects of her family life:

> T: I was wondering about your mother. Uh you mentioned a long time ago that you thought you might feel terrible when she dies because you might feel guilty. (C: Yeah) And I wonder how you feel about her these days? You haven't seen her?
>
> C: No. (Pause = 3 seconds) I feel pretty, I feel that same way for a long time that (Pause = 4 seconds) I won't feel guilty. (T: Oh you won't.) I don't think so (T: Well good) because she never, she never, she, made any sacrifices for me (T: Ahh) that, I feel she gave birth and she raised my older brothers and sisters. She did that and they're there for her if she were needy. If she needed me, I think then I'd feel guilty if I didn't give. (T: Hmm) I don't, she's better off with them than with me.
>
> T: Hmm, hmm. (Pause = 3 seconds) So you don't think you're going to feel guilty when she dies.
>
> C: No. I, I did, (T: Hmm) I, I worried about that for a long time in my adult life and then I (T: MmHmm) came to the conclusion that I don't know whether she gave me anything when I was little.
>
> T: You can't remember?

C: She gave me some initial love and I believe that (T: Hmm) and that's kind of a treasure and (T: Hmm. She likes babies.). Yeah, she likes babies. (T: MmHmm) I mean it didn't have a whole lot to do with me. (T: MmHmm) I didn't feel that (T: Hmm) and, and I was her champion. I wouldn't let anybody talk badly about her. My older brothers and sisters, after my dad died, my older brothers and sisters used to come on the farm and criticized her in front of us. She was never there. I mean, she was to be criticized, but I'm not sure by whom, maybe by us who she neglected rather than they who were gone. And at the time I thought that they were being busybodies because they never helped her at the time. That's what I thought at the time. Later I was told that they did try to help her and she shunned all their help, which is a possibility. (T: Hmm) That's neither here nor there to me, but what, but what I did feel greatly hurt by her, because she gave me away in particular. (T: Hmm) I was the only girl at home. They were all boys, except for my little tiny sister and they were babies, E. was 2, C. was 4 maybe. And uh I took care of those babies. (T: MmHmm) I did the laundry. (T: Yeah, Mm-Hmm) I cooked. I did all this stuff and she was never there. And I wouldn't let anybody talk bad about her, but she gave me away without a thought (snaps fingers).

T: Well, who took care of the kids, the little one when, after you were go-, gone?

C: She gave us all away en masse. We were removed from her. Actually she was given warnings after warnings (T: I see) about child welfare. Child welfare removed us. (T: I see, I see) Yeah.

T: I see. So where did they all go?

C: To various brothers and sisters. (T: MmHmm) I think 6, 6 were already married and had a home and uh various children went to various homes. (T: Oh, MmHmm. Did anybody go with you?) Yeah, my little sister came with me (T: Hmm) temporarily and then, then the next year, (C laughs) okay the next year, my mom took everybody back. (T: Oh) She figured she had straightened herself out and she requested her children back.

T: Did she? You too?

C: No, uh, how, how it went was everybody was supposed to come home and I think that I wouldn't forgive her for giving me away, (T: MmHmm) so I went to my sister. And the first year at my sister's house really wasn't really so terrible because she was working and her husband was working and she was getting money for my welfare and uh, and I had white underwear for the first time in my life. (C laughs) And I was in 8th grade and the kids at school liked me and I was no longer looked down upon and called poor and all those things. (T: MmHmm) And I liked that. And the nuns all liked me very much because I was one of the best kids in the class. I worked. (T: Hmm) And so I had a lot of good stuff there. (T: Hmm) And uh so when everybody went home, I told D. [older sister], "I don't want to go home" and she said, "I will, I will ask mom for you." So I was not meant to hear this, but all the kids were there and D. took C. [younger sister] in and C. was just in kindergarten or 1st grade maybe, she's that much younger than me, and uh D. says, "Mom, well here's C. but uh Sophia asked me to see if you might let her stay with me." And my mother said, she said, "Well, that's all right." She says, "I expected that from Sophia, but I want my C. back." (C laughs, Pause = 11 seconds) I think that's the only time in my life that I felt that my mother preferred one of the other children to me.

T: Well, she obviously did.

C: Oh yeah. C. was her baby. She was not the younger one. There were 2 boys younger than her, but she always petted C. C. was always on her lap. (Pause = 4 seconds) I was shocked by that. (T: Hmm) I was very young, but I was shocked. (T: Hmm) Even though I, I was the one who asked not to go home, (T: Right) I was surprised at the words. (Pause = 6 seconds) Maybe I wanted her to beg me. (T: Could be.) Never thought about that.

T: (Pause = 5 seconds) You surely wanted her to want you. (C: Yeah. Yeah) It must have been a deep hurt.

C: (Pause = 7 seconds) And I put her out of my life probably then sort of. I never realized how, how young I'd done that. (T: Hmm. How old were you then?) Twelve maybe.

T: Hmm. (Pause = 7 seconds) You haven't said much about your father.

C: I have very few memories of him. Um, he was in an institution from my 1st grade off and on. Um let's see, no maybe 2nd or 3rd grade. (Pause = 5 seconds) The memories I have of him are very loving. Um he was a hard man. He was a German and very stern, you know the stereotypical thing, but I think he had a warm heart. I felt his warmth, um . . . (T: Pause = 9 seconds. What institution was he in?) He, he died in a state mental institution. (T: Hmm) M-, my mother had him committed because he tried to commit suicide. (T: Oh!) He uh, he had several strokes, and uh . . .

T: (Pause = 15 seconds) Must be very hard to think about.

C: (crying) He tried to commit suicide while I was babysitting.

T: When you were babysitting? (C nods) When you were babysitting outside the house or inside the house? (C: Outside) You remember that? (C: Yeah) (C crying) What do you remember about it?

C: I remember he took pills out of the medicine cabinet (C sniffs) and uh (C sniffs) I saw him do it. He took a whole bunch of pills. And uh I said, "Daddy, you shouldn't take so many pills." And he said, "Oh, I'm just taking them upstairs, so I have them when I need them in the night." And uh I said, "Okay" and I, (Pause = 5 seconds) I was in the 2nd, maybe 3rd grade. (Pause = 6 seconds) And uh he went upstairs. He said he was going to take a pill and sleep. He, he had been sick. He had strokes and he was paralyzed for a while. (T: Oh) And then he worked his way back and, and uh he was better, but not well. (T: Hmm) And uh when my mom and sisters came back from town, my mother went upstairs and started to scream and he tried to cut his wrists.

T: Oh he had. He didn't, (C: He did cut his wrists) rely on the pills then? (C: He had cut his wrists) He had cut his wrists. And so she started to scream. He, he was conscious? (C shakes head no) But he must have recovered consciousness? (C nods head yes) And she called what, an ambulance? She must have.

C: Yeah, I think, I don't remember.

T: But what do you remember? You remember her screaming?

C: And my brother-in-law brought (C crying) the, the razor in the kitchen. (C crying)

T: (Pause = 16 seconds) I wonder if you could put into words what it is you're really crying about now?

C: (sniffs) (Pause = 6 seconds) I'm scared.

T: You are? Scared? Of what? For yourself?

C: Yeah, of what will happen to him (T: To whom?) and what my father, what'll happen to me.

T: I see. Your father's soul and you said what will happen to him.

C: No, him, his body. I never wanted him to leave. (T: I'm sorry, I didn't . . .) I thought, I didn't want him to die. I thought he was dead. I didn't know he was still alive at that point. (T: Yeah, but he did die later.) Yeah, but it was years, a couple years later, but my, after that, after he tried to commit suicide my mom had him committed.

T: Yeah. (Pause = 5 seconds) And he stayed the rest of his life at an institution?

C: Yeah, it was awful, it was awful there. (C sniffs) (T: You saw it. What kind of awful?) Oh, everybody screaming. It was horrible, horrible screams and, (C sniffs) and people walking around us and they were all, all out of it and that I was frightened for my father to be there.

T: You must have been frightened to be there yourself. (C: Oh) You, you're talking about seeing this with your own eyes, right?

C: Yeah, they scared me, but I didn't want to be there with, but I did want to be there with him. I wanted to see him. (T: Your mother took you?) Somebody. (Pause = 4 seconds) He didn't know us. (T: He didn't?) He didn't remember who we were, not, he called us, our older brothers and sister names, the ones he couldn't remember I think.

This catharsis was a powerful experience for Sophia. They returned to talking about it for the final session, but Sophia still felt "unglued" and expressed some concerns about being able to function on her own. The therapy stirred up feelings that could not be resolved immediately. Sophia had little choice about termination, however, since both she and Dr. R were going to be away for the summer.

Client Behavior

In the sessions, Sophia spoke slowly and deliberately, almost as if she had rehearsed what she was going to say. She related endless details of various situations in her life in a melodramatic style. Interestingly, although she was very emotional, her stories seemed shallow, superficial, and lacking in genuineness. Everything was expressed in extremes; for example, people were either extremely wonderful (like her daughter) or extremely bad (like her middle child, a son), she was either extremely happy or extremely depressed, and others were either perfect or awful. Further, Sophia often contradicted herself, but seemed unaware of these inconsistencies. For example, she would first say that she wanted to have nothing more to do with men. When the therapist would try to clarify, she would change her story and say that she did want a relationship. It was as if she were unsure what she actually felt.

As a client, Sophia was very motivated. She was always on time and initiated topics and seemed genuinely involved in the therapy process. In a case write-up, Dr. R reported that Sophia seemed to understand, without much explaining, what to do with the interviews. In most sessions, she told about the preceding week, what had happened, and how she felt, concentrating mainly on her relationships with men, including her ex-husband.

Therapist Behavior

For response modes, Dr. R used primarily closed question, information, and paraphrase. Compared to the other therapists, she used less direct guidance and more closed question, reflecting her probing, clarifying style. Further, Dr. R was relatively inactive, speaking little during sessions. When she spoke, her voice was very soft and guttural (due to throat surgery) and her comments were brief and somewhat cryptic.

In her case write-up, Dr. R described her own behavior:

> I found myself being inclined to be very supportive of all her efforts to provide herself with a better life, including finding a suitable partner, suitable work, pleasant living conditions, and adequate financial support from her wealthy ex-husband. She responded very well and very openly to an accepting attitude on my part. I let her go at her own pace, which she did, and I rarely found it necessary or desirable to prod. I tried to make some of her present problems more tolerable to her by increasing her understanding of the difficulties which she had gone through in childhood and adolescence without a supportive mother figure. My effort has been to increase her self-confidence by pointing out her strengths in overcoming obstacles in her life and in the good relations she has with friends, her children, and with me.

Thus, Dr. R's approach was to sit expectantly waiting for Sophia to talk. Dr. R listened carefully, probing to make sure that Sophia expressed herself clearly. Rather than provide answers, Dr. R encouraged Sophia to think through her options. Dr. R then reinforced Sophia for knowing herself what she wanted to do, thus trying to build Sophia's confidence in her ability to be a competent problem-solver.

Dr. R expressed strong opinions. At one point when Sophia said she felt guilty about taking money from her ex-husband, Dr. R told her she shouldn't because "he owes you a lot more." In a post-session review, Dr. R said that Sophia could get a lot more money from the ex-husband. She felt that since the ex-husband was wealthy, he should support Sophia without her having to work at all given that she was raising the children. At another point when Sophia was angry at men in general, she said, "Who needs men?" Dr. R replied, "You do," to which Sophia indignantly said, "I do not." Dr. R changed it to say, "You want one."

Analyses of Therapist Techniques

Sophia and Dr. R talked about their reactions to the therapist techniques in the post-therapy interviews:

R: *How did the changes occur?*

C: She respected me as an individual. She seemed to like me and approve of me. Her acceptance enabled me to come out of myself.

T: I don't think anybody ever knows how change occurs in anybody, ever. And that includes her. But I can make something up. I think she had an experience of relating to a person whom she respected and whom she probably looked at, as an authority figure, namely me, over a period of 3 months. She experienced pretty much unqualified respect and this new experience was beneficial to her. *So the relationship that you had with her allowed her to make the changes on her own?* Yes. I think of myself as a kind of midwife. I don't do the birthing, she does.

R: *What did Dr. R (or you) do best with Sophia (her)?*

C: She remembered things I told her. That was very important to me. It gave me a feeling of importance to her. I wasn't just another client. I felt I could trust her. That was big. I really believed that she would help me. *She,* not the therapy. I really feel that she worked with me. *So the relationship was important?* Yeah. It never seemed like a relationship to me. When I thought about coming here, I didn't envision her. I thought about coming to a session. I was all very selfish and wrapped up in myself. I did not think about her much at all. When the session was over, I would think about her more. *What were some specific techniques that were helpful?* She was very subtle. I wasn't aware of techniques except she would say, "How did that feel?" That was a great tool because when somebody interrupts you to ask how you feel, you're honest and you have the feeling with you. It's not something you think about and label. It's there and it comes out of you. Another thing that was very good is that she brought up my highs and lows.

T: I was able to let her go at her own pace in her own way without interfering more than what I consider necessary. I more or less kept quiet. I consciously and intentionally offered her a lot of unconditional support. With the average patient that I see I don't always feel unconditionally supportive, but I really did with her. It seemed to me that that was what she needed. I was on her side, without any question of wavering. I gave her this strong impression that it was consistently hers to be respected. To some extent, I thought it was important for her to cathart, particularly when she was talking about her father. I tried to encourage insight. I tried to reinforce change. Sometimes I challenged her, although not as much as with other patients. *Were there specific techniques that were helpful?* I don't believe in techniques. One simply has to be, as a therapist, free to be themself.

R: *Were there any specific therapist interpretations or feedback that helped you (Sophia) view yourself (herself) or your (her) situation in a different way?*

C: It took her maybe 3 or 4 sessions till I got it. She kept commenting about how there were no proper parents around. I was talking about my fear of going to the beach, but it's my fear of everything involved with my family, that I'm not capable, when she started with this parenting stuff. Every week, she started saying very subtly at some point, "There was no proper parent," or "Will there be no proper parent?" After the third or fourth week, I got it. That really helped me because I never made the connection. I've done a lot of thinking and studying about me and my family, how I've gotten from there to here and my hang-ups and why they are, but I never connected the fact that I had very poor parenting to explain why I am like I am, in terms of my fears and lack of self-esteem. I'm pretty bright, but I never knew that I'm not just stuck with having such low self-esteem all my life. *What route do you see out?* I have decided to be my own mother, my own parent. I never had satisfactory parenting. I'm a terrific mom, a terrific parent. So I decided I'm going to parent myself until I get strong enough to say, "I've had good parenting, I've given it to myself" and see how far that takes me. Counsel myself, like I do my 16-year old daughter and give myself credit for being there for me. Mrs. R started that. She told me that I can do that for myself, but since I've never done that for myself, I couldn't make the connection. I had a big fight with my daughter and we were putting our relationship back together and it struck me. I love her [daughter] so much and I can do this for her. I can love her and discipline her. All that she needs, I have it in me to give. That's what I always wanted. That's why I'm so tuned into their needs because I always had those needs even though they were never satisfied. I decided if I know what I need so much, then why don't I do it for me? But the crossover came from what Mrs. R said.

T: I'm sure I said to her in various ways that she had dealt with a very difficult situation and done it very well, going through childhood before her father died and her sister took her in. She probably never saw herself as having dealt with hard things very well. She had seen the hard things all right, the poverty of her father's death and her sister's meanness, but I don't think she had seen that she had dealt with them well. My saying it to her at various times was a different way of looking at it for her.

How did she demonstrate that she heard the interpretation? She agreed that she had strengths that she was now using with her children.

R: *Try to recall one session that was particularly satisfying?*

C: The stuff with my father was so powerful and there's a lot of answers in that session. It was a turning point for me personally. That's why I came here, for this to happen. I knew there was something deeper. It was the core of my anger and feelings of worthiness. I think it was a major trauma, because the anger has been coming out of me uncontrollably. I've always known that there was more anger inside me than any situation warranted. The first week I cried and my feelings were real tender and sad and then the second week I started feeling like this is really valuable and I started to look at what was going on. Maybe this is the seed, maybe you can work with this, if you keep your wits about you, you can dig yourself a whole new hill to climb. I'm feeling very relieved and calm and I'm taking charge. I think she led me in the right direction with my father's stuff. Letting go of that old pain has let me feel more responsible for myself and more in control.

T: It was a session close to the end where she expressed a lot of emotion about going to the beach for the summer.

R: *What did Dr. R (you) do least well with you (Sophia)?*

C: I envisioned more challenging from the therapist. I don't think I ever deliberately told Mrs. R a lie because I'm basically not a liar. But I held things back and I felt like she knew I wasn't telling her all. But she didn't ask me and I wanted her to. It would have been a lot more constructive if she had asked me more questions. I was real open to her and she could have asked me more. In the first 6 or 8 sessions, I just came in and talked and that was kind of stupid. She could have asked me questions and given us other places to go. I was somewhat bored with what wasn't going on. I got very little out of the early stuff except that I learned to trust her. She never said one critical word and I'm so used to people criticizing me. The other thing that bothered me at first was that she sat too still. I wondered if it was an innate bearing or if she held herself back. Also, in one of our first sessions, she said, "Are you going to have trouble with me because I'm a woman?" I felt like that was a big challenge. She was daring me to give her a hard time. I thought that was very peculiar and I still don't understand where she was coming from. I was totally confused and asked her why she said that. She knew I disliked my mother and sister and she was trying to get a feel for things. I don't hate all women, but I'm much more careful making a female close to me than a male. I'm more accepting of men's little stupidities than I am of women's.

T: The least helpful thing I did occasionally was to talk. If I had spoken less, it would have left more room for her. On the other hand, I probably let her go on too long with recounting details that were not so important. That was one weakness of letting her pace herself, that I would let her go on too long sometimes and couldn't shut her off. It wasn't really detrimental, just a waste of time.

R: *Recall one session that was particularly unsatisfying?*

C: It's the same session, the one I cried at and told her about my father's trying to commit suicide. I was angry with her for making me tell the story. And the last week, I had the feeling that she didn't understand the depth of what went on the week before. I was disappointed in her because she and I opened me up and when I came back in the following week, I expected her to help put me back together. I felt like I was on my own. Maybe that's good because anything you do for yourself usually lasts longer. But when I was here in the session, I wanted something from her that she didn't give me. *What did you want?* She treated the last session lightly and I got confused. I asked her where do I go with this now and didn't get any answer. She did recommend a book to me and I've read some of that and that has helped. It suits the stage of my life at this time. It has been a great help to have the book when I could no longer count on coming to her. But see, I asked for that, which is the way it should be, because I guess I wanted that. I should be doing it for myself. *Is there anything you wish the therapist had pursued further with you?* Feelings about my ex-husband. She accepted totally what I had to say about him on a given day. In my mind I gave her three different feelings. I told her I loved him, hated him, and was indifferent to him and she never once challenged that. Maybe she understands that I feel all those things, but I wanted her to help me sort through them.

T: I remember being bored when she recounted a lot of detail that was important maybe to her. *Is there anything you wish you had pursued further with her?* If I had been seeing her more often, I might have taken more chances to push for emotional material, but I didn't want to stir too much up without the possibility of her getting any help from me and anybody else in putting it together again. *If there were no time constraints, what would you have pursued?* How her relationship with her sister and mother were connected to her feelings about the lack of a man in her life, more about her ex-husband, and of course the thing with her daughter that came up at the end of the last session. I certainly would have pursued the matter with her father.

Quantitative Analyses

Table 10.1 shows the results of analyses comparing therapist response modes on client and therapist helpfulness ratings, client experiencing levels, and client reactions. Table 10.2 shows the codings of the post-session reviews. Both Dr. R and Sophia gave mostly positive comments, attributing the helpful events mostly to therapist techniques. The hindering events were attributed to client tasks by Sophia and to therapist techniques by Dr. R.

Combining the results of the post-therapy interviews with the quantitative analyses shows that the most helpful techniques were approval, interpretation, and direct guidance. No techniques were consistently viewed by Sophia as hindering, but she wished that Dr. R had used more confrontations, direct guidance, and interpretation. Dr. R felt that at time she used too much direct guidance, but that at other times she did not use enough.

Discussion of the Helpful Techniques

Interpretation. The major helpful interpretation was linking Sophia's inadequate parenting as a child to her present lack of self-esteem and overinvolvement with her children. These interpretations were infrequent, reinforcing the notion that the quality of interpretations is more significant than the frequency of use. Given slowly and gently throughout the second half of therapy, these interpretations allowed Sophia to open up and disclose her feelings about her father's attempted suicide and her feelings of abandonment by both parents. This interpretive theme is discussed fully in Chapter 12.

The use of interpretations was undoubtedly affected by Sophia's style. At the beginning of therapy, Sophia seemed "pseudo-insight-oriented," in that she presented a lot of explanations of why things were as they were. Dr. R seemed wary of providing Sophia with too many more explanations to use as weapons. She instead tried to engage the client in becoming curious about her behavior and saved the interpretations until later in the therapy when she judged that Sophia was able to handle them.

Approval. Dr. R felt that by providing unconditional approval, she created an atmosphere where the client felt encouraged to explore her concerns and come to her own solutions to her problems. Sometimes Dr. R acted like a parent who takes the child's side

TABLE 10.1 Proportion of Occurrence, Client Helpfulness Ratings, Therapist Helpfulness Ratings, Client Experiencing, and Client Reactions for Therapist Response Modes in Case 8

Response Modes	%	Client Help Rating		Therapist Help Rating		Client Experiencing		Most Likely Reactions
		M	SD	M	SD	M	SD	
Approval	.09	7.22	1.28	6.28	.84	2.52	.61	Supported
Information	.19	7.14	1.37	6.13	.96	2.35	.54	Supported
Direct Guidance	.02	7.04	1.08	5.81	1.06	2.23	.51	
Closed Question	.28	6.78	1.39	6.04	1.00	2.33	.54	No Reaction
Open Question	.12	7.11	1.31	6.31	.94	2.43	.59	Challenged
Paraphrase	.18	7.20	1.27	6.22	.93	2.40	.58	
Interpretation	.06	7.80	.98	6.76	.93	2.29	.53	Ther. Work
Confrontation	.05	7.48	1.24	6.70	1.05	2.24	.46	Challenged
Disclosure	.00	8.00		7.00		3.00		
TOTAL		7.12	1.30	6.22	.96	2.36	.55	

NOTE: Helpfulness was rated on 9-point scales (9 = extremely helpful); experiencing was rated on a 7-point scale (7 = high). ANOVAs indicated significant differences between therapist response modes for client helpfulness, $F (8, 1390) = 7.16, p < .0001$, therapist helpfulness, $F (8, 1390) = 8.94, p < .01$, and client experiencing, $F (8, 1390) = 2.90, p < .01$, although no post hoc differences were found for any of the three measures. The overall relationship between response modes and client reactions was significant, $X^2 (28) = 142.46, p < .0001$. There was only one therapist disclosure in the entire case.

against bullies, as when she encouraged Sophia to get as much money as she could from her ex-husband because she deserved it for raising the children. Dr. R encouraged Sophia to do for herself what she had been wanting others to do for her, pointing out that Sophia had a lot of strengths and had in fact been taking care of herself. Thus, Dr. R was able to be patient and caring and genuinely empathic with Sophia.

Direct guidance. Sophia liked it when Dr. R structured the sessions and wished there had been more structuring. Dr. R, on the other hand, sometimes thought she did a good job of keeping Sophia from

TABLE 10.2 Proportions of Helpful and Hindering Events Reported by the Client and Therapist in Post-Session Reviews in Case 8

	Client		Therapist	
	Helpful	Hindering	Helpful	Hindering
Therapist Techniques	.32	.02	.33	.08
Support	.11	.00	.13	.00
Direct Guidance	.06	.00	.08	.05
Closed Question	.01	.00	.00	.00
Open Question	.01	.00	.00	.02
Paraphrase	.03	.01	.04	.02
Interpretation	.06	.01	.10	.00
Confrontation	.02	.00	.00	.00
Disclosure	.00	.00	.00	.00
Therapist Manner	.10	.00	.06	.00
Client Tasks	.25	.17	.24	.02
Focus	.00	.04	.03	.00
Experiencing	.06	.09	.03	.02
Insight	.10	.02	.11	.00
Changes	.10	.02	.06	.00
Client Manner	.10	.02	.22	.00
Relationship/Alliance	.01	.00	.05	.00
TOTAL	.78	.22	.90	.10

rambling but felt that she was sometimes too active to the detriment of Sophia taking more control herself. Occasionally, Dr. R's direct guidance for outside the session was also helpful. For example, in the first session, Sophia was explaining that she was worried about returning to work because she was afraid that her boys would beat each other up. Dr. R asked her what her alternatives were and when she said to send them to after-school day care, Dr. R quickly rein-forced her for knowing what to do and told her to get child care. She cut off exploration about Sophia's ambivalence about going back to work and just told her to do it. On other occasions, Dr. R told Sophia that things would go more smoothly with her ex-husband if she tried to understand him more.

Perhaps the most profound advice that Dr. R gave Sophia followed the interpretation that she had been abandoned by her parents. Dr. R suggested that Sophia could parent herself. Paired with the interpre-tation, the advice was very useful for Sophia. Rather than pitying herself for her deprivation in childhood, she came away with a positive feeling that she could change her fate.

Discussion of Less Helpful Techniques

One specific confrontation that Dr. R used was mentioned by Sophia as confusing and unhelpful. After talking about her negative experiences with women in the first session, Dr. R asked whether Sophia would have trouble dealing with her since she was a woman. Sophia responded defensively that she respected her elders, but then came back the next session worried that she had offended Dr. R by labeling her as old. Dr. R confirmed that in fact she was old. The subject got dropped there, leaving Sophia feeling unsure of why Dr. R had brought it up.

Additionally, Sophia wished that the therapist had confronted her more about her contradictions, made her focus more, interpreted more, and provided more structure. Essentially, she was uncomfort-able with the responsibility she had to make something happen within the therapy. One could construe her wish for more as a bid for dependency, which Dr. R was not willing to fulfill. Dr. R was very supportive, but was also very clear in her limits and in telling the client she had to come up with her own answers.

Dr. R concurred that sometimes she let Sophia ramble too much about unimportant details. Sophia was quite dominant in her talking and Dr. R sometimes had to interrupt her to get a word in edgewise. However, Dr. R also felt that sometimes she talked too much herself. At those times, she felt that it might have been better to let Sophia go on with what she was talking about rather than be interrupted in her train of thought.

Process Issues

As important as what techniques were used are the ones that were not used. Given the client's histrionic style, it is interesting that Dr. R never gave feedback about how Sophia's behavior affected her. Rather than give feedback, Dr. R clarified exactly what Sophia was saying. Thus, when Sophia presented her typical contradictions, Dr. R would ask questions to force Sophia to be specific about what she really meant. Sophia would start with one extreme and then contradict herself by giving the other extreme, but would then come to some moderate point through Dr. R's persistent questioning. Thus, the closed questions were not used to gather information but to clarify and in effect challenge.

They also never focused on her target complaint of anger, even though the client specifically stated that she needed to work on expressing her anger. Dr. R felt that anger was not really a problem (see Table 10.3, Target Complaint ratings) and decided not to focus on it. Dr. R appeared to judge that Sophia's underlying problem was the damage from her childhood, with anger simply being the surface expression of her inability to cope with current problems.

One of the most fascinating issues in this case was that observers typically reported that they did not like watching the case. Sophia had a repetitive, hysterical, boring style that made it hard to empathize with her. Dr. R talked in a very low voice and was somewhat difficult to hear and understand. Often it seemed that Dr. R was just chatting with Sophia, asking questions and being supportive, as one might be with a neighbor over coffee. Her style was understated and subtle. Although observers felt that not much was going on in the sessions, the therapy was quite helpful.

Moderating Variables

Client Factors

Sophia had a chaotic family history and had been abandoned by both parents. She was a "victim" who had a fragile self-esteem and identity issues, although she was functioning moderately well and seemed to have adequate coping strategies in her current life. The therapist's supportiveness, encouragement, gentle probing style, and occasional advice seemed quite appropriate for this client. Sophia may have found a more insight-oriented approach to be too threatening. For example, Sophia felt distressed when the therapy terminated shortly after the sessions about her family, which suggests that she could not have handled more catharsis or insight.

Therapist Factors

Three issues about the therapist seem relevant to her use of techniques. First, her psychodynamic training influenced her to consider childhood events to explain the client's present behavior. Thus, Sophia's early deprivation, traumatic experience and shame at her father's attempted suicide and hospitalization, her mother's abandonment of her, and being raised by her sister, were seen as precipitating factors in her present difficulties in functioning.

The second influence that seemed equally potent was Dr. R's Tavistock background in dealing with the authority issues within the therapy. Dr. R communicated that Sophia was responsible for determining the course of therapy and her life, with Dr. R available as a consultant. Sophia had to take charge and ask for what she needed. This orientation is reflected in the data showing that both persons attributed a lot of responsibility to the client.

A third factor that influenced Dr. R's choice of techniques was her personal background. Her own father had died of an embolism when she was a year old and she had blamed her mother for his death. Further, as have most therapists, she felt some dissatisfactions in her own marriage. Although Dr. R never shared her experiences with Sophia, she felt that her experiences helped her to empathize with the client.

The Therapeutic Relationship

Based on WAI scores (see Chapter 2, Table 2.2), Sophia and Dr. R both rated the working alliance as moderately strong, and Sophia indicated that it became more positive across treatment.

In the post-session reviews, Dr. R mentioned that her liking for Sophia grew over time, beginning in the second or third session. The client mentioned the therapist's patience and said that she was "terrific." In the sessions, they appeared to like each other and the interaction seemed comfortable.

Interestingly, they seemed to agree implicitly on the tasks of therapy. The relationship was not discussed, even though Dr. R had emphasized the importance of discussing the relationship both in her theoretical statement prior to therapy and in a statement to the client during the second session about what she might want to talk about. Dr. R felt that discussing relationship issues could potentially have been too disruptive for Sophia given the brief contract of treatment. In fact, there did not seem to be any problems in the relationship that needed to be attended to. Both were happy with the relationship. Although she felt a strong bond, Sophia did not idealize nor denigrate Dr. R as she had other people in her life. Rather she was able to use Dr. R as a sounding board to help her solve her problems. Undoubtedly, Dr. R's approach to having the client take responsibility with the therapist acting as a midwife enabled Sophia to focus on herself instead of becoming dependent on the "good mother."

External Factors

Extratherapy involvement. Comments from the post-therapy interviews indicated that Sophia spent time outside of the therapy sessions thinking about the issues raised in the sessions:

R: *What did you (Sophia) do to help these changes come about?*

C: I tried to be honest with everything. I felt that was a main ingredient. *Sounds like you did a lot of work at home thinking about all this stuff.* Yeah, I did. I was honest and willing to do almost anything she asked me to do. I was totally committed. *How much of your changes were due to yourself compared to your therapist or outside influences?* It was more due to her than me. I've known for a long time that I was like that, so it was her or the therapy that made the difference. Outside influences didn't make much difference.

T: She worked hard and was conscientious about her appointments and agreements. She used what she heard from me during the sessions.

Support network. Most of Sophia's interpersonal relationships seemed to be with her children, with whom she was overly involved. Additionally, she was emotionally and financially involved with her ex-husband, even though she did not see him often. Sophia was also connected with several members of her family, particularly the sister who had raised her and her sister's children. During the course of the therapy, there were several visits from relatives.

At one point Sophia said that she had several female friends who were quite supportive, although at another point she said she had no female friends. In therapy, she discussed a couple of friends with whom she went to singles bars. She had a big fight with one of these friends because the friend felt that she had ignored her. The friendship dissolved over the fight, with Sophia feeling betrayed and angry at the woman.

Sophia met and dated a few men during the course of therapy, but was not involved with any one man. In sum, Sophia had somewhat of a support network outside of therapy.

External events. Several minor events happened during the course of therapy that influenced Sophia's moods and choice of topics within sessions. When a man made a date to meet her and did not show up, she got depressed and drank enough to have a blackout. About the same time, her daughter skipped school and got into a series of minor scrapes, which upset Sophia. Her ex-husband also started dating another woman regularly and wanted to be with the children more, which made Sophia jealous and upset. On the other hand, her ex-husband helped her out of a financial crisis and paid for a house at the beach for Sophia and the children for the summer. For the therapy process, it was useful that these events occurred because they provided real-life examples of the issues that Sophia needed to work on. Other than these minor events within the therapy, however, no major events occurred to either help or hinder the progress of therapy.

Outcome of Therapy

Session Outcome

According to scores on the SEQ (see Chapter 2, Table 2.2), Sophia and Dr. R both perceived the sessions as being moderately deep and smooth.

Pre-Post Changes

Sophia was somewhat improved after 12 sessions of treatment (See Table 10.3). She had improved significantly on five MMPI scales (Schizophrenia, Psychopathic Deviate, Psychasthenia, Paranoia, and Mania), bringing her profile into the normal range. She was

TABLE 10.3   Scores on Outcome Measures for Case 8

Measures	Pre	5th	Expect	Post	6 Mo	1 Yr
Client-Rated Measures						
MMPI						
Schizophrenia	77			58*		
Psychopathic Deviate	74			64*		
Psychasthenia	71			51**		
Depression	69			61		
Paranoia	65			50*		
Social Introversion	62			50*		
SCL-90-R	50			43	31*	[35]
TSCS	41			[33*]	41*	46
TC (1) Anger	10	—	6	6*	3*	3
(2) Men	9	[10]	5	6*	2*	[5*]
(3) Children	9	7	2.5	4**	3	[4]
(4) Project True Self		9	2	4**	1*	1
Satisfaction					10	10
Therapist-Rated Measures						
TC (1) Anger	4	4	3.5	4		
(2) Men	10	10	7	7*		
(3) Children	10	9	7	7*		
(4) Project True Self	10	7	7*			
Researcher-Rated Measures						
Hamilton Anxiety	20			15*		
Hamilton Depression	13			[15]		

NOTE: High *T* scores indicate high symptomatology on the SCL-90-R GSI, high self-esteem on the TSCS; worst functioning on the TC, higher satisfaction, and greater disturbance on the Hamilton scales. Expect = level expected after treatment. * = significant change at $p < .05$; ** = $p < .01$; *** = $p < .001$. Negative changes are in brackets.

also functioning better on her target complaints and was less anxious. She was unchanged in symptomatology and depression and was lower in self-concept, which was probably due to the last two sessions of therapy when she felt "unglued" from discussing her background.

In the post-therapy interviews excerpted below, both therapist and client felt that Sophia had changed during therapy, although they disagreed on the specific changes. The client claimed changes in her overinvolvement with her children, becoming more feminine, less symptomatology, and having lost weight. The therapist felt that Sophia was more self-confident, less depressed, and better able to deal with her children and ex-husband.

R: How have you (or has Sophia) changed as a result of therapy?

C: I feel more like an adult, not a little kid. I've been working on my overinvolvement with my kids. It's better now. I understand that I am what I am because my parents gave me away. So I've held on to my kids tight, like nobody's ever going to do this to them because I love them. That kept me overinvolved with them to where I feel their stuff and I hurt with them. To a certain extent that's normal and I don't want to get away from it. I want to know where they are and what they're into so that I can counsel, take care of, love, and give them what they need. Another change is that I was being tough and have come back to being the tender, sweet, feminine person that I want to be and I've always been. *Any changes in symptoms?* Yeah, less grouchiness, gritting my teeth, lack of sleep. I feel active. I feel like doing things. I've been dieting consistently and I've lost 15 pounds and I feel limber. *Any behavioral changes?* Yeah, when that friend dumped me, it was the first time in my life I have not taken it and beaten myself to death with it. *Any self-concept changes?* I bought some new clothes for myself. That's part of the mothering myself. *Any changes in relationships?* I feel better about them because I feel like I have something to offer.

T: She has become more self-confident, sure of herself and her own resources, and aware of various feelings as they come up. *Any symptom relief?* Since her major symptom was depression, I must say that at termination she did not seem greatly depressed. Now that doesn't mean that she won't be again because she is subject to mood swings. *Behavioral changes?* She handles her second child better, who she complained about considerably at the beginning. She also handles her ex-husband somewhat better in terms of not becoming so dependent and standing up for herself somewhat better. *Other interpersonal relationships?* Her relationship with her daughter has changed for the worse. She did not have any relationship with a man, except her ex-husband, which was improved. She may have a better idea of how to protect herself and go cautiously.

R: How satisfied are you with the nature and amount of changes?

C: I think where we've come in this short time is almost outrageously significant.

T: I am satisfied that the nature was good, but the amount was not enough. She may be able to get through the rest herself, but I doubt it. My guess is that she still needs help.

Six-Month Follow-Up

Sophia was improved at the six-month follow-up. Her symptomatology was lower; she was functioning better in three of her four target complaints; and she had returned to pre-therapy levels in self-concept. She had begun working as an accountant and office manager, was in a relationship with a man, and had lost an additional five pounds. Her relationship with her daughter was still rocky and Sophia had sent her daughter for therapy. She felt better about herself in general and felt that she had gained many new understandings about her life.

One-Year Follow-Up

Sophia maintained her gains on the outcome instruments and was substantially improved compared to pre-therapy. She had continued the relationship with the same man and said that even with his faults ("too tall, thin, and clumsy"), she would "keep him" because "he's good for me." She still had problems with her children, but felt that they were handling them. She had quit her job because it was "very bad" with a "truly crazy" boss. She had a new "terrific job" with a boss who was a "truly honorable man" and she was "well thought of and trusted by all the clients and my boss."

Long-Term Follow-Up

Three years after treatment ended, Sophia was still in a relationship with the same man and in the same job as she had been at the last follow-up. She had gotten large raises in her job because she was so important to the functioning of the business she worked in. She felt that her job had allowed her financial independence and an identity apart from her children. She was getting along better both with her oldest child, who had moved out of the house, and with her middle child, who was now in high school. She had a good friend who gave her feedback about her behavior and encouraged her. In our meeting, I found Sophia calmer, less histrionic, and easier to talk with than she had been before and during therapy. She had not sought further therapy since the termination of her treatment with Dr. R.

Summary

Therapist techniques were more helpful than other variables in this therapy. The most helpful techniques were approval, direct guidance, and interpretation. The therapist seldom gave the client feedback about her behavior or discussed the relationship. The only negative aspect was that both the client and therapist thought that the therapist should sometimes have been more active and structured the sessions more.

Client variables, therapist variables, and the therapeutic relationship all played significant roles in moderating the effects of techniques. The techniques worked because this client had a fragile self-esteem, the therapist was psychoanalytic and believed that the client should take responsibility, there was a good therapeutic relationship, and there were few external events that interfered with the process of therapy.

In short, Sophia was in a lot of pain at the time of therapy and was able to make good use of Dr. R's gentle, supportive, interpretive style. Once Dr. R helped her with the basic issues of her self-confidence and mourning her father, she was able to make some initial changes in getting a job and getting a relationship. These changes then helped foster further changes in independence and feelings of self-esteem. Because she could drop some of her more irritating behaviors, Sophia began to get along better with others and could then turn to them for more general support to continue the change process after therapy ended. In this way, she began an upward spiral stimulated by the therapy. Thus, all the factors worked together to foster continued change in Sophia.

PART III

SPECIFIC THERAPIST TECHNIQUES

11

Therapist Self-Disclosures

Humanistic theorists believe that self-disclosures can facilitate the therapeutic process (Archer, 1979) and build the therapeutic relationship (Rogers, 1957; Truax & Carkhuff, 1967). Similarly, interpersonal theorists (e.g., Kiesler, 1988; Strupp & Binder, 1984) advocate that therapists use personal reactions as immediate examples of how client behavior affects others. In contrast, psychoanalytic theorists (e.g., Curtis, 1981) generally hold that self-disclosures contaminate and interfere with the transference and demystify the therapist, reducing his or her status. Given the controversy around this therapist technique, it is interesting to examine how disclosures were used in these cases.

We were initially surprised to find in the overall analysis (Hill, Helms, Tichenor, Spiegel, O'Grady, & Perry, 1988) that although disclosures were used infrequently, they were not only rated by clients as the most helpful therapist response mode but that they also led to the highest levels of client experiencing. Therapists, on the other hand, rated them as the least helpful response mode. In pursuing this further, Hill, Mahalik, and Thompson (in press) found that reassuring disclosures were more helpful and led to higher client experiencing than did challenging disclosures. This study, however, provided few clues about how disclosures were used in individual cases. Thus, the purpose of the present chapter was to explore the use of disclosure in the two cases (1 and 3) in which disclosures were used most frequently.

I was dissatisfied with the categories we used in the past research because they did not seem to fit the type of disclosures used by our therapists. Therefore, all the disclosure events were categorized (by Jim Mahalik, Barbara Thompson, and myself) into six new categories: (a) *Immediate reassuring:* Reassuring the client with the therapist's immediate feelings or reactions to the therapy or the therapeutic relationship; (b) *Immediate challenging:* Challenging the client by presenting the therapist's immediate feelings or reactions, (c) *Disclosing facts:* Presenting facts or credentials, (d) *Disclosing similarities:* Disclosing similarities between the therapist's and client's past experiences, (e) *Disclosing feelings:* Disclosing similar feelings or reactions, (f) *Disclosing strategies:* Disclosing strategies that the therapist has used that the client could use to change.

Examples of each type of disclosure event are excerpted to show how disclosures were used in each case. In the excerpts, the disclosures are underlined.

Case 1

Most of Dr. A's disclosures were immediate rather than disclosing, indicating that Dr. A often discussed his feelings about the relationship.

Immediate Reassuring Disclosures

Dr. A used immediate reassuring disclosures to reinforce the client's expressiveness and encourage Sandy to keep up her good work. They were used most often when Sandy was exploring herself in a productive manner. These disclosures were used: (a) to establish rapport and relieve anxiety during the first few sessions and occasionally later, (b) during the process of therapy to deal with issues in the relationship, and (c) during termination.

To establish rapport. An example from the end of session 1:

T: How, how did you find yourself reacting uh to the, just to the, you know us meeting in sort of this little corner of the room (C: Yeah) and stuff?

C: Uh, actually I didn't, I didn't, I didn't feel uh like I should be in a nicer space. (T: MmHmm) I felt like what, what we were doing just had to do with you and me. And so (T: Yeah, yeah) it didn't really matter where we were.

T: *I felt a lot more anxiety than I expected to feel in some ways, especially at first. And* (C: Uh huh) *uh I guess that sort of dissipated as we began to focus in on what was going on.* How, how, how did you . . .?

C: Well I think initially (T: Yeah) when we first sat down (T: Yeah) and you and I were trying to kind of figure out who each other was (T: Yeah, right) I felt anxious. Like (T: Yeah) I felt like how could I, I'm sitting here with this man I don't even know (both laugh) and I'm going to start telling him all the intimate details of my life here. And, but I feel very I felt very comfortable with you.

In this disclosure, Dr. A communicated to Sandy that he too had anxieties and that the research situation was likely to be difficult for him too. He tried to alleviate Sandy's fears and modeled how to talk about feelings. Sandy reciprocated by talking about her feelings, so the disclosure had the desired effect.

Issues in the relationship. The best example of this type of disclosure occurred in the third session:

T: How did you feel about the session?

C: Uh I felt, I felt comfortable with the session. (T: Okay) Uh I felt it brought up a lot of sadness for me (T: MmHmm, yeah) that I hadn't thought about (T: Yeah, yeah) for awhile, but I . . .

T: *I shared that with you. I don't know whether you could see that or not. I didn't, somehow I, I didn't know how to communicate that. But as you talked about especially the last couple of weeks and your coming home and finding your mother and so* (C: MmHmm) *forth, I really was, I found it really very sad.*

C: Well, I thank you for telling me that. I couldn't, I didn't know. (T: MmHmm) And uh, but I think it was probably good for me to tell you that, so that I somewhat listened to what I was saying (T: Sure) and it gives me more input.

On her Post-Session Questionnaire, Sandy mentioned this disclosure as the most helpful event in the session. She had been unsure about how Dr. A responded to her sharing of deep feelings.

Termination. Dr. A dealt with termination extensively in the final two sessions, so that both participants had time to process what gains had been made in therapy and to talk about how they felt about the termination. In the final session:

> C: I also thought if I went back to therapy, would I go to a male therapist. (T: MmHmm) I haven't come to a decision (T: Yeah) because initially I wouldn't have gone to a male therapist because like I told you when we first started out (T: Yeah) I was kind of shocked that they gave me a male therapist (both laugh) but now I give it, I'd give it more consideration.

> T: MmHmm, yeah. (Pause = 5 seconds). *I feel sadness in some ways, in some ways. I'm really glad you didn't end last week because I guess I feel that, that more of a feeling this week of having joined each other for awhile,* (C: Yeah) *you know, but our lives will go on separately. And that's just kind of a loss in not being able to stay with things that we would have been able and so forth. Yet I know you will in your life, but it's sort of a loss for me in not being involved in that.*

> C: Yeah, do, I mean you, I would think that, that would, well I don't know what it would feel like for you. On the one hand, I view it as this is your profession (T: MmHmm) and maybe sad like this is what you do, so you can't get too connected you know to the, to your clients.

> T: Yeah, that's true. *In the sense of, it's not a sense of, of, of, of desperation or sense of saying I need you* (C: MmHmm) *to somehow stay in touch or something like that, because that's not the feeling. It's more of an immediate sort of feeling of, of your having sort of gone with you for a while. Part of it's how, how will you do this and how will things work out.* (C: Yeah) *It's not so much a feeling of having to have contact as much as ah, you know you're bright and talented and an interesting lady. And it would be sort of interesting how you worked out your life.* That, you know, ah, ah, but in some ways that's not terribly realistic because sort of keeping in touch doesn't make a lot of sense. You're welcome to call me. I don't know what [the researcher's] constrictions are. *One of the, one of the things that is different in this than most of my therapy is that, that probably the thing I fear most in therapy is keeping people longer than you need to be kept.* (C: MmHmm) *So that part of what I'm not feeling is that you need to stay.* (C: MmHmm) *That's, that's not what I'm feeling. I mean the sadness is sort of giving up something that has been interesting and part of it. Also there's the sense that the whole situation has been interesting.*

When Dr. A first said he felt sad about the relationship ending, Sandy reacted as if there was something wrong with his professional capacities. In response, Dr. A backtracked and tried to explain himself. His low rating (3 on a 9-point scale) was probably due to her strong reaction to his statement and the fact that he felt vulnerable and exposed. Interestingly, Sandy rated the whole sequence as extremely helpful (9 on a 9-point scale). Thus, there was a discrepancy between Sandy's behavior in the session and her ratings. Initially, when Dr. A seemed vulnerable, she seemed frightened that he was inadequate and dependent on her, causing her to push him away. When Dr. A reassured her that he did not need her and when she had the hour intervening between the therapy and watching the videotape, Sandy seemed to relax enough to feel that he had indeed said something positive. Dr. A later said that he had used the disclosure to help Sandy get into her feelings of loss, which also may have been very threatening for her.

Immediate Challenging Disclosures

These disclosures were rated as the least helpful of all the types, probably because they were all delivered when Sandy was not exploring herself. Dr. A felt a need to do something to get Sandy into a more exploratory state, which he did by confronting her about what was happening in their relationship. Although Sandy did not like these challenges at the time, they seemed helpful in the long run for making her aware of maladaptive behaviors. It is important to note that Dr. A delivered most (85%) of these disclosures in sessions 7-19, indicating that he waited to use them until he felt a strong bond with Sandy.

Dr. A used three types of immediate challenging disclosures: (a) confrontation, (b) admitting being stuck, and (c) persuasion.

Confrontation. Dr. A used these disclosures to give Sandy feedback about her behavior. For example, in Session 7, Sandy was angry at her sister for hanging up on her when they were talking on the telephone. She was indignant that her sister would treat her that way and seemed to lack any understanding of her sister.

T: *I react to that in some way. But I'm not, I c- can't really put it into words very well.* It's sort of (sighs) sort of like, okay you don't do that, and that sounds, and it sounds important that you don't do that. (C: Yeah) But other people have different styles.

C: Yeah, other people have different styles. Yeah, that's true. (laughs) That's true, yeah. I just wish she was nicer to me. (laughs) I mean if I did that to her, I'm sure she'd be shocked. Maybe I ought to try it out. (laughs) It wouldn't accomplish anything.

This disclosure confronted Sandy about how she came across. Dr. A was very tentative and vague in his presentation, which may partially account for the lowered helpfulness ratings.

Stuck. Dr. A was the only therapist to use this particular type of disclosure. When he did not know what to do in a session, he candidly admitted that he was stuck. Prior to the example from session 7, Sandy had been talking about feeling unsure of how she felt about a former boyfriend.

C: Pause = 10 seconds. So I feel like I, I get stuck.

T: MmHmm. *That's the way I feel right now.* (C laughs) *Yeah, uh yes, is that, I assume that's, that's coming from you, that somehow it's just hard to know* (C: Yeah, cause I . . .) *where to go with that.*

C: Yeah cause I'm stuck. (T: Yeah, okay) I, I just don't know where to go with it. (T: MmHmm) I feel like on the one hand uh I want to maintain a friendship . . . (goes on to explore productively)

About three minutes later, Dr. A returns to his feelings:

C: How are we doing for time?

T: We're a couple of minutes over. *I'm, in fact, I've been thinking more about time in the last 10 minutes. And I think, somehow I have a feeling that we're not going to get a sense of closure today. It sort of bothers me, but I'm not sure there's anything we're going to be able to do about it.*

C: It doesn't bother me.

T: Yeah, *well it bothers me.*

C: It bothers you?

T: Yeah, yeah. *It's, only in the sense that it's not closed* (C: MmHmm) *you know uh, uh, uh and I don't, I don't know exactly where to go with this thing with [boyfriend]. I guess I'm feeling a little sort of direction-less at this point. And I don't know where we need to go, like next time.*

C: Well, maybe just to discuss it more. But I, I would like to get some feedback from you in terms of what you hear me telling you, (T:

MmHmm) you know in terms of what kind of sense you get from this.
(T: MmHmm) because I, I feel like I, I need that.

These "stuck" disclosures received the lowest helpfulness ratings
of all the disclosures from both Sandy and Dr. A. In the post-therapy
interview, Sandy said that she had felt frustrated when Dr. A was
stuck and could not help her get unstuck. She had hoped that Dr. A
would have more advice and would put things together for her more.

From another perspective, however, these "stuck" disclosures
seemed to have a paradoxical effect. The metacommunication of
"I'm stuck" seems to be "I do not have the answer, you'll have to
help me struggle for it." On the one hand, "I'm stuck" sounds like a
weak position. On the other hand, it is strong to admit that you feel
weak. It may have the effect of letting the client feel more competent,
realizing that all of us struggle for answers. This may be a good way
of dealing with dependency issues, at least for a client who has the
capability of coming up with her own answers.

Persuasion. In these instances, Dr. A used his personal power to
persuade the client to do what he wanted her to do. These disclosures
were uniformly rated negatively and may have been reflective of a
power struggle in their relationship. Interestingly, in all cases, the
therapist "won" and the client complied with his requests. For example, early in the therapy, Dr. A wanted Sandy to go a doctor to check
out her health concerns. She did not want to go because of past
negative experiences with the medical profession. He used his immediate personal feelings to persuade her to go. On another occasion
in session 11, Dr. A wanted to change the time of their appointment:

T: *I usually have 7 o'clock appointments* (C: Oh) *which means that, that
only gives me an hour and a half to get home, get dinner, get set up,
and, and start* (C: Yeah) *seeing people there. So that's really, uh that
would be I think a problem for me.*

C: Okay, is Wednesday the only day that you're available?

T: It's the only day that they're available. (C: Oh) That's uh.

C: Pause = 6 seconds. Well uh (Pause = 5 seconds) if 2 is the only time
that you can do it, then I I'll arrange my schedule. It, it it's not the best
thing for me.

T: It really is. (C: But uh . . .) Yeah, *the, the problem is, with me is that
if I, if I really cut it tight on the other end,* (C: MmHmm) *uh, uh it means*

I get home at 6 for, at, at 6 fif-, at uh at 6:15 or something like that. (C: MmHmm) *And it, after a couple of those I begin to resent it.* (C: Yeah) *And I, and I, that would, that doesn't make any sense for us.* Now are you in a comparable. . . ?

Sandy explained that by coming earlier she would lose a whole afternoon from work. After a few minutes of discussion, however, she gave in and changed her schedule.

Disclosing Feelings

On several occasions, Dr. A acted as a model discussing his feelings to encourage Sandy to identify and experience feelings. These disclosures seemed similar in intent to reflections of feelings. Rather than saying, "You feel angry," Dr. A said, "If I were you, I would be angry" or "When that has happened, I have been angry." One was never quite sure if Dr. A was saying something about himself personally or giving a hypothetical disclosure in the service of a reflection of feelings. For example, in session 5 when Sandy described how her sister hung up on her, Dr. A disclosed how he would have felt if he were Sandy:

T: *If I put myself in that position, if somebody hangs up on me, I can think of being angry. But I can think of a lot of other feelings I'd have too.* (C: Like what?) *Well, helplessness. Like I mean, all of a sudden* (C: Oh, like you can't do anything.) *Yeah, all of a sudden here I'm, I'm sort of trying to do something. Maybe, maybe I screwed up, maybe I didn't. I feel sort of anxious about, you know, maybe I did something wrong and I'm angry and I feel sort of helpless. I can think of all sorts of . . .*

C: Yeah, I feel a lot of, yeah, I feel all those things.

The use of a disclosure in this instance appeared to make it easier for Sandy to accept that she had negative feelings.

Disclosing Strategies

In this type of disclosure, Dr. A shared problem-solving strategies that had worked for him in the past. He did not directly say that Sandy "should" do these things. Instead he presented advice in a tentative manner, by suggesting alternatives that had worked for him. For example in session 11:

C: I found the same thing with [roommate]. So I have toned down. And it's hard for me to tone down (T: Yeah, yeah) because I'm not a toned-down type of a person. (T: MmHmm, yeah) But, so, but I've been trying. And I've (T: MmHmm) really been trying not to give suggestions, (T: MmHmm) like, well, why don't you try this or why don't you try that, but just listen.

T: *You know one of the things that's worked for me and has been helpful for me, uh is this concept of active listening, which is uh communication.* (C: Right) People and marital therapists and so forth use it all the time. Which is that we think of listening often as being very passive and rather than being passive is really sort of involving yourself with the other person. You know repeating back, maybe reflecting back, sort of letting them know that you really understand, really trying to understand the situation. So that basically listening can be very hard (C: MmHmm) not just because you're restraining yourself from giving advice, but it can be really hard because you're really getting in and trying to understand what's going on with the other person. That (C: Yeah) *that's been helpful for me a lot of times in, in sort of toning down my wanting to tell people how it is they should live their lives* (C laughs) *which they're not asking me at all* (C: Yeah) *and, and helpful then for me to feel like I'm doing something.* (C: MmHmm) Right?

C: Well, I, I, I'm familiar with this (T: Yeah, okay, good) concept of active listening. So I, and I've read part of this PET book. (T: Yeah, mmhmm, yeah) And um so I've been trying to incorporate that. (T: Good, good, good) I've been listening to my sister. (laughs) (T: Yeah, good) And it, like I say, you know I think it's working. I think our relationship is changing. (T: MmHmm) And it's changing for me too a lot. (T: MmHmm) And it's also teaching me a l-, a lot in terms of, you don't have to (T: Yeah) give people suggestions. They're going to change when they want to change. (T: Sure, yeah) And you're just there to listen (T: MmHmm) and provide whatever type of comfort you can (T: Yeah) to them.

This is a good example of how Sandy took what Dr. A said, expanded on it, and used it.

Disclosing Facts

There were only two disclosures of facts. Both seemed innocuous but perhaps necessary. The following vignette was the very first interaction in the therapy and appeared to be intended to structure treatment and ease the client into therapy:

T: *I'm a clinical psychologist. And uh, uh I work, I do work here full time. I also have a practice of probably about a day a week. I see individual clients and also see couples uh for marital therapy and some for sexual therapy. Worked in a medical school setting for about 10 years and then came here in 1972 and been here and teach graduate and undergraduate courses, those sorts of things.* (C: MmHmm) *Uh I'll also give you a card in case you need to get ahold of me* (C: Oh all right) *at any time. Any questions about me that you've got?*

C: Uh, well, I, I'll tell you my first reaction. (T: Okay) My first reaction was when they said that, uh they told me your name. My, my reaction was "oh, it's a guy" (both laugh) like ugh.

By telling about himself and then asking if Sandy had questions, Dr. A immediately established that he was open and that their relationship could be discussed. Sandy responded by revealing her initial reaction of not being sure she could relate to a man, which was one of the core themes of her life and of the therapy. Thus, although the disclosure itself was not rated as helpful, the resulting opening up of the core theme for the entire therapy is an indication of its effect.

Disclosing Similarity

There was only one disclosure of similarity, which was actually a set-up for a confrontation in session 18:

C: There's certain core things that I need out of the relationship. (T: MmHmm) But I'm willing to, like I'm willing to sacrifice certain things out of the relationship. (T: MmHmm) You know, but I guess, like there's like the core. Why have a relationship if you're not going to have an extremely intimate relationship with somebody? I mean there just, uh for me I, I guess that's it, you know maybe that's it. If you can't have an extremely intimate relationship with someone, you know, why have the relationship? And maybe that's an, uh I don't know, maybe that's unrealistic. You know how intimate a relationship can you have with someone? (T: MmHmm) Maybe it can't be that way.

T: *I sort of share with you the, the, the view that in a lot of ways, it's a lot easier for women to talk intimately and openly about their feelings and about things that are going on inside of them and to be able to process those things and to just be open about uh, about a lot of things generally than men are. Uh and, and you know in some ways that's a, that's a, a real tragedy and a loss for men.* You know, in other ways it may also be something (C: Mm) that at times keeps them task-focused and may be helpful for them in other ways. And it's a, it's not a question of which is better or which is worse in a way, but the, there may well be some differences. But that (sighs) somehow then what you're describing is sort of a, you know, is finding a sort of a, a, a man who can do these things or sort of, if you really want a relationship with a guy, you'd be giving up something about what you need (C: Yeah, yeah) for other things. But whatever they are, you haven't really talked about other things. You haven't really said "but as far as men are concerned this is what I do like" I haven't heard anything about that.

C: True. (both laugh) That's true. Well, uh that's a tough one. (both laugh) Um I mean there's a, well let's see, what do I like about men? I don't know. It's hard to generalize about this.

By establishing that they were similar in their perceptions that women were more open than men, Dr. A may have made it easier for Sandy to hear the confrontation about whether she liked men.

Summary of Case 1

The effectiveness of self-disclosure in this case was probably due to both client and therapist factors. Sandy was open, articulate about her feelings, and insight-oriented. She wanted feedback from Dr. A and asked him how he felt about various things. Sandy had a lot of issues about her relationships with men. She did not have a very high regard for men, generally choosing as partners men who were passive. By using self-disclosure, Dr. A showed her that not all men were like her stereotype and that he could both be strong and comfortable talking about his feelings.

In the first two sessions, Dr. A quickly established an equality in the relationship by sharing how he felt and asking her to tell him how she felt. Every event in the therapy was open for discussion. Disclosures fit with Dr. A's approach to treatment, which he characterized as interpersonal (e.g., Kiesler, 1988).

Perhaps the ratings of helpfulness were so much lower for Dr. A than for Sandy because the disclosures were anxiety-producing for him. He was using his own personal feelings and reactions in the treatment, sometimes opening himself up to challenges and questions from the client. Whereas open discussion may yield a productive relationship, it is not necessarily easy to pull off. Because of his interpersonal style, he opened himself up more than did the other therapists, taking more risks with his personal reactions.

Case 3

Most of Dr. H's disclosures were disclosing types, particularly disclosures of similarity.

Disclosing Similarities

Dr. H had a unique way of using this type of disclosure that appeared to be disarming to Lucille, who was whiny, complaining, and self-pitying. When Lucille would say, "I am a terrible person because of such and such," Dr. H would use disclosures to convey the indirect message, "I am just like you in that regard, but I accept myself." Dr. H obviously enjoyed being somewhat eccentric, a characteristic that Lucille wished she could allow herself to be. Lucille was dramatic and wanted to act and write poetry, but often stopped herself for fear of what others would think. Dr. H communicated that you have to accept yourself, in spite of what others think.

Dr. H chose not to confront Lucille directly about her cognitions, as a cognitive therapist might have done, but by his acceptance of himself on what she considered negative traits, he indirectly challenged her way of looking at herself. As a result Lucille became less whiny and began to explore herself in productive ways, indicating that the disclosures had a powerful effect. Several examples illustrate this type of disclosure.

Session 1   C: So how do you go about finding a partner? How do you find a companion?

T: *I don't know. I'm a worse recluse than you are.* (C: You're the worst recluse?) *I'm a worse recluse than you are.*

C: Oh you are! Wow! So you know, I mean it's, uh, when you get to be my age if you chose. . . .

Session 2   C: Because I don't have anybody to go on the road with. Here again we go to this companionship.

T: Pause = 7 seconds. *Well, I'm having a hard time because* (C: Now, now) *when I go travelling I almost always want company.* I think that's what you're saying.

C: MmHmm, yeah. It's not all that much fun to do everything by yourself. Not that I don't appreciate time alone, you know, when you're too much with everybody, you need to get away. But uh I've had too much time alone.

Session 5   C: In other words you're saying you have to start with one step, you can't make quantum leaps. (T: Yeah) Well, I understand everything you've said so far. It's, but, it is difficult.

T: *I don't do it much. I indulge in a lot of bad habits.* (C: MmHmm) *And I know they're bad habits, just as you know you're into bad habits.* (C: MmHmm) *And I, I don't change them much.*

C: I can break a bad habit. I don't know if you consider smoking a bad habit? (T: Yeah, it's a bad habit.) Yeah, I smoked for maybe 20 years. I've been quit now for 15. So I can break a bad habit.

Following these disclosures, Lucille's experiencing levels went up and she was able to view herself in new ways. Thus, these disclosures were helpful to disrupt her negative self-statements.

Disclosing Strategies

The first example occurred in session 14. Dr. H began with a similarity disclosure and led into his strategy disclosure.

C: I'm not, I haven't had enough experience on these and computers, I can do the computer to have my check okayed at the store. I have a little mini-computer that I double check my uh, my own figures with but . . .

T: Pause = 5 seconds. *Uh, I share some of you inadequacy feelings in the face of these contemporary, uh, devices of the devil.*

C: Devices of the devil (both laugh) then again . . .

T: *However, I've, I've made myself sit down at them and they, they do work pretty simply actually.*

C: Yeah, they work as long as when you put the plug in, the power source is there.

In an example from the final session, Dr. H begins with a feelings disclosure and then moves on to a strategy disclosure:

C: Although um, there's still a little bit of me that is like a cat with a mouse, won't let it go, two or three things that I just stuck, I can't forgive and forget. I'd be (laughs) better off if I could. And I've noticed that time really makes it easier.

T: You, this is terribly abstract. But usually those stickers, those, those events that stick with us so, so because they represent an injury to our sense of self. (C: Yes) *They, they were situations where I felt humiliated, ashamed. And um, situation might have put me in where I felt guilt-type conflict, where I, basic sense of goodness, your worth at risk might have stimulated some very deep anger that I find uncomfortable. It doesn't fit with me.* So those kinds of wounds just seem to take an awfully long time to heal. And I, I don't know if, I don't think there's anything, no there isn't anything, including *Psychology Today* which offers a more uh, uh, rapid way of viewing (C: Mmm) those hurts.

C: Well, I, I do know that time makes them less livid (T: Yeah) because I don't get as turmoiled (T: Yeah) about things that happened some years back (T: Yeah) as I did at the time.

T: *What, what I don't do myself with those is look back. And, and I recall when, I'm usually recalling the scene.* And, and because, as you are something of an externalizer and attention goes out first, rather than in. *Um, I reexperience some of the pain or anger at the other or others, whatever and uh can let myself have that. It's there. It's not going to go away, not just cause I suppress it. Then I stop and think, "Okay now, what part of me was I experiencing in, in that memory."* (C: MmHmm) *And just being able to step back into the observing positions and look at that need, that part of me calms me down faster and helps me let go of the, any anger, rage inside much, much faster. Again, I don't think it speeds the healing so much as allows me to feel more balanced more quickly after* (C: MmHmm) *getting back in touch.* Now that may be what religious people mean by forgiveness. I'm not sure. *I know I don't feel terribly humble* (T laughs) *as a result of doing that.* (C: MmHmm) *I don't feel I can keep from suffering by doing that. But I, but I do notice a calmness seems to come from observing, finding a part of me in that scene.*

C: Well, I think it's for your own peace of mind to have, to not let it eat you. (T: Yeah) So I'm able to, things don't eat at me as long as they used to.

Lucille seemed to hear what Dr. H said. She indicated that she had tried to allow herself to experience her feelings more often rather than to just ignore them.

Disclosing Feelings

Dr. H only used three disclosing feelings disclosures, as illustrated by the following example from session 5:

T: Okay, so I think what your associations just told you is that, yes, even when it's a person you like very much and you feel likes you, it's still unpleasant to feel obligated.

C: It may be, uh yes. Why?

T: There's something about it that doesn't feel good.

C: Why?

T: Pause = 5 seconds. What, what do you think?

C: I don't know. Um . . .

T: *I know it's hard for me. It's a curb on my autonomy. I can't spend all my time doing just what I want to do when I want to do it if I'm obligated to other people.* (C: Yeah. That's part of it too.) That sound like you a little bit?

C: Yeah. MmHmm. Well, I don't like demands made on me when I'm not willing to, you know, (T: Right) in other words I distance myself (T: Right) from demands on me that I don't want to fill.

Lucille was demanding an answer from Dr. H, who chose to deal with this demand by revealing how he would feel in a similar situation. Whether it actually would make Dr. H feel this way or whether he is simply phrasing it as a disclosure to encourage her to express her own feelings is unclear. In either case, Dr. H's strategy was to model his feelings, with the implication that Lucille was to follow suit and reveal her feelings. Lucille did respond with her feelings, so the strategy was effective.

Disclosing Facts

There was one disclosure of facts when Lucille asked about Dr. H's upcoming vacation during session 14:

C: Hope you enjoy whatever it is you're planning to do.

T: *A trip to the North Maine and the Gatts Bay.*

C: Oh, I love Maine, New Hampshire, and Vermont. Nice country.

T: *Home town. That's where I grew up.*

C: Oh, is it in Maine?

T: *No, northern New Hampshire.*

C: Oh, really, that's part of my favorite, the prettiest place, I remember a place called Joe's Pond, Vermont.

T: Right. I've been there once.

Dr. H revealed some personal information about where he was born and where he was spending his vacation. He did not ask how this information affected Lucille, but did "gratify" her wish to know more about him, making himself less distant.

Immediate Challenging Disclosures

Dr. H used only two immediate challenging disclosures, for example:

Session 4   C: I can't believe the time has gone by. (both laugh)

T: Careful. *I'm not too, I'm not too good with time.* Remember you throw yourself into self-doubt and we could be here for two hours.

C: Well, it seems it's passed awful quick.

Dr. H seemed uncomfortable with this disclosure (as he did with the other one of this type). He shifted the blame to Lucille, rather than dealing with her comment openly. It should be noted that Dr. H was always quite late for sessions, but Lucille never complained and in fact said that the lateness did not bother her. Perhaps Dr. H was feeling apologetic when the subject of time came up, because instead of dealing with Lucille's comment as a reflection of the session being good and going fast, he responded defensively. Lucille felt unheard and repeated herself, after which Dr. H changed the topic.

On the other hand, Dr. H may have been doing something like a similarity disclosure, in which he essentially said, "This is just the way I am. You'll have to accept me as is." Hence, Dr. H communicated to Lucille that he did not think he was perfect, but accepted his flaws, which subtly encouraged her to do the same.

Immediate Reassuring Disclosures

The therapist used only one immediate reassuring disclosure and that was at termination during the final session.

T: We, we have reached the end (C: MmHmm) now. And I'm, and I'm, you shared with me some very meaningful feelings about our work, right at the beginning of this hour. (C: MmHmm) And I wondered if there's any others that you need to share with me as we finally . . .

C: No, well I sa-, I said it so that I would be sure to get it in. (C: Laughs) So that was the main . . .

T: And I appreciate very much the kindness and courtesy you've put into that work. It's been very useful to me. *And I've enjoyed working with you. It's been a real pleasure. I've had my secret ups and downs not knowing for sure how well we were doing. Taking responsibility for that of course.* (C: MmHmm) *But I feel increasingly positive and strong* (C: MmHmm) *in my convictions about* (C: MmHmm) *the way we worked and that the nature of our relationship* (C: MmHmm) *has felt quite companionable to me.* (C: MmHmm). *And I appreciate that.* (C: I do too) Great. I, I'm quite confident that things will continue to go well.

Dr. H seemed to want to leave Lucille feeling positive about the therapy. He revealed that he had experienced some doubts, but apparently did not feel that it was appropriate to deal with those doubts with Lucille during the therapy. Alternatively, Dr. H may have revealed these doubts at the last minute, not so that they could work on them, but so that Lucille would realize that he too felt unsure of himself occasionally.

Summary of Case 3

Dr. H seemed comfortable and expert in using indirect disclosing interventions that subtly challenged her to accept herself. He was less comfortable using the immediate disclosures.

His greater use and comfort with disclosing rather than immediate disclosures did not seem to be related to Dr. H's theoretical orientation, given that he employed both psychoanalytic and behavioral techniques where he felt them appropriate. Rather his preference seemed to be related to his somewhat indirect style of communication, where he provided a message and the client had to struggle to understand its meaning, reminiscent of Milton Erikson's style (Haley, 1973).

Use of the disclosing type was also probably related to Lucille's style. She was rarely in an exploratory state, so immediate disclosures may not have been appropriate. Rather, she was typically in nonexploratory, particularly whining, self-pitying, "I can't do it" states. This type of client can be hard to deal with, because therapists might feel like giving up on them. Especially given her age, there might be a tendency for a therapist to feel that she could not change because her self-pitying style was so ingrained. Yet the similarity and strategy disclosures did work well for her, first to suggest that others felt as she did and then to suggest alternative coping mechanisms.

Conclusions

A comparison of the disclosures in these two cases is particularly interesting since two therapists used very different types of disclosures. Dr. A used mostly immediate disclosures, which fit his open, direct style. These immediate disclosures worked well with Sandy, since she was insight-oriented and willing to work on the relationship. Dr. A's unique type of disclosure was to admit that he was stuck, thus encouraging Sandy to take more of the lead in getting them "unstuck." Dr. H, on the other hand, used mostly disclosing similarity disclosures, which indicated that he had negative characteristics but accepted them within himself. These similarity disclosures fit his indirect style and worked well to disrupt Lucille's whiny, helpless stance. Both the "stuck" disclosures and the disclosing similarity disclosures appeared to have a paradoxical effect. Without directly telling the clients to do something, these disclosures indirectly suggested that the clients might consider taking more responsibility and changing.

Both of these therapists used themselves as models to encourage their clients to think in new ways about themselves. Perhaps their helpfulness ratings of their disclosures were lower because they made themselves vulnerable to their clients by revealing their own feelings. It is probably more difficult to judge how a client reacts to disclosures about oneself than to other interventions. Clients, however, really valued the therapists' disclosures. Not only did the objective data (helpfulness ratings, experiencing ratings) indicate their effectiveness, but the examples clearly indicated that the clients got unstuck and went on to explore feelings and coping strategies.

The caution should be repeated, of course, that disclosures, even in these two cases, were extremely rare events. Clients may have valued disclosures even more because they were allowed such few glimpses into the therapists' private worlds.

Types of Disclosures

The disclosure types seemed to function like other response modes. The immediate reassuring type of disclosure (reassuring the client with the therapist's immediate feelings or reactions to the therapy or therapeutic relationship) seemed similar to approval. The therapist, however, offered what he was feeling so that the client felt less isolated and alone in being the only one to reveal information. The immediate challenging disclosures (challenging the client by presenting the therapist's immediate feelings or reactions) seemed similar to confrontations, but may be a softer way to confront someone. In effect, therapists took responsibility for how they felt about the client's behavior. Disclosing facts were close to information; disclosing feelings functioned in the same way as reflections of feelings (paraphrase); and disclosing strategies seemed similar to direct guidance. The only disclosure type that was unique was the disclosing similarity type. When therapists revealed ways in which they were similar to clients, this appeared to enable clients to feel less alone. If others feel similarly, the client is not so different (Yalom, 1975).

Relation to Theory

In relation to the controversy over the usefulness of disclosure, these data indicate that disclosures can be a very effective way of intervening with some clients. Based on the clients' helpfulness ratings, experiencing levels, and comments about the disclosures, disclosures appeared to be very memorable and useful. There was no evidence that the "gratification" of the disclosures interfered with the transference in these brief therapies. Disclosures did seem to reduce the status of the therapist, which was positive in that the clients felt less scared and more equal with the therapist, thus enhancing the working relationship. Thus, these data provide some support for the humanistic theorists who advocate the use of therapist disclosure.

12

Therapist Interpretation

Clara E. Hill, Barbara J. Thompson, & James R. Mahalik

In psychoanalytic theory (e.g., Blanck, 1966; Freud, 1961 [1914]; Fromm-Reichmann, 1950), therapist interpretation has been viewed as the central technique for producing self-knowledge and change. In information-processing theory (e.g., Levy, 1963), therapist interpretation is thought to be effective because it presents a discrepancy between the view of the therapist, which influences the client to change in the direction of the therapist. This discrepancy enables the client to relabel and reconstrue his/her perceptions. Thus, although these two theories postulate different mechanisms through which interpretation influences change, both agree that interpretation is an important therapist technique.

In the present study, therapist interpretation was found to be helpful in every case, supporting past empirical and clinical literature (see Spiegel & Hill, 1989). The manner in which interpretation was used, however, differed across cases, once again confirming the need to study it within an individual case.

We will examine the interpretations within one case to gain a more in-depth understanding of when and how interpretation was used. Case 8 was selected for this chapter because the client, Sophia, provided the most dramatic example of how understanding an interpretive theme enabled her to think and behave differently. The theme (see Chapter 10) was that Sophia's difficulties were due to the inadequate parenting she received as a child. The resolution was that she could learn to parent herself.

In this chapter, we will excerpt every interpretation related to this theme in the therapy sessions, as well as references to the theme in the therapist post-session interviews. Using this data, we will speculate about why Dr. R chose to intervene when she did and assess how the client responded to the interpretations.

Two criteria were used to identify interpretations that fit the interpretive theme. First, an intervention had to have been judged as an interpretation by the response modes judges. In the response modes system (Hill, 1985), interpretation was defined as a therapist statement that goes beyond what the client has overtly recognized and provides reasons, alternative meanings, or new frameworks for feelings, behaviors, or personality; it may establish connections between seemingly isolated statements or events; interpret defenses, feelings, resistance, or transference; or indicate themes, patterns, or causal relationships in behavior or personality, or relate present events to past events. The second step was that the three of us had to agree that a given interpretation fit the interpretive theme of inadequate parenting. Of 89 interpretations used by Dr. R, 54 fit the interpretive theme and were included in this chapter. In the excerpts, the interpretations are underlined.

Session 1

The first session was spent covering Sophia's target complaints. Toward the end, in response to a question about her mother, Sophia gave a carefully edited glimpse of her childhood:

C: My mother had 16 children and my father died when I was 10. She had nine of us still at home and we lived on a farm and we didn't have much money. And she got social security and a welfare supplement and, but she didn't care for us. She didn't take care of us. She had been married when she was 14 and never had a young life and she didn't know how to handle money and didn't know how to discipline children. And, and the older three at home were all boys and they were big strapping teenagers. And she uh couldn't deal with us, so she just went on her merry way, had a good time and she went drinking and with friends and sometimes she'd not be home for three days. She didn't buy us food even. She was very poor. And uh eventually, my older brothers and sisters made an issue of it and we were taken from her by child welfare at that point. We were going to be placed in homes and our older brothers and sisters divvied us up and uh I went to live with my sister who was about, let's see, she's 13, 15 years older than me and that was a horrible experience for me.

T: Hmm. But you were 10? So that your life before that was, sounds rather miserable.

C: But I wasn't miserable. (T: Oh?) I was happy. I belonged. (T: Oh.) I belonged there (T: Yes) and I've never felt that since.

T: *I would imagine then you long back to that time before 10 when you, when you belonged.*

C: Yeah, right, cause there were all of us and we were, well, we were all in the same boat. We were poor and we were uncared for and we didn't have anything other kids did. But that never bothered me 'til, (T: Hmm) I never even thought about those things.

On the videotape review, Dr. R indicated that her intention for this interpretation was to clarify and intensify feelings rather than to promote insight. So, in this early exploration of the family history, Dr. R encouraged Sophia to talk about her childhood experiences but did not link these to her present troubles. Dr. R seemed to be gathering data to form hypotheses that later developed into the interpretive theme.

Sessions 2-5

During the next four sessions, Sophia talked extensively about her ex-husband and children. She did not talk about her childhood, nor did Dr. R make any interpretations related to the theme. In the post-session review after session five, Dr. R speculated about whether she should interpret the effects of the past to Sophia. She decided that bringing up the effects of Sophia's past would not be beneficial since there was not enough time to deal with it.

T: I keep seeing Sophia's face, which is a child's face. It seems to me that she's not allowing much into her consciousness. I have to remember that anger, which she now doesn't make much of, toward her mother and her sister. She keeps saying that her sister was a good woman and her mother couldn't help it or that they tried. I'm inclined to let sleeping dogs lie because they're not part of her present life really. It's not important to her, so let her leave them in peace. I may conceivably do that as a matter of fact because we don't have that much time together. I don't want to drag up mother and sister. I don't think bringing it up would pay off in terms of the time limit. I would do it without any question, I would keep my eye and ear peeled for anything that would be relevant, if we had indefinite time. But I wouldn't want to bring it up unless I could really have a chance to work with what I suspect is her repressed fury and that would take quite a bit of time. If it comes up, I'll have to deal with it, probably in a supportive way, along the lines of, "I don't see how you could help but be infuriated by the way you were neglected and treated."

Session 6

This segment occurred toward the end of the session and is related to Sophia's discussion of her fear of getting involved with a man who invited her out to dinner.

T: Is that what you mean when you say that you're afraid of getting out of control, (C: Oh no, oh no, no) afraid of getting out of control sexually?

C: No, emotionally, emotionally depending on somebody, (T: Mm-Hmm) um, (Pause = 10 seconds) having a need, and not for emotional stuff, and not being, and another person who is supposed to be capable of giving that to you, can't give it or won't give it or doesn't have it.

T: And that's what happened with your husband? (C: Pause = 4 seconds) You're afraid that might happen with this man?

C: Pause = 3 seconds. Any man.

T: And you don't have any confidence that you can do that for yourself?

C: Do what?

T: Well you know, uh you say you need it from another person. I don't know why you can't do that.

C: Yeah, okay. That's why, that's why I don't want to get involved because I'm okay when I'm alone. I'm not dependent on anybody.

T: Pause = 6 seconds. But then you're lonely. And you want somebody.

C: Pause = 16 seconds.

T: *Is it like uh you're afraid that if you let a li-, a little trickle in, the floodgates will open?*

C: Yeah. Pause = 13 seconds.

T: *It's something I guess you wanted so much as a child.* (C: Pause = 17 seconds) *And now it's really hard to learn that other people are just, just grown up people like you and not mothers or fathers to you.* (C has a puzzled expression) You don't understand?

C: Yeah, I understand. I uh, (Pause = 3 seconds) you, you mean that I want somebody to care for me, take care of me like a father would? I uh, I, I don't think that's uh . . .

T: You don't think you want that?

C: No. (T: You just want uh . . .) Cause [ex-husband] was kind of like that.

T: He was?

C: Yeah, he, he took care of me, sort of physical needs and all and would pat me on the back every once in a while when I did something. But he also disciplined me and disapproved of me and . . .

In the post-session review, Dr. R said,

T: I related some of that back to her childhood and wanting to be taken care of when she was saying that she was afraid of being in charge and the "normal parental relationship" of somebody in charge, she really had not had. God knows about this father, I think that's so complex that I don't want to spend time going into it. But she surely didn't have somebody she could rely on and sort of snuggle into. There was something about the interpretation that she rejected, but I'm not sure what it was. I would expect she would forget the interpretation really. I don't expect her to jump up and down with glee to interpretations. I think it will come up again only if she finds herself in a relationship with somebody or if she were in therapy long enough to let this relationship with this man who invited her out to dinner continue, then it might come up, but it depends on what he does.

The context for this first interpretation was the discussion of the fear of becoming involved in a relationship. Dr. R took Sophia's stated fear of losing control, amplified it, and then linked it to the inadequate parenting theme. This was the only time since the first session that Dr. R made an interpretation related to the effects of Sophia's childhood. Sophia's initial reaction to the interpretation was confusion, perhaps because the interpretation was too deep or far from her experience. She could not understand what Dr. R meant about her wanting parenting since the parenting she had received from her ex-husband was so clearly inappropriate. After "planting" the idea that Sophia's problems in relationships were related to her childhood experiences, Dr. R dropped it. Rather than clarifying the interpretation further, she shifted the focus because she felt Sophia was not ready to deal with her childhood issues in the therapy.

Interestingly, although Dr. R had just stated after the last session that she would not pursue the parenting theme because of the short-term nature of the work, she tentatively began to approach the theme in the very next session. We would speculate that Dr. R felt that the material presented by Sophia was too central and important to ignore. Further, Sophia seemed genuinely interested in trying to understand why she was so afraid of getting into a relationship.

Session 7

This segment came towards the end of the session. Sophia was talking about her ex-husband:

C: I guess he really can't say or do all that much (T: Hmm) except criticize me.

T: Is that so terrible? Look at how you criticize yourself.

C: Not really, it's not very terrible.

T: It can't be worse, can it?

C: I'm not so critical of myself.

T: Oh? You said you're spoiled rotten.

C: It, well sometimes I feel, sometimes not always, (Pause = 7 seconds) uh my life is easy and that's what it is, my life is easy. I mean, I've been coasting for years (T: Well, that's great!) and that's spoiled rotten to me. (laughs)

T: *Well, you certainly had a hard enough childhood, so that it doesn't uh,* (C: Well, that's probably why I feel this way) yeah, *you can't take it for granted that that's the way life is* (C: Yeah) *easy.*

C: Yeah, I'm sort of always waiting for something bad to happen.

Four minutes later, continuing the same theme:

T: *I wonder if this uh feeling that it's hard to wait is what you mean really when you say you're spoiled rotten?* (C: Mmm) *You know, that you, you have to have it right away the way you want it. And that sounds a little like a spoiled kid,* (C: Yeah) *even though you were not a spoiled kid.*

C: Yeah, I do want it right now and all of it. (laughs) (Pause = 4 seconds) But I do wait. (T: Yes) I do wait. (T: MmHmm, Yeah) So it's just my internal feelings.

T: MmHmm, yeah, so you know you can wait. (C: Yeah, Pause = 6 seconds) I notice you just sat back and relaxed.

C: So I'm not as impatient as I feel myself to be.

Dr. R was again the one to bring up the interpretive theme and this time expanded further on it. Dr. R interpreted Sophia's self-criticism as a reflection of a difficult childhood and a desire to be satisfied immediately. Sophia accepted this interpretation ("That's probably why I feel this way") and became more relaxed, showing that the interpretation gave her control over her feelings.

Session 8

In the middle of the session, Sophia was talking about what it was like for her to go to bars to meet men:

C: Just being put down like that (T: MmHmm) and made to feel like, (T: MmHmm) it wasn't cool to love your kids and want to be around them or to go home because you had to get up in the morning to get your kids off (T: Hmm) or, or not invite men to your house because that's just something you don't do because you've got a houseful of kids. (T: MmHmm, MmHmm) I mean, you know, those, that's how I am. (T: MmHmm) And I don't want to change that. I mean, I, I made a decision about those things. I don't want those things in my life and, and yet I've been put down for them and I think maybe I don't fit anywhere, you know.

T: Is that, is that how it feels sometimes?

C: Yeah, (T: Hmm) yeah. Pause = 10 seconds.

T: *Well, I should think that you might have felt like that as a child quite a lot with your sister and all.*

C: Yeah, I, I think that's probably why I'm so sensitive to (T: Yeah) fitting in and being part of a group and feeling accepted. (T: Yeah) But, but what I do (sighs) because I'm so sensitive, if someone hurts me, I stay away. (sighs)

Sophia shifted slightly to talking about her fears of being away for the summer in a segment 10 minutes later:

> C: What if something happened to one of the kids (T: Hmm) and their doctors weren't by or that, the medical facilities in Ocean City aren't terrific, or what if I'm working and somebody got careless, you know, just junk. I know that's junk. Those, those things don't happen. And I, and I take all the precautions. And that's all I can do.
>
> T: Pause = 15 seconds. *There's nobody there who will take care, hmm?* Is that your feeling? *There's no good mother or father around to be sure that nothing happens to the kids or you?*
>
> C: Yeah, maybe that's it. (Pause = 5 seconds). It's, my house is like my (sighs) security blanket.
>
> T: Hmm. Well, I regret to say that it's time for us to stop. But I'm really curious about this feeling of uh, being nervous. And maybe you could notice it and see what comes uh of being nervous. And maybe you could notice it and see what comes to your mind about what it is you're afraid of.
>
> C: Okay. It might just be, you know, being very tired and having a lot on my mind too.
>
> T: Could be part of it. But it, it's too bad if you can't get to sleep, isn't it? (C: Yeah) Yeah. I think it would be helpful if you would notice if there are some more dreams and what goes through your mind when you can't sleep. You say you were like this in your marriage (C: Yeah) before your divorce. (C: Yeah, yeah) *And that there it was very clear that there was no good father and good mother around except you.*
>
> C: My ex-husband was there. (T: Yeah) Un certainty, the uncertainty.

In the post-session interview, Dr. R said,

> T: She surprised me at the end of the session by saying that she'd been extremely nervous since Sunday. I really don't know what that's about. I did all I could with it since it was so much toward the end. Just put it off til next time. But I'm still kind of unhappy that we had to leave it. I said to her what seems to me the crux of it and that is the uncertainty of not having had any adult that she can rely on in her life. That includes me since I'm obviously going out of her life fairly soon. I went on a fishing expedition into her childhood and it did not result in anything and so I did not pursue it. But I noticed that I had gone on a fishing expedition and had failed to get a fish and so let it go. But the reason I

thought of it just then is that I suspect I will have to go fishing again and that it will have to do with the lack in her life of a benevolent parental figure. In fact, I'm really curious that she's not psychotic. I think that probably if one took enormous time to take a history, one would find something better in her life, like some aunt or uncle and also that the father must have been a more stable character. What she really said, which impressed me at the time and still does is that while she was at home before her father died, there was a huge group of kids that seemed to have taken the place of what is ordinarily parents. The fact that they didn't have any good clothes or anything and that they were much poorer than the other kids didn't matter because "we were together."

Dr. R's first interpretation around the parenting theme in Session 8 involved how Sophia's early experiences with her sister and parents may have influenced her present feelings of not belonging. Later, Dr. R reintroduced the interpretation that Sophia rejected in Session 6 that Sophia had missed out on "proper parenting," but expanded the interpretation to include Sophia's fear that there was no one around to take care of either her or her children. Although Sophia did not reject these interpretations as she had in the sixth session, neither did she enthusiastically embrace them or elaborate on the content of the theme.

Session 9

There were several interpretations in this session. The first excerpt came from near the beginning of the session after Sophia mentioned that her ex-husband gave her $500 to help her with a financial problem. In the segment, they also refer to a situation that had occurred during the week in which a man asked Sophia to meet him at a bar and then didn't show up, sending Sophia into a depressive tailspin.

C: I was greatly relieved [when ex-husband gave her $500]. I cried.

T: You cried? (C: Yeah) From relief?

C: From gratitude.

T: Oh, I notice you made a little face when you say gratitude.

C: Something else.

T: What else?

C: I felt cared for.

T: Yes and that was a good feeling.

C: It's so rare that I have that feeling. (Cries)

T: *Hmm, I guess it's not, it's rare in your life that you've had it, especially when you were a child and needed it the most.*

C: (cries) Yeah, it was like I was paying my own way always.

T: I guess you were. You haven't allowed that to really strengthen you as mu-, as much as it might.

C: (cries) I, yeah, that's right. That's right. I think you're right, but why? What did I miss?

T: *Well, you missed being cared for as a child, which I'm sure every child h-, wants.*

C: Well, how come it hasn't made me, what, I forget your word.

T: *Well, I said that you didn't allow that fact that you, you cared for yourself and paid your own way, so to speak, to strengthen you as it might have, to know in yourself that you're a strong person and can do a lot of the caring that you need for yourself.* Of course it's not as nice as having somebody drop by and give you $500. I think that was very nice too, hmm? Even though he could well spare it, hmm? And he owes you a lot more.

C: I get what you mean finally. Sometimes (T: You do?) I'm like that and I'm proud of it.

T: Yes, sometimes you are. (C: Pause = 4 seconds) But when you need it most, you tend to forget it, hmm?

C: (crying and sighing) Pause = 19 seconds. I-, it's emotional things that I need that I can't get out of myself. (T: Mmm, sure) The other things, you know, the physical things and all . . .

T: You can do for yourself.

C: I can do it, yeah.

T: But we can't uh get the affection that you want from somebody else. You think (C: Yeah) you do though get it? I mean even though this man didn't show up, uh God knows why, he certainly did like you the first time.

C: Yeah. (Pause = 6 seconds). And the guy was confused. (T: Who?) The guy I snuggled up to (T: Oh) and he pushed me away cause I've always been very hard on him about being married and going out. (T: Pause = 13 seconds) Why, why am I feeling like this now? Why?

T: *It doesn't take much, I think, to remind you, I think to remind you of how you felt when your sister was nasty to you.* (C: Pause = 5 seconds) Well, I don't know if she was nasty, but she was cruel.

C: Yeah, she was cruel. And that, are you saying that, then that brings back the feelings of helplessness and hopelessness?

T: Yes, *and that brings back, brings back also the, the desertion that you must have felt from your mother.*

C: And my ex-husband.

T: Yes, *so you have a lot to be angry about really (C: Yeah) about having been deserted by people you could expect to be cared for by.*

C: Yeah, but instead of getting angry, I get low, (T: Yeah) depressed. (T: MmHmm. Pause = 17 seconds) Uh I, I've been depressed for a long time now.

This was the first occasion that Sophia expressed curiosity in the effects of her childhood, when she said, "What did I miss?" When Dr. R responded that she missed realizing that she could care for herself, Sophia responded that she finally understood. The interpretive theme began to make sense to Sophia.

They continued talking for a few minutes about Sophia's anxiety over leaving the safety and haven of her own home for a temporary home for the summer. When they picked up again on the theme in the next excerpt, Sophia seemed more accepting of the interpretation and elaborated on it.

C: When I'm feeling like this, I, I can just stay home or I can run home. (T: Oh) And if I'm there and have problems, I'm not sure it would give me the same feeling. (T: Oh) I haven't been there, I don't know. I haven't run to it.

T: Maybe you could run to yourself, regardless of where you are.

C: Pause = 3 seconds. How does that work? I, I know people who do that. (T: MmHmm, MmHmm) Are there tricks? Can you be taught to do that?

T: I don't know any tricks. But perhaps if you can just remember that you have been an extraordinarily strong person in spite of the fact that you were deserted by your mother and then that your sister really treated you badly, that in spite of that you've come through. And that your husband also treated you badly, you came through anyway. And maybe you can simply remember those coming through times.

C: Pause = 18 seconds. Then when I felt threatened or hurt, I could give myself a mental uh cue like or words to say to remind me that I will survive this too? I don't want to just survive.

Again, in this segment, Dr. R reassured Sophia that she could begin to parent herself. About five minutes later, Sophia shifted to talking about the sister who raised her:

C: I always wanted to forgive her desperately, (T: MmHmm) needed to forgive her (T: Yeah, sure) that I hated her. And I did hate her.

T: *Well and maybe there is some forgiveness in your heart when you think that she was treated very badly by your mother just as you were.*

C: She wasn't. (T: Oh, she wasn't?) She was married when my father died, already gone from home.

T: *But your mother doesn't sound as if she'd been a very warm mother to anyone.*

C: My mother's much warmer than my sister. (T: Oh?) Yeah, she has, my mother has the capacity. (T: She has?) She has the capacity. She's, she's a stupid woman. She's not bright. And she's easier to forgive (T: MmHmm) because there is warmth from her. (T: MmHmm) Um when she takes a new baby in her arms, (T: MmHmm) you can see that she really feels (T: MmHmm, MmHmm) this.

After talking more about her sister and mother, Sophia asked,

C: So you think that when I, when I'm rejected or my feelings are hurt, I become my child again?

T: Yeah, *I think it must bring up all those memories that, of a very difficult childhood.*

C: What can I do about that?

T: I think you can remember that you're not that child anymore, (C: Hmm, Pause = 7 seconds) that you're a very strong person that put up with your sister and left home. And you got out of your marriage when it got too much.

C: Pause = 13 seconds. So even going to the beach is threatening me. (T: Yes, apparently) And I am acting like a child.

T: No, no matter how old you get, even when you're old like me, there is still a child in everybody.

C: I, I, I, I know that. And that's cute sometimes. I mean that's very attractive. I like that. And that's part of you. You can't, you can't get rid of that child.

In the review of session 9, Dr. R said:

T: I referred more to her past in this session than I have for a long time, except when she gave me a brief history. It seemed to me that her past was showing and really having its toll on her. One of the most useful things that I could do was point out how inevitably her past must come up and make her more aware of her feelings and the origins of them in an extraordinarily difficult past. It's my experience, and therefore belief, that heightened awareness of one's feelings is by itself helpful. The ability to observe one's feelings automatically without taking control is a helpful thing to a person.

In this session, Dr. R presented the proper parenting theme several times and interpreted Sophia's lack of being cared for as a child as influencing her present feelings and reactions to people and situations. Sophia indicated that she finally understood the interpretation and asked Dr. R a lot of questions about why and how this all came about.

Further, Dr. R went beyond the interpretation of the relationship of her present difficulties with her inadequate parenting and suggested that Sophia could run to herself, giving her some solutions rather than allowing Sophia to use the inadequate parenting as an excuse for her difficulties. In conjunction with these solutions, Dr. R continually focused on Sophia's strength and ability to come through difficult times. That is, once the interpretive theme was heard, Dr. R moved into an action or planning stance, which probably made it safer for Sophia to stay with the interpretation.

Session 10

Again, there were several interpretations in this session. This segment occurred at the very beginning of the session.

C: I've been thinking about why it hurts me to love [ex-husband]. Sometimes it doesn't hurt. Sometimes it's okay. (T: Mmm, MmHmm) It hurts when I'm needy and I want more from him. That, that's . . .

T: Okay, so it hurts when he doesn't give what you want.

C: Yeah, right. (T: MmHmm) But, but only then, so that, (T: Mmm) so that . . . Pause = 3 seconds.

T: *It isn't the loving,* (C: That's right) *it's the need.*

C: Um and it's not him either that hurts me. It's just my lack of having what I, not having what I need from somebody.

T: Or you think you need it from somebody. (C: Yeah, right, right) You don't know that you can give it to yourself. (C: Pause = 5 seconds, Oh) *You don't really think you have that much to give to anybody, including yourself.*

C: Pause = 4 seconds. I feel like I give it to other people.

T: Yeah, I know you do. You give it to your children.

C: And friends. (T: MmHmm, Pause = 8 seconds). See, I think I'm good to myself.

After some more discussion of Sophia's strengths, Dr. R reminded Sophia that they would be ending in two weeks and suggested that Sophia could get in touch with her after a six-month break imposed by the research team.

C: Thank you. I'm glad you told me that because I was feeling like well, (T: Well, I'm . . .) like it's gonna end (T: Yeah) and I, and it's been good for me.

T: Well that's good. I'm very glad that it has. Uh but I, I, I think that you have felt a little bit stronger in yourself. (C: Yeah) And that's uh, really what we can do in this short term is to uh make you aware of the uh tools that you have in yourself. (C: Yeah) *And I think uh you did a very good piece of work on this question of your husband, uh your feeling that loving him hurts you. And then you discovered that it isn't the loving him that hurts, it's the need* (C: Yeah) *that you think you have.*

C: Yeah, and that surfaces when he is around.

The next excerpt begins 20 minutes later. Sophia has been discussing her relationships with men:

C: I need to be liked (T: Hmm) and (Pause = 4 seconds) enjoyed and appreciated. Well, um I like people to enjoy my intelligence or my sensitivity (T: MmHmm) or . . .

T: *Well, what I'm thinking is that you don't really know enough that they do, that you're not sure enough that they do. And that makes you then somehow feel very depressed.* (C: MmHmm) *And if somebody doesn't show up for what was possibly a date or it seemed that it was* (C: Yeah) *when he didn't show, then you felt terrible. You forget all the intelligence that other people think you have and that you know you have.*

C: Sort of goes out the window.

T: Yes. *It's not surprising that it goes out the window when you um think back on your history uh with your sister being so mean to you and your father dying and your mother being not much comfort.* Or am I wrong about that?

C: Yeah, you're right. Um. (Pause = 6 seconds). (T: Hmm?) I have self esteem, (T: Mmm) but it's newfound. (T: MmHmm) And it's easily shattered.

Dr. R continued linking Sophia's present with her past and also reinforced Sophia's strengths. Sophia seemed more able to accept and elaborate on the interpretations in this session. Further, Dr. R seemed to be preparing Sophia for termination and being on her own, encouraging her to rely on herself.

Session 11

This segment occurred right at the beginning of the session. This is the first time Sophia clearly expressed a full awareness and acceptance of the interpretive theme. She was able to make the cognitive shift from seeing herself as spoiled to an awareness that she was too hard on herself.

T: I was wondering whether um you felt that what you had come for was in any measure at all accomplished or whether it, it had changed, that what you had really wanted?

C: Well, I, I think I'm getting there. I think the, the (T: MmHmm) sessions (T: MmHmm) have been very helpful for me. (T: MmHmm) Last week didn't seem to be so powerful, (T: Hmm) but when I got home I was relating the things you said last week to the things you said previously (T: Hmm) and you keep going back to something uh parent-child thing. (T: Hmm, MmHmm) And that makes sense to me (T: MmHmm) that my parent is really too tough on me and, (T: That means you?) Yeah, yeah, my own, yeah, my parent is tough on my child, right? And uh, and that's true. It's, I've never seen myself as being so hard on myself, (T: Hmm, MmHmm) always was more aware of my child in me

(T: Hmm) being spoiled or not doing the things that I'm supposed to do. And yet I do.

T: Yes, you do.

After just a few minutes, Dr. R asked,

T: What do you attribute it to that you feel better?

C: Um, well, you're never negative with me. And I, and I, I respect that you, (T: Hmm) I mean that helps. (T: Hmm) You don't ever seem to disapprove of anything. And there are very few people around me who are like that.

T: Hmm. And you could be that way yourself.

C: That's right, that's right.

Thus, Sophia essentially said that being reparented in a better way helped her, to which Dr. R quickly reaffirmed that Sophia could also parent herself.

Sophia then shifted the topic to relating some long, detailed, somewhat boring descriptions of interactions with her daughter. After letting Sophia go on for a long time, Dr. R finally changed the topic to asking about Sophia's mother. All the interpretations about her childhood seemed to have "chipped away" Sophia's defenses and she poured forth the real story of her father's attempted suicide and subsequent hospitalization in a mental hospital prior to his death and her mother's neglect and abandonment of her after her father's death. (See Chapter 10, pages 241-5.) During this portion, Dr. R did not interpret, but used open question and paraphrase to help Sophia cathart. They continued:

T: So you feel that you have that potentiality [suicide] in you?

C: Yeah. (T: Yeah) That's strange for me to think that, but I do.

T: *Not so strange.* (C: No?) *Well, is your mother uh and, and your father were very depressed I gather* (C: Yeah) *from time to time,* (Pause = 6 seconds) *hmm, so it's no wonder that you fear.*

C: Pause = 5 seconds. That I fear depression?

T: *Yeah, that you fear depression and that you fear ending up like your father.*

C: Pause = 8 seconds. I don't see myself anywhere near as good a person as my father.

T: Oh really, you don't? He was so warm-hearted you said.

C: No, he was such a hard worker.

T: Oh, and you're not?

C: I'm all but decadent, (T: Oh) I mean physically, you know, but other things . . .

T: Do you look like your father?

C: No, (T: Hmm) no, I look like my mother's family. (T: Hmm, Hmm, Pause = 6 seconds) More I'm, I'm scared of ending up like my mother.

T: Ah, and that's what you think about that you could be an alcoholic?

C: Or stupid (T: Oh) or noncaring.

T: Well, you know you're not stupid. And you know you care. (T: Pause = 4 seconds) *But I guess you forget it sometimes cause your memory of your mother must be very potent.*

C: Yeah, my, my sister said something, my oldest sister said something to me one time which was minor. And I got very upset about it. And I kept trying to figure out why it upset me so. And it was because of my mother. It reminded me, she made me feel like my mother. (T: Hmm) And I hated that.

T: Yes, sure, you hated that. *And you felt so sorry for your father I guess, felt guilty toward him somewhat because you should have stopped him from taking the pills, from slitting his wrists somehow.*

C: I feel sorry for my mother mostly. I mean, I don't hate her. I hate what she was like and what she did to me. (T: Hmm) But I feel sorry for her because she's not bright. And she doesn't, she never had the opportunities.

T: Hmm. I, I regret it is time for us to stop.

C: I had, I had never thought about these things. I've thought about them, but I've never shared them, with very few people. And I never tried to make any sense out of them for me.

In the review, Dr. R said,

T: It was very important and charged and emotional for us both. It's too bad it comes so toward the end. I'm sure that's always true, always too late in life. During the first three quarters of the session I had the feeling that we were marking time. I didn't want to stir up too much, but I brought up mother because it seemed like it was time that we should move on. I was surprised there was so much emotion about all this because we had not stopped that long over history in the beginning and I hadn't gone into detail. I remember making a conscious decision that we couldn't spend too much time over history. So I was surprised to hear about these dramatic events with the father's death. I felt a kind of horror for her, of how terrible that must have been. I thought it was important for her to be as honest as she could with herself. How she remembered and what she thought now about these things. I wanted her to come as close to her feelings that she has when she lets herself think about these things and to remember them because it seemed to me that she doesn't do that with anybody at all. I wanted to draw out her feelings so that she wouldn't be so scared. It's very natural that she must be worried about herself having an inheritance, genetic as well as example of a father and mother neither of whom were very cheery characters. Naturally she must worry about herself, but she has enormous reservoirs of strength which she's proved. I think it was helpful that I went back to her mother which led her to talk about father and brought her back to the disappointments of her early life when the mother said she wanted her sister, not her.

It is interesting that all this material came out so late in the therapy. In the sessions leading up to this, Dr. R was helping Sophia tie things together and figure out a direction for her life. Undoubtedly, all the interpretations about the parenting theme leading up to this session uncovered a lot of the layers of defense that Sophia had built up around these childhood experiences, so that a simple question about the mother unleashed all the pent-up emotions. In this session, Dr. R tried to give Sophia a framework to help her make sense of how her childhood experiences affected her, providing her with an explanation for her fears.

Session 12

This segment occurred at the beginning of the session.

T: It was very, something very important that you brought up though I thought, (C: Yeah) very important. I'm glad you did. Are you?

C: I don't know if I can, (Pause = 9 seconds) if I can use it, (T: MmHmm) yeah, but so far I haven't come up with anything positive. I just feel bad.

T: Bad? (C: Bad) What kind of bad?

C: Uh sad.

T: Hmm, yeah, that was really a terrible loss for you to lose your father. *I think it's important that you should grieve it because I don't know if you did as a child enough.* And I had this feeling I'll tell you. Uh, uh I'm gonna have to check this out with you. *But I have this feeling that you must have blamed your mother for, have for, for your loss of your father.*

C: Pause = 4 seconds. I, I definitely blamed her for committing him and (T: Yeah) didn't think that, that was fair. (T: MmHmm, MmHmm) But, but I've been thinking a lot about it. And in my mind that day he tried to commit suicide was the day he died to me.

T: For you, (C: Yeah, to me) for all intents and purposes. MmHmm.

C: Yeah, yeah, yeah, and I remember very vivid-, vividly. And I've always been upset by his death, any mention of it. (T: MmHmm, MmHmm) I remember trying to sneak down to see him alone. (T: Oh, did you?) He was waked in the house. And I stayed up real late. And I didn't hear any noise. I wanted to go down and see him alone, but (T: Oh) there was always somebody there.

T: Oh, I see. Oh, who was there?

C: S-, uncles and aunts. (T: Mmm) They sat up all night with the body, somebody did.

T: Oh, I see. After he was dead, you went down there to see (C: Yeah) him gone?

C: Yeah, and I remember at the funeral when they put him into the ground, it was awful.

T: Yes. (Pause = 7 seconds). It's, it's uh very natural indeed that a little girl is very attached to her father. *Uh and you, you must have been.* And he had some very good qualities you tell me. (C: Pause = 5 seconds) And then after that in a, in a sense, pretty soon anyway, your home broke up.

C: Pause = 10 seconds.

T: You're shaking your head like.

C: Yeah, like what happened?

T: Pause = 5 seconds. It was a bad loss.

C: Pause = 10 seconds. There were so many of us. And we were treated like, like a herd. Nobody got any kind of (T: Yeah) individual attention.

T: Yes. Pause = 7 seconds. Also not from him, surely not from your mother or your sisters?

C: I, I remember certain ti-, a couple times when he in particular was very tender with me. (T: MmHmm) And I did have an older sister who I counted on who was affectionate with me. (T: MmHmm, MmHmm) And uh, (Pause = 5 seconds), the sister who raised me doesn't like her, that sister. And I was by myself having to keep my mouth shut about that because I think, (Pause = 5 seconds) I still appreciate (T: Yeah, of course) the time she spent with me.

T: MmHmm, MmHmm, well it must be very sad to remember those times when your father was tender with you.

C: Pause = 4 seconds. No, it's not. (T: Yeah) No, it's sad to remember that he was gone.

T: Yeah, MmHmm, (Pause = 6 seconds). *In, in a way, it must have felt to you as a child like a desertion, that he abandoned you, left you behind.*

C: That's what a friend of mine said. And uh (T: It doesn't?) it just felt horrible. I don't remember ever having one thought that I blamed him. (T: Hmm, Pause = 7 seconds) But then, I, I'm trying to think what, you know with my religion, (T: Yes) e-, religion at my house is so harsh. And (T: Yes) you didn't blame people for things. You just sucked it up. (T: MmHmm) And I might have repressed all those feelings because I thought they were bad, really bad to have.

T: Could have been. Could have been. *Anyway uh y-m you were abandoned.* When whoever did it is another question. Of how, whether somebody was to blame or not is another question. *But you were abandoned.*

C: Pause = 7 seconds. I was thinking he was rather a coward (Pause = 4 seconds) to do it when there was a 7-year old in charge at the house.

T: MmHmm. (Pause = 14 seconds.) Yeah, it must have been pretty bad for you. Or you wouldn't probably, hmm?

C: Pause = 7 seconds.

T: Did he have strokes before he uh tried to commit . . .

C: Yeah, he had like 11 strokes all told. Some of them were fairly minor. And some of them were pretty (T: MmHmm, MmHmm) hard. He had been paralyzed. And then his potatoes had frozen in the fields. That was right before he slit his wrists. And he, I knew that he was very upset about them (T: Yeah) because that was his main source of income (T: Yeah) at that point.

T: Yeah, it was very tough. *He may have figured of course that you'd be better of-, you all would be off if he were dead.*

C: Uh that's wonderful. (T: Yeah, Pause = 5 seconds) He could never have thought that, (T: Hmm) intelligently have had that thought (T: Hmm) because he knew what my mother was. My mother was very, very weak and couldn't handle anything.

T: Pause = 14 seconds. You know you, one of the things that you wanted when you came here was to understand better your relationships with men. *And that surely has something to do with your father.*

C: I, I've been thinking, I've been trying to put (Pause = 4 seconds) feelings about my father and the feelings that I've repressed about him, (Pause = 4 seconds) I've tried to see what they do, what they have done in my marriage. And (Pause = 15 seconds) I think every time [ex-husband] let me down, (T: MmHmm, Pause = 5 seconds) I had that same horrible feeling. (T: MmHmm, Mmm) And I reacted on the feeling (Cries). (T: MmHmm, sure) And sometimes it was out of proportion to the act.

T: Pause = 15 seconds. *W-, w-, was it like reliving the loss of your father when he uh let you down?*

C: Yeah, like when, when he wouldn't come home at night. I would, I would sit at the front door and wait for him and be scared to death (T: MmHmm) about what was going to happen (Pause = 4 seconds) (Cries) every night, night after night.

T: *Like that little girl who was abandoned by her father.*

C: Pause = 6 seconds. So then what he was, what he was doing wasn't right to do, (T: Yeah) but my feelings might have been easier to handle if they hadn't been tied up.

T: *Yes, your feelings were the same as that little girl's.*

C: Yeah, Pause = 6 seconds. Will, can I change that now? Can I . . .

T: Pause = 5 seconds. You can change yourself. You don't have to go through it all again.

C: (Cries) Pause = 11 seconds.

T: *It sounds in a way as if you'd married a man who had never grown up himself.* He was, he was so attached to his parents that I think you told me that he had to go home every weekend at first.

C: And he was kind of like my father. (T: He was?) Yeah, (T: Oh) he was brilliant. My father was a self-taught electrical engineer. (T: Yeah, yeah) And [ex-husband] had that in him too. He doesn't have a college education, but he's one of the (T: MmHmm) smartest people I know.

T: MmHmm, MmHmm. (Pause = 13 seconds.) *But it sounds as if you uh needed to marry somebody who would in a way mistreat you and abandon you, treat you badly.* And I don't mean that your father treated you badly. *But his death did.*

C: Hmm, and I should have known that about [ex-husband].

Thus, Dr. R made another link between Sophia's deprived childhood and her current functioning, specifically to her relationship with her ex-husband. They expand that to talking about her relationships with men:

T: It does seem to me that we have barely scratched the surface of uh, of your relationships with men. And that was one of the things that you came about. And we really haven't had time to go in for it because this is the first time that came out your really your grief about your father. And I'm sure that's important, terribly important.

C: Like what, (T: Like . . .) like what can it mean?

T: Well, it's a terrible loss for a little girl (Pause = 7 seconds) that a father in a sense abandoned her in w-, in a way, in a way by his own hand. His suicide was his, his own doing. And that was awful for you. *And then to, to boot to have mother really take him away from you.*

C: And then give me away. (T: Yes) Somebody called me an orphan once. (Laughs) (T: Yes) And I think that's not so. I'm not an orphan, but in a way I am.

T: Yes, MmHmm, yes. (Pause = 12 seconds.) *And so in a way it's not really surprising that uh you expect more of people than they can deliver, like more of your husband, uh, ma-, maybe not more than a normal expectation. But he was a baby in a lot of ways when he married you.*

C: Pause = 12 seconds. Yeah, the men, the grownup men who I've had relationships with since then don't want them from me and I find that refreshing (T: Hmm) I don't have to be their mother.

In the review, the therapist said,

T: I was most helpful by reinforcing the idea that it is better for her to be aware of and grieve about her father and about how she had one hell of a time as a child growing up, that nobody bothered much about her. She told the story about the aunt who said, "It's good to get rid of the kids, to have them out of the way." That hurt. It was important for her that she had one more session after bringing up the thing about her father, to chew it over a little bit and to recognize some more about her two sisters. I heard for the first time about this second sister that she liked. The way that the sisters came in was perhaps the most important of all because they're still alive and part of her life. She can recognize that there are important ties there and that she can exploit these ties.

This session was very painful for the client, as was indicated by her pauses and crying. Dr. R tried to mop up all the feelings brought up in the last session. They continually went back and forth between the present and the past. Sophia again asked Dr. R what she should do and seemed to need the reaffirmation that she was strong and could take care of herself.

Sophia was upset at having to terminate at this time, as indicated by her comments in the session and post-session questionnaire and low scores on her outcome tests at post-therapy. Since so much came up at the end of therapy, it was not possible for Dr. R to leave Sophia with everything resolved. Rather, Dr. R suggested that what Sophia needed to do was to grieve over her father and also to get angry. Although this was scary for Sophia, she reported in the long-term follow-up that the grieving was one of the most important outcomes of the therapy.

Issues Related to the Use of Interpretation

Interaction with Other Techniques

In conjunction with interpretations, Dr. R used approval, closed and open questions, and direct guidance as her intervention strategy for this theme. First, Dr. R was tremendously supportive throughout all interactions related to this theme. Dr. R would continually say that Sophia had come a long way and that she was very strong. Dr. R believed in and accepted Sophia.

Within this supportive context, the rough sequence of events was of catharsis, interpretation, and direct guidance. Through closed and open questions, Dr. R encouraged Sophia to explore and uncover her feelings and reactions to childhood events and present difficulties. During this phase, Dr. R was totally focused on helping Sophia to talk about the situation and reexperience her feelings. The first half of therapy was devoted to this catharsis phase, as was the beginning of each interpretive event within the final sessions. When Sophia had completed the exploration, Dr. R interpreted how Sophia's present difficulties were linked to her troubled background and then followed it immediately with direct guidance about how Sophia could parent herself. So the interpretation of the improper parenting was quickly followed up with how Sophia could compensate for this lack. Thus, exploration led to insight and action, in much the way that Carkhuff (1969) and Egan (1986) postulated. However, for the client to get into exploration, Dr. R used primarily closed and open question rather than reflection of feeling.

Timing

Other than the single interpretation in the first session, Dr. R waited until the middle of therapy before she interpreted the material about Sophia's past. Even then, she was somewhat hesitant to bring it up. She mentioned in the post-therapy reviews that she was worried that there was not time in such a brief therapy to deal with such heavy issues. Sophia kept bringing up related material and made many self-defeating attributions (e.g., "I'm spoiled"). Dr. R began slowly and tentatively to make interpretations. Sophia did not respond enthusiastically to these first interpretations, so Dr. R did not pursue them, but continued to plant the seeds and later developed them more fully.

There was a strong correlation between session number and the number of interpretations, $r(10) = .83, p < .001$, indicating that more interpretations were used toward the end of treatment. The use of more interpretations in the final portion of treatment supports our previous findings (Hill et al., 1983; O'Farrell et al., 1986). These data suggest that a therapist needs time to develop a good relationship, time to generate data to form adequate hypotheses about a client, and also time to assess what the client can tolerate in terms of the type and depth of an interpretation.

Client Incorporation of Theme

The first few times that Dr. R interpreted the parent theme, Sophia resisted and had a hard time accepting it. After a while, however, she not only accepted it but began to use it herself, indicating that she had incorporated the idea as her own.

In session 9, Sophia said, "Then when I feel threatened or hurt, I could give myself a mental cue to remind me that I will survive this too?" Later, in the same session, she said, "So you think that when I'm rejected or my feelings hurt, I become my child again?" In session 11, she said, "I was relating the things you said previously and you keep going back to something uh parent-child thing and that makes sense to me that my parent is really too tough on me." These examples indicate that Sophia had absorbed Dr. R's statements and was beginning to use them. The process was thus educational, in that Dr. R taught Sophia a new way of looking at her situation. Sophia had a lot of questions about the fit, but once she accepted this framework, she could apply it to various portions of her life to make more sense of everything.

Stiles, Elliott, Llewelyn, Firth-Cozens, Margison, Shapiro, and Hardy (1988) proposed a similar assimilation model. They hypothesized that problematic experiences pass through several stages as they are being assimilated by clients: being warded off, entering awareness as unwanted thoughts, becoming clarified as a problem, attracting insight and understanding, and finally contributing to adaptive changes in everyday life. As a result of these cognitive changes, the client goes from feeling vaguely disturbed, to experiencing the content as acutely painful, then as problematic but less distressing, then as merely puzzling, then as understood, and finally as confidently mastered.

Repetition

The client rejected the initial interpretations around the parenting theme. The therapist let the interpretation go for that session, but repeated it throughout the course of the treatment. Dr. R would present the interpretation on the theme almost as an afterthought following a piece of therapeutic work. After a time Dr. R would bring the interpretation more and more into the foreground. Sophia gradually got comfortable with the interpretation and began to respond to it and even expand upon it.

Intuition as a Strategy

Dr. R did not plan to interpret this theme in her treatment plan. Rather, she did what she felt was right at the moment in the therapy. In fact, she mentioned that she did not believe that therapist techniques were particularly useful, believing instead in the curative role of the relationship (See her post-therapy review in Chapter 10).

Interestingly, even though Dr. R did not plan her interpretations, she used them according to common guidelines, such as waiting until the client was ready, using interpretations of moderate depth, and repeating them until Sophia could incorporate them. Thus, although Dr. R seemed to think of the therapy process as an art rather than a science, we would argue that her use of interpretations followed a logical, scientific process. Probably because of her extensive experience, Dr. R could intervene without having to think about the specific components of the response. She had an intuitive grasp of timing and client readiness developed over many years of dealing with clients so that it was second nature with her to know when and how to intervene.

Therapist Initiation of Theme

Dr. R was almost always the one to initiate talking about the childhood, which is interesting given that Dr. R indicated in her reviews that she felt that the client should be the one to determine the topics. Despite her initial reluctance to delve into childhood issues, Dr. R apparently came to believe that Sophia needed to deal with the residuals of her childhood. Perhaps Dr. R felt that Sophia would not bring up her childhood if left on her own, especially given the time limits. Further, Dr. R may have needed to give Sophia permission to discuss her past before Sophia would bring it up, given how shamed she felt by her past. She had rarely if ever mentioned her complete family history to anyone.

Type of Interpretations

Depth of interpretation. The interpretations were not far beyond what the client already recognized. During the first session, Sophia talked about how bad her family background had been, so she was clearly aware that she had not had a wonderful childhood. Further, she was certainly aware that she had problems in her current life. She had not, however, made the connection between her childhood experiences and her current functioning. The interpretations, then, were just slightly beyond what Sophia was aware of and helped her relate previously unconnected parts of her life. This supports the notion that interpretations of moderate depth are more helpful than superficial or deep interpretations (Speisman, 1959) and the psychoanalytic notion of interpreting just beyond the limits of the client's awareness (Fenichel, 1941).

Accuracy of the Theme

Many have questioned whether interpretations need to be accurate or just present a discrepant view from that of the client (e.g., Kelly, 1955; Levy, 1963). In our judgment, the interpretive theme fit with the data presented by the client. A further clue as to the accuracy of the theme was Sophia's obsession with her own and other's parenting styles, which was evidenced in the topics she chose to discuss.

The search for whether an interpretation was accurate does not seem to us to be a fruitful way of looking at the issue. Liebert and Spiegler (1987) indicated that an interpretation can be validated partially by the degree to which the client accepts it as true and partially by whether it leads to changes in the client's behavior. In this case, Sophia clearly accepted the interpretive theme as true, as indicated by her comments in Session 11 and in the post-therapy interview. Further, she made major behavioral changes, in that she lost weight, got a job, and was able to form a lasting relationship with a man. Thus, given that the interpretive theme met both criteria, it was therapeutically valid.

Conclusions

The way in which the interpretive theme developed in this case fits with the literature. Interpretations were presented in a context of approval and support and were interwoven with questions and paraphrases aimed at catharsis and followed by direct guidance. The interpretations themselves were of moderate depth, presented mostly at the second half of treatment, were repeated many times, and seemed to be accurate. The client not only accepted the interpretations but slowly began to incorporate them into her own cognitive system and own them as her own. The interpretive framework helped her to understand herself in a new way and freed her from some of her self-defeating attributions. Further, by being paired with direct guidance, the interpretations enabled the client to change in some fundamental ways.

PART IV

CONCLUSIONS

13

Integration of Findings

In this chapter, I will draw some conclusions about why each of the nine techniques was either helpful or hindering across the eight cases. Further, based on studying these cases intensively, I will present some observations about psychotherapy process that might lead to future research areas.

When interpreting the review of techniques that follows, the reader should remember that the therapists were all experienced and had been nominated by their peers because they were highly regarded for their therapy skills. Although generally eclectic, the therapists tended to be psychoanalytic in orientation. The clients were all women who had never been in therapy before and who were motivated, able to form relationships, anxious and depressed, and had problems with self-esteem and relationships.

Each of the nine techniques was used by all the therapists, albeit in differing amounts and in different ways. Thus, although some of the techniques occasionally stood out as particularly helpful or hindering, each of them seems to have an important place in a therapist's repertoire of interventions.

Interpretation

As predicted based on the literature (see also Spiegel & Hill, 1989), interpretation was helpful for all clients, although it was used in different amounts for different dyads. Insight-oriented clients (Cases 1, 3, and 8) liked interpretations most. They did not necessarily agree with the interpretations, but the new explanations made

313

them think about what was causing and maintaining their maladaptive behaviors. Insight-orientation may be related to intelligence or to a personality style of investigative as opposed to realistic or conventional (Holland, 1973).

Interestingly, Molly (Case 2) was not insight-oriented at the beginning of therapy, but Dr. B was able to stimulate her curiosity about motives behind her behaviors. Although Molly was very defensive, Dr. B's gentleness enabled her to feel safe enough to hear the interpretations. In contrast, the clients in Cases 4 and 7 were not insight-oriented at the beginning of therapy and did not become more insight-oriented across therapy, perhaps because they were more passive, dependent, and psychologically disturbed than the client in Case 2. Because of the clients' lack of insight-orientation, the therapists in Cases 4 and 7 used fewer interpretations. The interpretations that they did use tended to be mild (i.e., close to the data) rather than deep.

Client acceptance of interpretation seemed to depend heavily on the client's trusting the therapist sufficiently to allow them to get into deeper material. Many of the most helpful interpretations were used later in therapy after the relationship was established and after the therapist had enough information from which to derive the interpretation. This fits with Carkhuff's (1969) theory that exploration should precede interpretation.

Interpretive theme. It was helpful when therapists used an interpretive theme, which involved developing a consistent thematic focus over the course of the therapy, slowly interpreting the theme, and repeating the theme in various ways, and applying it to a number of situations so that the client could work it through. This interpretive theme is conceptually similar to a dynamic focus (Strupp & Binder, 1984). Interpretive themes emerged in Cases 6 and 8 (see Chapter 12). These cases were similar in that the fathers of both of the clients had died when the clients were children. This suggests that it is feasible to develop an interpretive theme when clients present problems that can be traced back to a central traumatic event. In Case 5, Dr. S formulated a theme about Diane's controlling behavior, but the reasons for the controlling behavior were never understood.

In several cases, a theme emerged for a few sessions but was not continued throughout the treatment. In Case 1, Dr. A interpreted Sandy's behavior as maternal and related it to her role in her family of origin. This theme was followed for about two sessions, examining the effects of Sandy's maternal behavior in a number of relationships, but was then dropped. In Case 2, a theme emerged in the last three sessions about the function of Molly's reading horror books in fueling her anxiety. In Case 3, the theme of linking Lucille's current dependency issues to her relationship with her husband was developed in the seventh session, but was not referred to after that.

In all cases, interpretation was used to explain whatever was being discussed at the moment, although the interpretation was not necessarily tied back to a major interpretive theme. For example, interpretations were used in Case 4 to explain why others acted as they did. In Case 7, Jane found it helpful when Dr. E interpreted that she married her husband for security.

The three cases in which the therapists developed interpretive themes were not more successful than other cases, indicating that it was not necessary to develop an interpretive theme. Rather, the data support the use of an interpretive strategy in general.

Use of transference interpretations. Malan (1963, 1976a, 1976b) found that high rates of transference interpretations, which link the client's behavior with the therapist to his or her behavior with his or her parents, led to favorable outcome. His assertions have stimulated a number of studies (Azim, Joyce, McCullum, McCullough, & Piper, 1988; Marziali, 1984; Marziali & Sullivan, 1980; Piper, Debbane, Bienvenu, De Carufel, & Garant, 1986), which have not supported his original findings. In the field, however, there is still great interest in the use of transference interpretations in brief therapy (Davanloo, 1978; Sifneos, 1979). Thus, it is instructive to examine how transference interpretations were used in these eight cases of brief therapy.

Transference interpretations were used minimally if at all. In Case 7, Dr. E linked Jane's discussion of keeping her house clean with her desire that the therapist not see any of her "emotional mess." Jane did not understand this interpretation and could not understand why Dr. E was bringing up their relationship when she was talking about something else. In the first session of Case 8, Dr. R asked if Sophia would have trouble with her as a therapist since she was a woman and Sophia had had so much trouble with her mother and sister. Sophia felt misunderstood and confused by this question, perhaps because it came too soon within the therapy. In Cases 1 and 5, therapists discussed the therapeutic relationship, but did not link it to past relationships.

Our therapists seemed to understand intuitively not to use transference interpretations. Transference interpretations are probably most helpful for long-term clients who have passed the first phases of therapy and are interested in understanding their behavior at a deeper level. Given that these clients were therapeutically naive and unsure of what was expected in therapy, it is not surprising that they were frightened of such intensity.

Approval

Although approval was only used sparingly (6% of all responses), it was helpful in every case. At first I was surprised that approval was such a helpful technique, because I was operating on the values that Carkhuff (1969) proposed that a therapist should not give reassurance because it stunted self-exploration and tended to minimize the client's problems. Psychoanalytic theorists (for example, Greenson, 1967) would also not approve of using approval because they assert that it interferes with the neutral stance of the therapist and "gratifies" the client too much, orienting the client to please the therapist rather than to examining him or herself.

A closer examination of how these therapists used approval reveals why it was so helpful. None of these therapists used sympathy, for example, "That's so awful"; or minimized the clients' feelings, for example, "Everyone feels that way"; or dismissed them, for example, "Time will cure all," "Don't worry, be happy."

Instead, the typical type of approval that these therapists used was reinforcement and encouragement. Like coaches cheering on their players, these therapists would support their clients and assure them that they were doing a good job. When clients were unsure of what their therapists wanted them to do, therapist encouragement helped them know that they were on the right track. Sandy (Case 1) used an apt metaphor to describe her feelings. She said that she felt like she was out on a cliff alone and needed to know the Dr. A was there to share the risks with her.

Frank (1973) theorized that client distress is due to demoralization or loss of hope. Frank's view suggests that one task of the therapist is to instill hope or re-moralize the client, which these therapists did through the use of approval statements.

Self-Disclosure

Self-disclosure was used infrequently, but was helpful when it was used. The variety of self-disclosure used was not the kind that is often found in "friendships," for example, "You think you have it bad, let me tell you about my experience." Rather, these disclosures kept the focus on the client and helped to clarify the client's experience. In about half of the disclosures, therapists revealed something that they were experiencing immediately, whereas half related to previous experiences of the therapist. These disclosures generally helped clients to become more aware of their own feelings or behaviors.

Seven of the eight therapists gave a disclosure in the last few minutes of the final session in which they talked about how much they had enjoyed working with the client. In the one case (Case 5) that the therapist did not use a "goodbye" disclosure, Diane expressed her dissatisfaction that Dr. S had not made such a disclosure. Even for therapists who generally do not disclose, a disclosure at the end of therapy seemed to be very typical as a socially acceptable way of ending the therapy relationship on more equal terms. In general, both approval and self-disclosure seem to provide clients with a sense of universality (Yalom, 1975), so that they feel more normal and similar to other people.

Paraphrase

Paraphrase, one of the most frequently used techniques within these cases, was helpful in seven of the eight cases. Therapists used paraphrase to check out their understanding of what the clients were saying as well as to let the clients know that they were listening to them. Paraphrase was generally used to maintain the interaction by helping the client explore.

Paraphrase includes restatement of content, reflection of feelings, nonverbal referent, clarification, and summary, all of which are similar in that the therapist is actively trying to understand and tell the client how he/she perceives the client's frame of reference rather than imposing his/her own frame of reference on the client. Reflection of feeling was the type of paraphrase that was mentioned most often as being helpful in the first six cases. Therapist reflection indicated an acceptance of client feelings as well as suggested other feelings that clients might have been experiencing. The helpfulness of reflection of feelings for getting clients in touch with their feelings and experiencing supports the skills training theorists (Benjamin, 1981; Carkhuff, 1969; Egan, 1986; Ivey, 1983).

Direct Guidance

Direct guidance was helpful in some of the cases, but not in others. To discuss these findings, two types of direct guidance need to be distinguished: (a) structuring within the therapy, and (b) advice for what the client should do outside the session.

Structuring within the therapy. Structuring occurred primarily in the first session, at the beginnings of sessions, or when the client was rambling or floundering. Since these clients were "naive" to therapy and to their therapists, they did not know what was expected of them in therapy. Hence, when therapists told them what to expect and gave them clear guidelines for their behavior, clients tended to feel relieved. Further, structuring helped them know how to behave appropriately in the situation. Because therapy was brief, time could have been wasted if clients were allowed to flounder. Given their high levels of anxiety, these clients might have dropped out if less structuring was done.

In Case 5, where Dr. S did not structure the therapy as much, Diane was very confused and upset and wanted more structure. In Case 8, Sophia felt like she rambled too much without the therapist helping her determine a direction. Dr. R, who generally felt that Sophia should determine the direction of the therapy, also felt that she wasted time by letting Sophia ramble too much.

The only case in which structuring was less helpful was in Case 6. Sometimes when Dr. C suggested a gestalt exercise, such as talking to her dead father, Gloria would comply and would get something out of the exercise. Other times she resisted and kept jumping and changing topics to avoid doing the exercise. Generally she seemed to want to comply because she liked and trusted Dr. C, but she also felt very vulnerable and awkward doing the exercises. Although at first, Gloria seemed very articulate and "together," it quickly became apparent that her articulateness was a defense against her feelings. The gestalt exercises were a powerful way of forcing Gloria to get in touch with her feelings, but she was not ready to cope with feelings that had been hidden away too long.

Thus, all of the clients seemed to like at least a minimal structuring of the therapy so that they knew what was expected of them. Problems occurred when the structure was too loose (clients allowed to flounder) or too structured (gestalt exercises).

Advice. Direct guidance for outside the session was more difficult for therapists to use effectively. In three cases, it was generally positive. In Case 1, Dr. A suggested that Sandy do relaxation exercises to combat stress and practice communication skills to resolve her interpersonal difficulties. These suggestions came after a thorough exploration of Sandy's problems. In Case 7, Dr. E seemed comfortable giving Jane the advice that she wanted after they had explored the situations. Dr. E's advice to Jane typically was that she be more direct in saying what she needed from other people. Direct guidance was also helpful in Case 8. Dr. R's typical advice to Sophia was to trust herself because she knew what she needed to do.

In other cases, direct guidance was less helpful. In Case 3, when Lucille asked for advice, Dr. H responded with a lot of direct guidance in the early sessions. Lucille usually resisted with "Yes, but . . ." for why she could not do what he suggested. Dr. H seemed to jump too fast to solutions for problems without an adequate base of exploration or understanding of the problem (Egan, 1986). The advice that Dr. H gave later in the therapy was accepted more readily by Lucille, although it should be noted that at the long-term follow-up she had come to accept her lifestyle rather than alter it in the direction that Dr. H had suggested. The progress in this case suggests that Dr. H had an agenda for how Lucille should be, for example, working or volunteering and having a large supportive network of friends, whereas she felt she needed to work through her grief over her husband's death and accept the lifestyle that she had developed. Lucille's case highlights the potential problems associated with imposing values on clients rather than facilitating their exploration of what they want from life.

In Case 4, the client was psychologically unsophisticated and wanted advice. Because challenging her to change her style would probably not have worked, Dr. M occasionally gave Marie advice when she solicited it. The most helpful advice was to be more direct in communication. Although Marie thought this advice was helpful and remembered it even at the long-term follow-up, she felt it was trivial and not related to her core conflicts.

In Case 5, Dr. S determined that although Diane wanted him to tell her what to do, she would get very angry at him if he took over for her, as she had with other people in her life. So rather than telling her what to do, he reflected her conflict over being taken care of. Diane felt very frustrated with Dr. S's approach, but that does not necessarily mean that the approach was "wrong." Diane clearly had dependency issues. Perhaps with a therapist who told her what to do, Diane would have become more dependent. More likely, she would have quit, as she had with two other therapists in the past. I think, however, that Dr. S could have been somewhat more gratifying in giving Diane advice, especially if he had then processed Diane's reactions to getting the advice.

Taken together, these results suggest that the value of advice depends on many variables. First, a client has to want advice. Second, a therapist has to understand the client's problem enough to be able to give advice that is consistent with the client's values and goals. Third, a therapist has to be helping a client decide what is right for him/her, rather than imposing his/her own values on a client. Finally, passive/dependent clients may want advice, but relying on an authority rather than learning to believe in themselves may create a dependency relationship. Like the old adage of teaching a person to fish rather than giving them fish, direct guidance may serve to foster dependency rather than help the person overcome it. If, however, a therapist chooses not to give the advice that the client so desperately desires (as in Case 5), the control struggle will probably become a central focus of the therapy. In such cases, the therapist might need to discuss his or her reasons for not giving advice to the client, so that the client's independence becomes a shared goal within the therapy. If a client does not desire to become more independent, the therapist's forcing the issue may be imposing his or her values on the client.

Open Question

Open question was helpful in some cases, but not in others. In Case 1, open questions allowed Sandy to explore new parts of herself. She liked the challenge in questions like, "What do you like about men?" or "What do you need from men?" because they helped her to see that she might not really like or need men as much as she thought she did. In contrast, Gloria (Case 6) felt very uncomfortable with open questions, which caused her experiencing level to go up and made her feel scared, suggesting that she felt out of control. The open questions challenged her defenses in a way that left her feeling anxious and vulnerable.

This suggests that open questions may be very challenging for some clients. With an open question, the therapist is basically trying to enable the client to explore. There are not necessarily any "right" answers, but the therapist is urging the client to examine aspects that he or she may not have looked at before. If the client has a lot of defenses and has held back on looking at feelings, open questions can be experienced as opening "Pandora's box" and can be very frightening. Open questions may be more helpful for clients with less symptomatology who enjoy exploring themselves and learning new information. Open questions might be experienced as more helpful if they are used in the context of approval, with the therapist demonstrating an understanding of the difficulty of the task of exploration.

Confrontation

Confrontation was helpful in some cases, but not in others. As with open questions, Sandy (Case 1) liked confrontation and wished that her therapist had used more of it because she enjoyed learning new things about herself. In contrast, confrontation was experienced negatively by some clients, even when it was presented in an even-handed, kind manner by therapists. The clients in Cases 3 and 7 felt mixed about confrontation. Although the clients recognized the need to be confronted, they did not like the immediate feeling of being confronted. In Case 2, Molly clearly did not like confrontation and said that she would have terminated if she had been paired with a confrontive therapist. Dr. B picked up on Molly's demand not to be confronted and was very gentle with her, which helped to establish a trusting relationship.

Thus, although perhaps necessary for clients who have a lot of defenses, confrontation can be uncomfortable for clients. Further, a therapist always has to be careful that confrontations are not vehicles for the covert expression of hostility toward the client or for imposing his/her own values and needs on the client.

Closed Question

Closed questions are attempts by the therapist to gain information, facts, or data from the client. Statements that were phrased in the form of closed questions but had the intent of another technique were categorized as the other technique; for example, "Are you sure about that?" would be categorized as a confrontation.

Although one of the most frequent therapist techniques, closed questions were never mentioned as helpful and were occasionally mentioned as hindering. This finding supports suggestions of counseling skills training (Benjamin, 1981; Carkhuff, 1969; Egan, 1986; Ivey, 1983) regarding the negative effects of closed questions. Although therapists apparently needed to gather information, it was not a particularly exciting aspect of therapy. In Case 1, Sandy found closed questions boring. Dr. A did a lot of assessment and sometimes asked the same questions in different sessions when he was stuck. In Case 5, Diane disliked closed questions about whether she masturbated. These questions seemed important based on Diane's target complaints, but Dr. S may have been too abrupt in his presentation style due to his anxiety.

Closed questions were used in a slightly different way in Case 8, although they were still not rated as particularly helpful. When Sophia presented contradictory information, Dr. R used closed questions to clarify exactly what Sophia meant and force her to communicate more clearly.

The most typical client reaction to closed question was "No reaction," which was accompanied by a low helpfulness rating. Closed questions typically created a feeling of being interviewed rather than being invited to become emotionally involved.

Although closed questions provide needed information, the therapist may have to balance his or her desire for the facts with the need to get the client involved in the process of therapy. Further, therapists need to be aware that sometimes questions can be too intrusive. As therapists, we sometimes become so accustomed to asking about the intimate details of people's lives that we forget that people regard some information as very personal.

Information

The most common therapist technique was providing information, although they were hardly noticed in the therapy process. Only one client (Case 7) found information helpful. Given Jane's passivity and desire to be told what to do, it is perhaps not surprising that she found the therapist's educational role to be helpful.

As with direct guidance, there was information related to the therapy process itself and information related to outside of therapy. Information about the therapy consisted primarily of establishing what to expect from the therapy, for example, the number and length of sessions, expectations for the client and therapist roles, the therapist's credentials, or telling what the therapist knew about the client from reading the assessment data prior to the first session. Information for outside the therapy consisted of educating the client about something external. For example, in Case 3, Dr. H told Lucille about various volunteer activities that she could get involved in. In Case 4, Dr. M provided information about many things, including death and dying, hospice programs for Marie's dying mother, and the university for Marie's daughter, who had just begun college. In Case 7, Dr. E educated Jane about the role of communication in marriage.

Integration of Techniques

Although some techniques were viewed as more helpful than others, the data do not suggest that therapists should use the most helpful techniques exclusively. In fact, therapists used the most helpful techniques only a small proportion of the time (interpretation, 8%; approval, 6%; self-disclosure, 1%).

The only helpful technique that was used frequently was paraphrase. Along with questions, paraphrase was the primary method therapists used to enable clients to explore their problems. The evidence suggests that, as the skills trainers (Benjamin, 1981; Carkhuff, 1969; Egan, 1986; Ivey, 1983) advocate, paraphrase (primarily reflection of feelings) is the most helpful way to enable clients to explore their concerns.

Although for the most part in this book I have explored the effectiveness of the individual techniques, I believe that the patterning of the different techniques is important. For example, in Chapter 12, we found that interpretation was used in a context of approval, preceded by open and closed questions, and followed by direct guidance. Thus, interpretation might have been helpful because it was used in conjunction with these other techniques. Further research on the patterning of the different techniques for different clients would be useful.

The Role of Moderating Variables

Client Factors

Even with this group of relatively homogeneous female clients, client factors played a large role in determining which therapist techniques were helpful. For example, passive/dependent clients liked directive techniques such as direct guidance and information, but did not like confrontation, even though it seemed useful to get them mobilized. All clients found interpretation helpful, but therapists used more interpretation with insight-oriented clients. In addition, although interpretive themes were useful to structure therapy, they were only developed in the three cases.

We cannot determine whether other clients would react in the same way to the therapist techniques. Clients of other diagnostic types or cultural backgrounds might have very different reactions to specific techniques. An exciting direction for future research is to determine which techniques work best for specific clients.

Therapist Factors

The use of particular techniques was influenced by theoretical orientation. These therapists, most of whom were psychodynamically oriented, used a fair amount of interpretation. The therapist who was most behaviorally oriented (Case 1), however, used less interpretation. The use of self-disclosure was also to be influenced by orientation, with the less psychodynamic therapists (Cases 1, 3, and 6) using more disclosure.

A therapist's awareness of a client's reactions and needs seemed to be an important factor in determining which techniques a therapist used during a session. We observed that when a therapist accurately perceived the client's reactions to his or her interventions, the therapist seemed to be better able to plan the next intervention. This observation was substantiated in a further study (Thompson & Hill, in preparation). In addition, we found that therapists were more accurate in predicting positive than negative reactions, suggesting that clients may hide their negative reactions from therapists.

The Relationship

With the exception of Case 4, the data for the WAI indicated that the alliances in all the dyads were within an average range compared to a normative sample. Interestingly, even though we picked expert therapists and "good" clients, the relationships were not stellar according to the Working Alliance Inventory (WAI) data.

Based on the data (WAI, ratings of satisfaction with therapy, and comments from the post-therapy interviews), the therapeutic relationships in three cases (2, 6, and 8) were close to ideal. In Case 2, Molly said that Dr. B was just what she wanted in a therapist. Dr. B was also very satisfied with the match. The relationship progressed very smoothly with no disagreements over what should occur, even though the relationship was never discussed. Molly returned for one session of crisis intervention during the six-month follow-up. In Case 8, Dr. R was remarkably supportive and able to provide a warm, accepting relationship that seemed to be exactly what Sophia needed. Interestingly, the relationship was never discussed in this dyad either, even though Dr. R's typical style was to discuss the relationship. The relationship was probably not discussed because no problems arose to keep the dyad from working productively. Sophia did not seek further therapy, but she probably would have contacted Dr. R if she had needed help. In Case 6, the relationship was good enough for Dr. C to push Gloria to visit her father's grave four times and for her to do some gestalt exercises even though she was reluctant to do them. The supportive atmosphere helped Gloria begin to feel comfortable enough to let down her "walls" and allow Dr. C to see some of her "craziness." Gloria sought 10 sessions of further therapy from Dr. C during the one-year follow-up period.

In three other cases (1, 3, and 7), the therapeutic relationships were adequate for accomplishing the work of the brief therapy, although the participants probably would not have chosen to work with each other. In Case 1, Sandy and Dr. A were able to discuss and negotiate their relationship (see later discussion) so that they found mutually agreeable problem areas to work on productively. When Sandy returned for further therapy, however, she sought out a gestalt therapist. In Case 3, Dr. H and Lucille found some commonality in their humor and theatre interests. However, Dr. H pushed Lucille to get out and make new friends and become involved in volunteer activities, which she was not inclined to do. In Case 7, Dr. E helped the client to become more direct in her communications, but the therapeutic relationship often seemed strained and uncomfortable.

Two relationships seemed less satisfactory. In Case 5, Diane complained that Dr. S was too technical and rigid. They talked about Diane's expectations and the therapy relationship frequently, with Dr. S taking a therapeutic stance of not gratifying Diane's opposing desires to be controlled and to be controlling. In Case 4, Marie was very unhappy with Dr. M. If the therapy had not been part of a research project, Marie said that she would have dropped out very early in the therapy.

Our research team reflected about how we would have rearranged the dyads based on our perceptions of what clients wanted from therapy and what type of therapy the therapists wanted to offer. It would have been fun to watch the interaction between Sandy (Case 1) and Dr. E (Case 7) because both were dynamic women who liked confrontation. Because Marie (Case 4) and Jane (Case 7) wanted answers to their problems, each could have been paired with Dr. A (Case 1) who liked to do problem solving. Diane (Case 5) could have been paired with Dr. B or Dr. R, both of whom were older, supportive women. Lucille could have been paired with Dr. C because his gestalt approach fit with her melodramatic style. Our observations would suggest that matching might be more effective if it were based on shared expectations and approaches to problem-solving, rather than on demographics or personality characteristics as has been done in the past (see Highlen & Hill, 1984). Whether such matching could be done prior to therapy based on testing or whether it involves issues that do not become apparent until the process is underway is an important question for future research.

External Factors

Outside of therapy, all the clients put considerable time and energy into thinking about the issues discussed in the sessions as well as trying to implement suggestions that the therapists made. This extratherapy involvement was an indication of their motivation in the therapy process.

Further, all eight clients had at least one person outside of therapy to whom they could turn for support. Except for Sandy (Case 1), however, most of them seemed somewhat isolated and lonely. The same behaviors that brought them into therapy may have made it difficult for these clients to maintain satisfying relationships with other people. Perhaps because they had at least a minimal support system, none of the clients got so dependent on the therapists that they had difficulty terminating, as did the client we reported on in Hill et al. (1983).

One way in which clients used their support system was to check out the therapist's feedback. In Case 1, when Dr. A told Sandy she acted maternal in her relationships, she asked her friends how they perceived her behavior. When they verified that indeed she did act maternal, she was more convinced that Dr. A was on the right track. In Case 5, Diane's women's support group served a similar reality-testing function. When Diane complained that Dr. S was not giving her enough answers to her problems, the group members laughed and said that she was up to her old tricks of trying to get everyone else to take care of her. Although clients often use their outside relationships to sabotage the therapy endeavor, that did not seem to occur in these cases.

Finally, external events often served either to facilitate or impede progress in therapy, indicating that external reality is an important factor. In several cases (4, 6, 8), getting jobs after the therapy terminated seemed to help clients consolidate their learning and continue changing. For Marie (Case 4), the illness and subsequent death of her mother and the imminent departure of her daughter for college caused Marie enough anxiety to impel her to seek therapy but also may have made it hard for her to form a relationship or focus on any other issues. In Case 5, Diane's unresolved relationship with her husband interfered with her progress in and after therapy. As Diane would get stronger and decide to leave her husband, he would want to reconcile the relationship, throwing her into a state of ambivalence.

Other Important Process Events

In the section that follows, several features of the therapeutic process that add to understanding the use of techniques within the cases will be discussed.

Negotiation

During the first four or five sessions, the therapist and client *negotiated* their implicit contract and determined the rules by which they would operate in the treatment. This involved both participants making concessions about what they had expected and desired from treatment. This negotiation process was not an explicit part of the treatment for any of the cases, but rather was a process which all the dyads went through in varying degrees.

Sandy (Case 1) came in stating that she wanted insight into her problems and that she was not particularly pleased that she had been assigned a male therapist. Dr. A's preferred style was to do problem-solving therapy on very focused concerns. Through negotiation, they both compromised. Sandy brought in some specific concerns with her sister and roommate that Dr. A could help her resolve. Dr. A then shifted to a more insight-oriented approach to help Sandy come to some understandings about her difficulties in relating to men. Both were satisfied with the results of the negotiation and productive work was accomplished in the therapy.

In Case 4, the opposite pattern occurred. Marie, an Asian woman, wanted some specific answers to concerns she was having, but Dr. M's style was more oriented to feelings and insight. Dr. M shifted her style to meet Marie's needs, but was not able to shift enough to please Marie.

In Case 5, Diane wanted explicit direction, but Dr. S determined that such directiveness would be detrimental for her and chose a more passive stance. In this case, the negotiation process became the focus of the entire therapy. Given Diane's basic issues over control, we might hypothesize that clients (or therapists) who have control or power issues will have more difficulty with the negotiation process.

The data suggest that therapists and clients both have a range of behaviors. Within that range, each person chooses behaviors that he or she expects to work in a specific relationship. If behaviors are called for that are outside the persons's range, the match will probably be unsatisfactory. The process of negotiation is undoubtedly a trial-and-error process, where both persons test out what the other person wants and can tolerate. Earlier I stated that a match on expectations was desirable. Given these findings about negotiation, it appears that negotiation can augment a mismatch on expectations.

Thus, if a client and therapist do not have an initial match on expectations, they need to be able to negotiate the relationship for successful outcome.

Secrets

Therapists and clients did not always have the same perception of events within the therapy. For example, a client might report negative reactions on the research measures, but not disclose these feelings to the therapist within the session. Hence, the therapist would not necessarily know about the negative reaction. This happened particularly in cases in which the therapist did not ask the client about his or her immediate reactions (e.g., Cases 4 and 7). When the therapist made it clear he or she wanted to hear about the client's immediate reactions (e.g., Case 1), there were few secrets between therapist and client.

When therapists asked, clients seemed willing to talk about their reactions. Further, as mentioned earlier, clients were quite willing to reveal negative reactions on the research instruments. Hence, the secrets did not seem to be a result of the client's inability to be aware of his or her feelings, but rather that the therapists had implicitly communicated rules to the clients that their immediate reactions were not relevant to the therapy process. Such behavior led me to become interested in metacommunication (Kiesler, 1988; Strupp & Binder, 1984), in which a therapist talks about his/her immediate reactions to the client and encourages the client to reveal his or her feelings. When a client is given permission to talk about feelings and the relationship is discussed openly, fewer secrets seem to be present and the relationship can be negotiated more easily.

Changes in Areas Not Discussed in Therapy

For the most part, the changes reported at outcome were related to issues that had been focused on in the treatment process. We noticed in a couple of the cases, however, that some changes occurred in areas that were not focused on in the therapy. In Case 1, Dr. A only rarely discussed Sandy's relationship with her father. Yet, during the post-therapy review Sandy was able to see that many of her difficulties were related to her feelings about her father. In Case 2, Molly's phobia about driving on the beltway was never discussed in therapy, yet she reported in one of the final sessions that she no longer had the phobia.

Apparently, therapists do not need to address and resolve every issue directly in the treatment. Rather, therapists do one of several things: (a) they provide support so that the client's problem-solving abilities are unstuck, (b) they teach problem-solving skills that clients can use in future situations, or (c) they teach clients to think about their problems differently by using insight or cognitive restructuring, which can then be applied to other problems.

Thus, clients do not need to discuss every problem within therapy, but rather bring problems in as exemplars. Instead of becoming dependent upon therapists to solve their problems, clients learn methods for solving their problems. The exemplars are worked on in therapy to facilitate the learning of coping and problem-solving skills and to remove things that block the client from using the skills. Once the skills are incorporated and blocks are removed, the learnings generalize to other problems.

Effects of the Research

The research probably influenced the results of all eight cases. First, clients knew that they had been selected out of a large number of applicants to participate in an extensive research project. Several clients told us that this made them feel special. They also felt that they were contributing to a larger effort than just their own personal mental health. Second, the clients participated in more activities than just the therapy sessions. Clients were given an extensive battery of pre-tests, a clinical interview with a researcher, 12-20 50 minute sessions, post-session evaluations, videotaped replays of their sessions, extensive post-testing, and follow-ups. As noted by Sloane, Staples, Cristol, Yorkston, and Whipple (1975), these additional contacts were probably therapeutic in and of themselves.

Another issue is that the research team formed friendly, although not therapeutic, relationships with the clients to ensure cooperation with the research. We had contact with the clients during the selection process and the videotape reviews. They also interacted with the secretary and research assistants while they waited for their sessions. Marie (Case 4) frequently called the secretary and the researcher. She remained in therapy, even though dissatisfied, to fulfill her obligation to the research project. Cordial researcher/client relationships were crucial for obtaining good research data but may have changed the therapy somewhat, particularly by diluting the therapist-client relationship.

The role of the videotape review deserves further mention. The clients varied dramatically in their response to it. On the one hand, Sandy (Case 1) thought the videotape review was as helpful as the therapy itself. She said it gave her a chance to review, in a more relaxed atmosphere, what Dr. A had said. If she had not heard or understood something the first time through, she was able to listen to it again during the review. She took extensive notes during the review so that she could remember things that she wanted to think about or bring up again in another session. Lucille (Case 3), who had done some acting, did not mind the videotape review. In contrast, Molly (Case 2), Diane (Case 5), and Gloria (Case 6) disliked the videotape review. Molly disliked it because she saw herself as complaining and whining. Diane disliked it because she was so aware and critical of her appearance. Gloria was so self-conscious and embarrassed about seeing herself on the videotape that she hid her eyes. She viewed the videotape as one of the drawbacks that she had to put up with to get the therapy that she could not have afforded otherwise.

Another issue with the videotape review was that it became tedious after a few times. The task itself was time-consuming and not always rewarding. For example, Dr. R (Case 9) complained that stopping the tape so often interfered with her ability to get much out of watching the session.

Finally, the research required three hours every week plus travel time, which both therapists and clients sometimes felt infringed on other activities. No one (except perhaps Lucille in Case 3) seemed sorry to give up that aspect of the project at the time of termination.

The Process of Observation

One thing that all of us on the research team noticed was that as observers behind a one-way mirror, we felt freer not to like aspects of the client's behavior than the therapists did. When we questioned therapists about client behaviors to which we had negative reactions, they would often respond that those behaviors did not bother them. Remembering ourselves in the role of therapist, we realized that we had likewise seldom felt strong negative reactions to clients. The role of therapist ideally requires a suspension of judgment to produce unconditional positive regard for the client (Rogers, 1957). Therapists generally try to understand the reasons for a client's negative behavior rather than reacting as one would socially. This blunting of negative affect, however, may make it difficult for therapists to identify when they are getting pulled into the client's maladaptive interpersonal scenarios (Kiesler, 1988).

A Final Word on Techniques

To be able to analyze therapist techniques from a number of different perspectives (therapist and client helpfulness ratings, client reactions and experiencing levels, and post-session and post-therapy comments), I operationalized techniques as verbal response modes, which refer to the grammatical structure of the therapist's verbal behavior independent of the content of the speech. My response modes system (Hill, 1985) has nine categories of therapist behavior (approval, information, direct guidance, closed question, open question, paraphrase, interpretation, confrontation, and self-disclosure). Response modes are an approximation of the way therapists think about their interventions and also represent the way therapists are trained (Benjamin, 1981; Carkhuff, 1969; Egan, 1986; Ivey, 1983). By defining techniques as response modes, I was able to examine the context in which the techniques were used and use evidence from the entire case to discuss the helpfulness of specific techniques.

Obviously, however, this definition encompasses only one dimension of therapist behavior and ignores other important dimensions, for example physiological or nonverbal behaviors, covert behaviors such as intentions, and larger clinical strategies (Hill, 1982). I do not mean to imply that therapist techniques and the therapy process is as simple as my choices would suggest. In fact, I believe that therapy is enormously complex, but to be able to have a manageable project, I had to select a piece that I could study from the overwhelming amount of information.

Conclusions

In the introduction, I hypothesized that therapist techniques were moderated by the effects of individual differences between clients, client and therapist factors, the relationship, and external events. Based on the findings from this study, I have reconceptualized the interaction between these variables.

I postulate that for change to occur in therapy, a therapist has to deliver the appropriate techniques for a particular client within the context of a "good-enough" relationship, which means that there must be a bond or "clicking" between the therapist and client. Once instigated or sparked by therapist techniques, change is facilitated through a client's efforts outside of therapy, a supportive network, and facilitative external events or at least a lack of interfering external events. Thus, none of the factors in isolation is necessary and sufficient for change to occur. Rather, all the factors work in concert to facilitate change.

In the form of propositions for future research:

1. Client motivation and involvement determine who seeks and participates actively in the therapy process.

2. Therapist factors, based on personality, training, and theoretical orientation, determine what techniques are in a therapist's repertoire. A therapist's awareness of a client's reactions and needs is an important factor in determining which specific techniques a therapist will use during a session.

3. The relationship (i.e., bond) between the therapist and client has to be at a minimally acceptable or "good-enough" level for clients to hear or accept any of the therapist interventions.

4. There must be an initial match between client and therapist about expectations for what should occur in therapy or the client and therapist must negotiate a mutually agreeable process.

5. Techniques are differentially helpful for different types of clients. Based on this small group of clients, the results indicated that: (a) Passive/dependent clients preferred direct guidance and information

but may not have progressed when these techniques were used, (b) Vulnerable, fearful clients found open question and confrontation helpful but threatening, and (c) Insight-oriented clients preferred and got more therapeutic value from interpretations. Further research with a greater variety of clients is needed to elaborate the prediction model of what techniques are most likely to work with different types of clients.

6. Patterns of techniques or the way in which a therapist interweaves the use of different response modes is important.

7. Although not included as one of the techniques investigated in the current study, metacommunication seemed helpful as a therapist technique to reduce the number of client secrets and amount of dissatisfaction with the process.

8. Once techniques have instigated the change process, influences outside of the therapy hour (extratherapy involvement, the support network, and external events) determine whether the changes will "take" and continue or will not be incorporated.

References

Alberti, R. E., & Emmons, M. L. (1974). *Your perfect right: A guide to assertive behavior.* San Luis Obispo, CA: Impact.

Anastasi, A. (1982). *Psychological testing.* New York: Macmillan.

Archer, R. L. (1979). Disclosure reciprocity and its limits: A reactance analysis. *Journal of Experimental Social Psychology, 14,* 527-540.

Azim, H. F. A., Joyce, A. S., McCullum, M., McCullough, L., & Piper, W. E. (1988, June). Antecedents and consequences of transference interpretations in short-term psychotherapy. Panel presented at the Society for Psychotherapy Research, Santa Fe, NM.

Battle, C. G., Imber, S. D., Hoehn-Saric, R., Stone, A. R., Nash, E. R., & Frank, J. D. (1965). Target complaints as criterion of improvement. *American Journal of Psychotherapy, 20,* 184-192.

Beck, A. T., Rush, A. J., Shaw, B. F., & Emery, G. (1983). *Cognitive therapy of depression.* New York: Guilford.

Benjamin, A. (1981). *The helping interview* (3rd ed.). Boston: Houghton Mifflin.

Bergin, A. E., & Lambert, M. J. (1978). The evaluation of therapeutic outcome. In S. L. Garfield & A. E. Bergin (Eds.), *Handbook of psychotherapy and behavior change* (2nd ed., pp. 139-190). New York: Wiley.

Beutler, L. E., Crago, M., & Arizmendi, T. G. (1986). Research on therapist variables in psychotherapy. In S. L. Garfield & A. E. Bergin (Eds.), *Handbook of psychotherapy and behavior change* (3rd ed., pp. 257-310). New York: Wiley.

Blanck, G. (1966). Some technical implications of ego psychology. *International Journal of Psychoanalysis, 47,* 6-13.

Bogdan, R., & Taylor, S. J. (1975). *Introduction to qualitative research methods.* New York: Wiley.

Bordin, E. S. (1979). The generalizability of the psychoanalytic concept of the working alliance. *Psychotherapy: Theory, Research, and Practice, 16,* 252-260.

Budman, S. H. (1981). *Forms of brief therapy.* New York: Guilford.

Budman, S. H., & Gurman, A. S. (1988). *Theory and practice of brief therapy.* New York: Guilford.

335

Carkhuff, R. R. (1969). *Human and helping relations* (Vols. 1 & 2). New York: Holt, Rinehart, & Winston.

Cobb, S. (1976). Social support as a moderator of life stress. *Psychosomatic Medicine, 38,* 300-314.

Cogar, M., & Hill. C. E. (in preparation). Therapist and client perceptions of the helpful and hindering components of psychotherapy.

Curtis, J. M. (1981). Indications and contraindications in the use of therapist's self-disclosure. *Psychological Reports, 49,* 499-507.

Davanloo, H. (1978). *Basic principles and techniques in short-term dynamic psychotherapy.* New York: Spectrum.

Derogatis, L. R., Rickels, K., & Rock, A. F. (1976). The SCL-90 and the MMPI: A step in the validation of a new self-report scale. *British Journal of Psychiatry, 128,* 280-289.

DiNardo, P. A., O'Brien, G. T., Barlow, D. H., Waddell, M. T., & Blanchard, E. B. (1983). Reliability of DSM-III anxiety disorder categories using a new structured interview. *Archives of General Psychiatry, 40,* 1070-1074.

Egan, G. (1986). *The skilled helper* (3rd Ed.). Monterey. CA: Brooks/Cole.

Elliott, R. (1985). Helpful and nonhelpful events in brief counseling interviews: An empirical taxonomy. *Journal of Counseling Psychology, 32,* 307-322.

Elliott, R. (1986). Interpersonal Process Recall (IPR) as a psychotherapy process research method. In L. S. Greenberg & W. M. Pinsof (Eds.), *The psychotherapeutic process: A research handbook* (pp. 503-528). New York: Guilford.

Elliott, R., Barker, C. B., Caskey, N., & Pistrang, N. (1982). Differential helpfulness of counselor verbal response modes. *Journal of Counseling Psychology, 29,* 354-361.

Elliott, R., Hill, C. E., Stiles, W. B., Friedlander, M. L.. Mahrer, A. R., & Margison, F. R. (1987). Primary therapist response modes: Comparison of six rating systems. *Journal of Consulting and Clinical Psychology, 55,* 218-223.

Fenichel, O. (1941). *The psychoanalytic theory of neurosis.* New York: Norton.

Fitts, W. H. (1965). *Manual for the Tennessee Self Concept Scale.* Nashville, TN: Counselor Recordings and Tests.

Frank, J. (1973). *Persuasion and healing* (2nd ed.). Baltimore: Johns Hopkins University Press.

Freud, S. (1961) [1914]. Remembering, repeating, and working through. In J. Strachey (Ed. and Trans.), *The standard edition of the complete psychological works of Sigmund Freud* (Vol. 12). London: Hogarth.

Fromm-Reichmann, F. (1950). *Principles of intensive psychotherapy.* Chicago: University of Chicago Press.

Fuller, F., & Hill, C. E. (1985). Counselor and client perceptions of counselor intentions in relationship to outcome in a single counseling session. *Journal of Counseling Psychology, 32,* 329-338.

Gelso, C. J. (1979). Research in counseling: Methodological and professional issues. *Counseling Psychologist, 8*(3), 7-36.

Gelso, C. J., & Carter, J. A. (1985). The relationship in counseling and psychotherapy. *Counseling Psychologist, 13*(2), 155-243.

Gottman, J. M., & Markman, H. J. (1978). Experimental designs in psychotherapy research. In S. L. Garfield & A. E. Bergin (Eds.), *Handbook of psychotherapy and behavior change* (2nd ed., pp. 23-62). New York: Wiley.

Greenson, R. R. (1967). *The technique and practice of psychoanalysis* (Vol. 1). New York: International Universities Press.

Haley, J. (1973). *Uncommon therapy: The psychiatric techniques of Milton H. Erikson, M.D.* New York: Norton.

Haley, J. (1976). *Problem-solving therapy.* San Francisco: Jossey-Bass.

Hathaway, S. R., & McKinley, J. C. (1951). *The Minnesota Multiphasic Personality Inventory Manual* (rev. ed). New York: The Psychological Corporation.

Hayes, S. C. (1981). Single case experimental design in empirical and clinical practice. *Journal of Consulting and Clinical Psychology, 49,* 193-211.

Hersen, M., & Barlow, D. H. (1976). *Single-case experimental design: Strategies for studying behavioral change.* New York: Pergamon.

Highlen, P. S., & Hill, C. E. (1984). Factors affecting client change in individual counseling: Current status and theoretical speculations. In S. D. Brown & R. W. Lent (Eds.), *Handbook of counseling psychology* (pp.334-398). New York: Wiley.

Hill, C. E. (1974). A comparison of the perceptions of a therapy session by clients, therapists, and objective judges. *Journal Supplements Abstract Service, 4,* No. 564.

Hill, C. E. (1978). Development of a counselor verbal response category system. *Journal of Counseling Psychology, 25,* 461-468.

Hill, C. E. (1982). Counseling process research: Philosophical and methodological dilemmas. *Counseling Psychologist, 10*(4), 7-19.

Hill, C. E. (1985). *Manual for the Hill counselor verbal response modes category system* (rev. ed.). Unpublished manuscript, University of Maryland.

Hill, C. E. (1986). An overview of the Hill counselor and client verbal response modes category systems. In L. Greenberg & W. Pinsof (Eds.), *The psychotherapeutic process: A research Handbook* (pp. 131-160). New York: Guilford.

Hill, C. E., Carter, J. A., & O'Farrell, M. K. (1983). A case study of the process and outcome of time-limited counseling. *Journal of Counseling Psychology, 30,* 3-18.

Hill, C. E., Helms, J., Spiegel, S. B., & Tichenor, V. (1988). Development of a system for assessing client reactions to therapist interventions. *Journal of Counseling Psychology, 34,* 27-36.

Hill, C. E., Helms, J. E., Tichenor, V., Spiegel, S. B., O'Grady, K. E., & Perry, E. (1988). The effects of therapist response modes in brief psychotherapy. *Journal of Counseling Psychology, 35,* 222-233.

Hill, C. E., Mahalik, J., & Thompson, B. (in press). Therapist self-disclosure. *Psychotherapy.*

Hill, C. E., & O'Grady, K. E. (1985). List of therapist intentions illustrated in a case study and with therapists of varying theoretical orientations. *Journal of Counseling Psychology, 32,* 3-22.

Hill, C. E., & Regan, A. (in preparation). The use of metaphors within a case of brief psychotherapy.

Hill, C. E., Thames, T. B., & Rardin, D. (1979). A comparison of Rogers, Perls, and Ellis on the Hill Counselor Verbal Response Category System. *Journal of Counseling Psychology, 26,* 198-203.

Holland, J. L. (1973). *Making career choices: A theory of careers.* Englewood Cliffs, NJ: Prentice-Hall.

Horvath, A., & Greenberg, L. S. (1986). Development of the Working Alliance Inventory. In L. S. Greenberg and W. M. Pinsof (Eds.), *The psychotherapeutic process: A research handbook* (pp. 529-556). New York: Guilford.

Ivey, A. E. (1983). *Intentional interviewing and counseling.* Monterey, CA: Brooks/ Cole.

Kazdin, A. E. (1981). Drawing valid inferences from case studies. *Journal of Consulting and Clinical Psychology, 49,* 183-192.

Kelly, G. (1955). *The psychology of personal constructs* (Vols. 1 & 2). New York: Norton.

Kiesler, D. J. (1988). *Therapeutic metacommunication: Therapist impact disclosure as feedback in psychotherapy.* Palo Alto, CA: Consulting Psychologist Press.

Klein, M. H., Mathieu, P. L., Gendlin, E. T., & Kiesler, D. J. (1970). *The experiencing scale: A research and training manual* (2 vols.). Madison, WI: Bureau of Audio Visual Instruction.

Klein, M. H., Mathieu-Coughlan, P., & Kiesler, D. J. (1986). The experiencing scales. In L. Greenberg and W. Pinsof (Eds.), *The psychotherapeutic process: A research handbook* (pp. 21-72). New York: Guilford.

Koss, M. P., & Butcher, J. N. (1986). Research on brief psychotherapy. In S. L. Garfield & A. E. Bergin (Eds.), *Handbook of psychotherapy and behavior change* (3rd ed., pp. 627-670). New York: Wiley.

Lambert, M. J., DeJulio, S. S., & Stein, D. M. (1978). Therapist interpersonal skills: Process, outcome, methodological considerations, and recommendations for future research. *Psychological Bulletin, 85,* 467-489.

Lambert, M. J., Shapiro, D. A., & Bergin, A. E. (1986). The effectiveness of psychotherapy. In S. L. Garfield & A. E. Bergin (Eds.), *Handbook of psychotherapy and behavior change* (3rd ed., pp. 157-211). New York: Wiley.

Lazarus, A. A. (1976). *Multi-modal behavior therapy.* New York: Springer.

Levy, L. H. (1963). *Psychological interpretation.* New York: Holt, Rinehart, & Winston.

Liebert, R. M., & Spiegler, M. D. (1987). *Personality: Strategies and issues* (5th ed.). Chicago: Dorsey.

Mahrer, A. R. (1983). *Experiential psychotherapy: Basic practices.* New York: Brunner/Mazel.

Malan, D. H. (1963). *A study of brief psychotherapy.* London: Tavistock Publications.

Malan, D. H. (1976a). *The frontier of brief psychotherapy.* New York: Plenum.

Malan, D. H. (1976b). *Toward the validation of dynamic psychotherapy: A replication.* New York: Plenum.

Marziali, E. A. (1984). Prediction of outcome of brief psychotherapy from therapist interpretive interventions. *Archives of General Psychiatry, 41,* 301-304.

Marziali, E. A., & Sullivan, J. H. (1980). Methodological issues in the context analyses of brief psychotherapy. *British Journal of Medical Psychology, 53,* 19-27.

Miles, M. B., & Huberman, A. M. (1984). *Qualitative data analysis: A sourcebook of new methods.* Beverly Hills, CA: Sage.

Minuchin, S. (1974). *Families and family therapy.* Cambridge, MA: Harvard University Press.

O'Farrell, M. K., Hill, C. E., & Patton, S. (1986). Comparison of two cases of counseling with the same counselor. *Journal of Counseling and Development, 65,* 141-145.

Orlinsky, D. E., & Howard, K. I. (1975). *Varieties of psychotherapeutic experience.* New York: Teachers' College Press.

Orlinsky, D. E., & Howard, K. I. (1978). The relation of process to outcome in psychotherapy. In S. L. Garfield & A. E. Bergin (Eds.), *Handbook of psychotherapy and behavior change* (2nd ed., pp. 283-330). New York: Wiley.

Parloff, M. B., Waskow, I. E., & Wolfe, B. E. (1978). Research on therapist variables in relation to process and outcome. In S. L. Garfield & A. E. Bergin (Eds.), *Handbook of psychotherapy and behavior change* (2nd ed.. pp. 233-283). New York: Wiley.

Piper, W. E., Debbane, E. G., Bienvenu, J. P., De Carufel, F. F., & Garant, J. (1986). Relationships between the object focus of therapist interventions and outcome in short-term individual psychotherapy. *British Journal of Medical Psychology, 59,* 1-11.

Porter, E. H., Jr. (1943). The development and evaluation of a measure of counseling interview procedures. *Educational and Psychological Measurement, 3,* 105-126.

Robinson, F. R. (1950). *Principles and procedures in student counseling.* New York: Harper.

Rogers, C. (1957). The necessary and sufficient conditions of therapeutic personal change. *Journal of Counseling Psychology, 21,* 93-103.

Russell, R. L., & Trull, T. J. (1986). Sequential analyses of language variables in psychotherapy process research. *Journal of Consulting and Clinical Psychology, 54,* 16-21.

Shon, S. P., & Davis, Y. J. (1982). Asian families. In M. McGoldrick, J. K. Pearce, & J. Giordano (Eds.), *Ethnicity and family therapy* (pp. 208-228). New York: Guilford.

Sifneos, P. (1979). *Short-term psychotherapy and emotional crisis.* Cambridge, MA: Harvard University Press.

Sloane, R. B., Staples, F. R., Cristol, A. H., Yorkston, N. J., & Whipple, K. (1975). *Psychotherapy versus behavior therapy.* Cambridge. MA: Harvard University Press.

Smith, M. L., Glass, G. V., & Miller, T. I. (1980). *The benefits of psychotherapy.* Baltimore: Johns Hopkins University Press.

Snyder, W.U. (1945). An investigation of the nature of nondirective psychotherapy. *Journal of General Psychology, 33,* 193-223.

Speisman, J. C. (1959). Depth of interpretation and verbal resistance in psychotherapy. *Journal of Consulting Psychology, 23,* 93-99.

Spiegel, S. B., & Hill, C. E. (1989). Guidelines for research on therapist interpretation: Toward greater methodological rigor and relevance to practice. *Journal of Counseling Psychology, 36,* 121-129.

Stiles, W. B. (1979). Verbal response modes and psychotherapeutic technique. *Psychiatry, 42,* 49-62.

Stiles, W. B., Elliott, R., Llewelyn, S. P., Firth-Cozens, J. A.. Margison, F. R., Shapiro, D. A., & Hardy, G. (1988). *Assimilation of problematic experiences by clients in psychotherapy.* Unpublished manuscript, Miami University.

Stiles, W. B., & Snow, J. S. (1984). Counseling session impact as viewed by novice counselors and their clients. *Journal of Counseling Psychology, 31,* 3-12.

Strupp, H. H. (1955). An objective comparison of Rogerian and psychoanalytic techniques. *Journal of Consulting Psychology, 19,* 1-7.

Strupp, H. H. (1980). Success and failure in time-limited psychotherapy: A systematic comparison of two cases (Comparison 1). *Archives of General Psychiatry, 37,* 595-603.

Strupp, H. H. (1982). The outcome problem in psychotherapy: Contemporary perspectives. In J. H. Harvey & M. M. Parks (Eds.), *The master lecture series: vol. 1. Psychotherapy research and behavior change* (pp. 39-71). Washington, D C: American Psychological Association.

Strupp, H. H., & Binder, J. L. (1984). *Psychotherapy in a new key: A guide to time-limited dynamic psychotherapy.* New York: Basic Books.

Sue, S., & Zane, N. (1987). The role of culture and cultural techniques in psychotherapy. *American Psychologist, 42,* 37-45.

Sullivan, H. S. (1953). *The interpersonal theory of psychiatry.* New York: Norton.

Thompson, B. J., & Hill, C. E. (in preparation). Therapist perceptions of client reactions.

Tichenor, V., Hill, C. E., & Helms, J. (in preparation). Female psychotherapy clients wanted: Who responds to the advertisements?

Truax, C. B., & Carkhuff, R. R. (1967). *Toward effective counseling and psychotherapy: Training and practice.* Chicago: Aldine.

Waskow, I. E., & Parloff, M. B. (Eds.). (1975). *Psychotherapy change measures* (DHEW Report No. 74-120). Washington, DC: Department of Health, Education, and Welfare.

Weiss, J., Sampson, H., & the Mount Zion Psychotherapy Research Group. (1986). *The psychoanalytic process: Theory, clinical observation, and empirical research.* New York: Guilford.

Yalom, I. D. (1975). *The theory and practice of group psychotherapy* (2nd ed.). New York: Basic Books.

Author Index

Subject Index

About the Authors

CLARA E. HILL received her Ph.D. from Southern Illinois University in 1974. She is currently a professor in the Department of Psychology at the University of Maryland. Dr. Hill has over 50 publications in the area of psychotherapy research, most of which have focused on the interaction between therapists and clients. Her particular interest has been in studying the effects of therapist techniques.

BARBARA J. THOMPSON and JAMES R. MAHALIK are students in the doctoral program in counseling psychology at the University of Maryland.

NOTES

NOTES

NOTES

NOTES

NOTES